BACKSTAGE WITH ACTORS

ALFRED LUNT and LYNN FONTANNE
They are seen here in the last act of "Amphitryon 38."

HELEN ORMSBEE

Backstage
With
Actors

*From the Time of Shakespeare
to the Present Day*

Essay Index Reprint Series

BOOKS FOR LIBRARIES PRESS
FREEPORT, NEW YORK

First Published 1938
Reprinted 1970

792.02
073b

70-9798
INTERNATIONAL STANDARD BOOK NUMBER:
0-8369-1934-3

LIBRARY OF CONGRESS CATALOG CARD NUMBER:
76-134123

PRINTED IN THE UNITED STATES OF AMERICA

To
MARY AND TOM

Preface

"THE actor is . . . a creature of sympathy," wrote John Bernard, comedian and manager, over a century ago. I have often thought of his pithy phrase when I have talked with Broadway stars in their dressing rooms. These people now at the top of their calling *are* creatures of sympathy—though most of them might shy away from the description, preferring to be regarded as proficient golfers, or farmers, or astute bidders at contract.

Somewhere within them, though, they possess a stratum like the emulsion on a photographic film. It is quick to take impressions and cannot stand over-exposure; it is their underlying endowment as players.

Here was the start of this book. I began to wonder whether famous performers of the past were like those of the present, and whether they went at their impersonations in ways that would be at all comparable. So I set about digging into the records. I would look at those men and women of long ago exactly as if they were busy in the theatre now. I would go backstage with them—not only literally, but backstage in their minds as well. And this excursion into other times would be for the purpose of coming back to today. I would try to see if there is anything in the actor's instinct that does not alter.

Before long I realized that I could select only a few players in each period. For example, Adelaide Neilson and Fanny Janauschek—two great geniuses—had to be passed over in favor of Edwin Booth and Joseph Jefferson. There are similar omissions in other epochs, including the present; but the only way to avoid writing an encyclopedia was to sift out instances. In doing so, I chose actors and actresses who illustrate the progress of the English-speaking theatre and its rhythmic variations in acting. The absence of a name from these pages does not imply any inferiority of gifts.

While I was working on this manuscript, I came upon notes by my father, Hamilton Ormsbee, concerning the stage of the 1890's and early 1900's. (He was dramatic critic of the *Brooklyn Daily Eagle* from about 1893 to 1910, his predecessor having been his friend Charles M. Skinner, brother of Otis Skinner.) Father dearly loved the theatre, and in my childhood I would sit at the breakfast table and listen to his talk about one play or another that he and my mother had seen on the preceding night. Thus these notes of his served to verify my recollections, and to extend my touch with acting further back than it would otherwise reach.

The first time I ever went behind the scenes was when I was perhaps nine and was brought to Mme. Modjeska's dressing room. She was then old and there was talk of her retiring; Father said we children might never have another chance to see her play. She was taking off her make-up with cold cream. So she wiped her hands on a clean towel and, with the utmost gentleness, held one of my hands between the two of hers. She said something —I have forgotten what. But while she spoke, a current of feeling seemed to flow right out of her; it made your heart melt inside you. I did not know what it was that I felt in her. But years later I understood; it was sympathy. She must have had it in a high degree. That was my first impression of the world backstage, and first impressions have at least a grain of truth in them.

HELEN ORMSBEE.

Brooklyn, New York.
March, 1938.

Contents

CONTENTS

HELEN HAYES in "Victoria Regina"

PROLOGUE

1.

What Makes Acting?

MORE than three hundred years ago, certain plays were put on by a company of actors at the Globe Theatre on the Bankside, in London. The company had no electric lighting for its stage, no scenery, no curtain to fall on telling situations and give them emphasis.

Suppose some strange visitor from the future could have approached the playwright of this troupe with an offer to film his dramas. "Sweet Master Shakespeare, your shows are swell—they'll be great for the pictures," the cinema's emissary might say. But such a suggestion would have no meaning for the author-player, so amazingly has the theatre expanded since he worked in it. Cameras and microphones? Close-ups, screen-tests, fade-outs? The terms would be blanks in his vocabulary. And could he believe that tall story, related with much detail by the man from Hollywood, about rolling up a performance on a ribbon of celluloid and shipping it around the world in a tin container?

Nevertheless, among endless innovations since Shakespeare's time, the theatre's most important unit of equipment is no novelty at all. It is still the actor. Without the player's instinct, Broadway and Hollywood would have to shut up shop. What actors bring into the theatre is their own peculiar bent for putting imagination to work; but they have no modern, labor-saving device for doing this. They must depend on mind, emotions and physique, just as their predecessors did centuries in the past.

This being so, are there resemblances in the output, even though styles of playing alter with every generation? The gifted actor's power over his audience is no new thing. It existed long ago. Is it the same power, whether it be used by Richard Burbage in 1600, or by Charles Laughton in pictures in the 1930's—by Mrs. Barry during the Restoration, or by Helen Hayes in "Victoria Regina?" In short, is acting a psychological art, with discoverable qualities of mind underlying all its differences? And what has that to do with the theatre of today or tomorrow?

To answer these questions, if possible, is the purpose of this book. Very early in the history of the English stage, people began to pass along fragmentary records of players' methods, and occasionally actors themselves made comments on their own and their fellows' performances. As time went on, these observations grew clearer. Little effort has been made, however, to examine such records in the light of present acting, in order to see whether there are similarities of spirit beneath a changing surface. That is the field of exploration for these chapters.

To examine acting is a good deal like trying to catch the proverbial greased pig. Ear or nose or tail—any place will do for a start, if you can just hang on and progress from there. So it may be as well to begin with a mark of good acting which is easy to put one's finger on. This is the player's ability to convince his audience that he *is* his part. "He just *was* that man," we say. Take George M. Cohan, for instance, as the perplexed father of an adolescent in "Ah, Wilderness," or Diana Wynyard trying to celebrate the Armistice in the film version of "Calvalcade," or Victor McLaglen caught in the toils of his own treachery in "The Informer." They seemed to be the people they were acting. They carried you along with them, and you never thought of them as separate from the story. So it was, too, with Burbage, Mrs. Siddons, Kitty Clive, and others of the old tradition, if we accept opinions of persons who watched their acting.

"His auditors . . . saw a *Richard*, not an actor of that personage," an annalist wrote concerning David Garrick's Richard III in 1741. In 1827 a New York critic said of Mrs. Duff, "You see before you only the character she is personating." Identification is one term that has been used to describe this gift of reality. Dramatic imagination is another. Transmigration was Salvini's word for it.

How does the performer come by this knack of putting himself so neatly inside the skin of somebody else? Once in a while, almost anybody can put himself into the other fellow's shoes. Jones can lie in his snug bed in the dark and imagine how he would feel if he were in the condemned cell, with the first light of his last morning stealing in upon him and the steps of the keepers coming down the corridor. . . .

Or, to use a happier illustration, he can lie there and feel himself in the office of the president of the company he works for. "Don't think we haven't noticed you," the president is saying to him. "You're just the man we want for—." Listening, Jones warms with a glow that would be his if this highly illusory scene were ever to take place. But such fancies are quite beyond Jones's control. They are generally silly and useless.

With a true actor, the case is different. He or she can be somebody else when he needs to, and for a purpose. At precisely nine-fifteen every evening, in the midst of the first act, he can find that letter on the table, and the fingers he reaches out for it will be the fingers of a person whose whole future hangs on the message in that envelope. He has got himself inside another skin.

The new covering fits him comfortably, delightfully. It even protects him. He is not standing there spiritually naked in front of an audience, going through gestures. He is somebody else, and that feeling sets him free. It is a most exhilarating experience; yet at the same time he is in control of it, knowing and directing what he is doing. That dual consciousness belongs to the actor.

But how does it come to him? Nobody can explain the process better than Constantin Stanislavsky, the great director of the Moscow Art Theatre, who still retains an emeritus connection with it. Here is a man who bases all his ideas about acting on having done it himself. He knows the player's state of mind.

Stanislavsky, whose French grandmother had been an actress, was born in 1863 into the rich manufacturing class of Russia. As a child, he went often to the theatre. He, his brothers, sisters, and cousins were always getting up plays and operettas.

After he had grown up, he organized his own group of semi-professional players. By the last decade of the nineteenth century, he became convinced that the general run of contemporary acting did not present life, but merely

Vandamm

GEORGE M. COHAN
This picture shows him at the Fourth-of-July dinner
in "Ah, Wilderness."

a set of cut-and-dried makeshifts. He felt that he must find better standards.

Accordingly, in partnership with Nemirovitch-Dantchenko, he formed the Moscow Art Theatre, in the late 1890's. It began as an experiment and a protest. It was, and is, an immense success. With the years, its influence has spread far beyond Russia.

In 1923 the Moscow Art Theatre company came to the United States, bringing Stanislavsky and others of its foremost members. From that event, dates the gradual infiltration of its methods here. There is scarcely any player in this country today who has not been touched, knowingly or unknowingly, by its ideas.

Stanislavsky believes that truth in acting is the thing which makes it persuasive. The actor must know what the person he depicts is thinking and feeling—and lip service, in place of this inward acquaintance, will get him nowhere. Though he speak with the tongue of men and of angels, he had better save his breath to cool his porridge. "You are not the real thing," Stanislavsky once said, in criticising a member of his company. "It is not the real feeling. It is not life! It is three kopecks."

Self-forgetfulness, concentration on the thoughts of the character to be portrayed—these were what Stanislavsky sought. In other words, he wanted the performer to follow the example of the village dunce who found the lost cow. "I says to myself, 'If I was a cow, where would I go?' And I went there."

The actor's secret, according to this Russian, is the ability to think, "If I were a cow, or an absconding cashier, or a girl in love, where would I go? What would I do? How would I feel?" To this power of imagination, every other talent is secondary. Acting grows from within, outward.

When the Moscow Art Theatre started in 1897 and 1898, Stanislavsky began to put the company through exercises in freedom from stage conventions. There were adhesions to be broken up. He wanted to get away from "stagey" customs of speaking, sitting, and standing; he wanted to use real life as the model for everything.

"During rehearsals you must remember, not your poses, but the feeling that produced those poses," was one of his instructions. "Eyes, eyes! Your eyes are empty," he complained—for he knew that behind empty eyes is an empty mind; and he placed dependence on the intensity with which the performer could think his rôle. The Russians have a very long word for this process. They call it "peregivanie." It is translated, "To live sincerely the feeling of another person."

Members of Stanislavsky's company were urged, too, to watch men and women on the streets or at home, to study them in instants of rage or grief. "Take your examples from life," he said.

He warned his players never to regard themselves as about to entertain the spectators; for an audience that catches an actor trying to please it, is never pleased. Like Queen Victoria, it is not amused. Neither will it cry because some actress is heaving and sobbing. Be true to the character, Stanislavsky urged, and let the effect on the audience take care of itself.

The director's suggestions were always practical. He could help a pupil to cling to that sense of being a real person all through a scene. He counseled the performer to put his attention on some object near him—on the table beside him, perhaps, laying his hand on it and noticing the feel of it under his fingers. Thus preoccupied, the actor could relax. His muscles could respond to his thoughts, instead of getting in the way of them. "In doing this, you will find yourself. Otherwise you will be rigid as steel."

These few illustrations of Stanislavsky's practice are not a thorough outline of his system, but they serve to show the root of his teaching. Gestures, inflections, bits of "business"—all those things are not appurtenances to be hung on acting like the tail on the donkey at a children's party. They are parts of a whole, and their beauty comes of their growing out of that whole.

All this seems delightfully self-evident while you sit in an armchair and think about it. But it is not easy in practice, or we should never have any bad actors.

There is, unfortunately, something about the stage, picture studio, or broadcasting room which tends to push the novice in the very direction he ought not to go. Mechanical requirements seize him and clamp him in a vise; he is no longer his own master. You think it would be quite simple to walk across a stage room, open a door and go out, conveying the impression that you were worried? But if you try it for the first time, the chances are that the reality and simplicity will elude you. The place will not seem like a room; you will feel stiff and silly.

The convincing actor has got beyond all this, and has learned to meet the artificialities without being owned by them. One of the charms of good acting is its apparent disregard of the difficulties. The experienced bad actor —and there are such people—complies with mechanical needs, and succumbs. He has nothing more to give. A test of fine acting is the abundance of reality which it has left to pour out, after fulfilling the rules.

Stanislavsky's method is of value because it helps to supply the player with that reality which sweeps him over obstacles. These ideas of Stanislavsky's were not of his sole devising. Long before him, individual performers sometimes used one or another of his processes; but until he came along no one had fitted them all together and put them into words. It took his genius to do this.

Here is a standard of acting widely accepted in the modern theatre. But can it apply to players of the old tradition? If we could call them out of the past and question them at a sort of histrionic committee meeting, would they agree that their aim was to live the feelings of another person?

There is no short-cut to becoming acquainted with players of the past. Since they cannot come to us, we must go to them. In due course, we must do this chronologically, seeking to see these people in the theatre as it existed in their eras. But first, let us dip indiscriminately into time, assuming that—as in "The Star Wagon"—one may turn the dial to any date one chooses. Among glimpses of acting thus drawn at random from past and present, will there be enough similarity in approach to the work to warrant further inquiry?

Take Sarah Siddons. Sir Joshua Reynolds painted her as the Tragic Muse, and in that guise she is legendary today. Yet as to what kind of acting she really did, prevailing notions are hazy. Stately and declamatory would be an average offhand guess. This is traceable to the fact that players who copied her lacked her greatness. Compared with her, they were like those dinner tables set up in show windows—elaborately equipped, and quite without nourishment.

But what of Siddons herself, according to people who saw her at Drury Lane in the 1780's? It was not her elocution that they remembered, on coming away from the playhouse; it was her true, sudden touches of feeling. When she said the single word "Oh," in "Venice Preserved," her audiences sobbed. She filled her rôles with a flood of reality which conquered.

An anecdote about Edwin Booth shows this same process in action. One night when he was playing "Hamlet," the man cast for the Ghost was someone who had never done the part with him. To the terrace came the Prince of Denmark, to watch for the apparition. The poor Ghost walked on, but the eyes Hamlet turned on him were so alive with horror that the Ghost backed off into the wings, frightened out of his wits.

Evidently other Hamlets had never given him such a look. Booth was a genius. He had the secret of entering so deeply into Hamlet's mind that his eyes were wholly imbued with it. There was no trace of Edwin Booth left in them. When a player is possessed by the character he or she impersonates, the eyes betray it. The actor becomes, to borrow St. Paul's phrase, a new creature.

Perhaps to an ordinary, hardboiled theatregoer, all this sounds far-fetched. But has he ever watched a performer who was one hundred per cent *unable* to become a new creature? I once played in a company, the business manager of which suddenly had to go on as an understudy. He knew his lines—and right there his proficiency ended. He suffered so from self-consciousness that he was in torture. The part was good-humored, easy-going—but while he made those jolly speeches, his face froze with anguish. His legs twisted into knots. In his eyes was the sick, pleading look of a person who could not *get out of himself*. If he had been able to, his troubles would have been over.

If one sets this man's ability to enter into the mind of his part at zero, and Edwin Booth's in that moment with the Ghost at one hundred, it becomes plain that there may be every gradation of this endowment among people who act. Those whose percentage is appallingly low soon cease to exhibit their deficiency in public. (The business manager would have been only too glad not to exhibit his.) Next in the scale come performers who have plenty of confidence, but little imagination. These are the routine actors, always ready with what Mrs. Fiske called "that firm, sure touch on the wrong note." The firm touch gets them by, and they never have the least doubt about the note.

A higher rating than theirs may go to many an obscure player whose work has the ring of truth in it. But those men and women rank highest of all who, owning this power of identification, know how to apply it with the artist's stroke.

In classifying phenomena of any kind, extreme cases are the most readily recognizable, and finer shadings must be filled in later. Edwin Booth and the understudy suffering from stage fright represent such extremes. Side by side with Booth, one might add Eleanora Duse as another performer acting from within so unswervingly that she seemed to lend her own flesh and blood to the part.

George Bernard Shaw has given a vivid account of a minute or two in Duse's "Magda" when she played in London, in 1895. Shaw was then a dramatic critic. In the third act, she came to the scene where Magda was about to encounter the man who, many years earlier, had been her lover and had deserted her.

From the instant when she knew he was waiting to be shown into the room, the audience saw that this meeting would be difficult for her. However, she got through the start of it with composure, and she and her caller sat down to talk quite impersonally. Then, just as she believed she had herself in hand and might take the situation easily, she began to blush. She could feel it, and that made the blush worse. It grew deeper and deeper as she sat there —until at last she buried her face in her hands. The actress used no make-up; her flush was not a trick of cosmetics. Indeed, the astute observer who testified to the incident was convinced that he beheld a feat of the acting imagination.

This scene of Duse's is a flawless illustration of that "peregivanie" which the Russians aim at. They say that when their actor Moskvin first played the title role in "Tsar Fyodor," his face and eyes became transfigured, radiant. Reaching such heights as these, impersonation is an incarnation—the idea clothes itself in flesh.

Having caught sight of Duse, Moskvin, and Booth in some of their most realistic moments, one begins to acknowledge the things an actor can do if his abilities are great enough. The color fled from Garrick's face, it is said, when he saw the Ghost in "Hamlet." Then there was a pause, and when he managed to speak his exclamation came "not with the beginning, but with the end of a breath."

Does this seem like the tumult and shouting which we may incline to believe was the whole stock-in-trade of old-timers?

It may be necessary to modify one's notion about performers of the past. When a player is inspired, it matters little what generation he lives in. He will accept the outward standards of his time, but there is that within him which passes show and makes him great. He has the gift of acting in its acute form, as contrasted with the chronic acting around him.

Such a player was Edmund Kean. His voice, said an actor who heard him, was the cry of a despairing soul. And no wonder. He had been a miserable, ragged, unmanageable boy. While he was still a child, he was playing in poor, ill-paid, broken-down theatrical companies.

In 1808, being then twenty-one, he married an actress, and the two of them appeared in the provinces wherever they could get engagements. They knew hunger, cold, and disappointment. One of the two children born to them in these wandering years died of hardships. (The other lived to go to Eton—but that is another story.)

When Kean, playing Shylock at Drury Lane for the first time, burst into the lines

> Fair Sir, you spit on me on Wednesday last;
> You spurned me such a day; another time
> You called me dog—

nothing like the smouldering fire of his acting had been seen in London for many years. All his life, until this night in 1814, he had been spurned and spit on. He had so intimate an acquaintance with suffering that he knew all the secret channels it cuts. Temperament and experience had equipped him to re-live the emotion of others.

"Just returned from seeing Kean," [wrote Lord Byron]. "By Jove, he is a soul! Life—nature—truth, without exaggeration or diminution."

Clara Morris, a member of Augustin Daly's company

Vandamm Studio

LESLIE HOWARD as Hamlet

and a popular star in the 1870's and 1880's, was another genius of emotion. She had extraordinary power to make spectators weep. The plays in which she appeared were artificial, but people who saw her have insisted that she triumphed over all the claptrap. Her characterizations were real and compelling.

Her method, she recorded, grew out of an instinct for living her part. Starting as a young girl in a stock company in Cleveland, Ohio, she never had many rehearsals or gave many consecutive performances of the same rôle. However, when she came into sudden fame at Daly's Theatre in New York in the autumn of 1870, she found herself faced with a new problem. How could she keep repeating the same emotion night after night, for weeks on end? Long runs were then coming into vogue.

Just here was Miss Morris's difficulty. She could not make audiences cry unless she cried, herself. One night she caught sight of Daly standing in the wings, waiting to see whether she was going to shed tears in her big scene. (Those tears were a box-office asset.)

Agonized for fear she could not do what was expected of her, she had a sudden recollection of something she had seen in a theatre years before. An old actress whose popularity had waned stood bowing and smiling to an uncaring audience. As she did so, comprehension came into her eyes—she realized that her day was over. It was the defeat in the old actress's face that came back to Clara Morris. She went on for her scene, and had no trouble about crying. This led her to the discovery that she could call on stored-up memories to release new feeling, which she might then translate into the actualities of some well-worn climax.

Hers was not that utter identification with her part

that Duse could arrive at. By comparison, Miss Morris practiced a psychological trick, like pulling a rabbit out of her hat. The rabbit was real and the hat was real, but the relation between them was not quite what it appeared to be. Still, the wrench of pain which she put into those scenes of hers sprang from something genuine, and her audiences divined it.

Katharine Cornell, in our own day, has more of Duse than of Clara Morris about her. Miss Cornell's flair for emotion is linked with restraint and with a sincerity which seems to be part of her. Anyone who talks with her can feel her habit of setting herself aside and putting all her attention on the subject under discussion. In acting, this is just what she does with a rôle. Not only the center of her attention but the outer fringes of it as well, are turned on the character. The reality she holds before the audience is greater than any incidental unrealities of the theatre. When she handles a cup of tea or a book, she is intent on it just as people are in life.

In "The Barretts of Wimpole Street," she had a scene in which Elizabeth Barrett sat puzzling over Browning's verse. One of her hands held the book, and the other a glass of medicine which had just been poured out for her. But she forgot all about it and went on reading. The hand holding the dose remained in a state of arrested motion, half way to her lips. The audience could feel her absorption in the printed page in front of her.

Ina Claire, who commenced her stage career by doing imitations, says that mimicry is based on this same sense of identification with the individual portrayed. "You start by feeling like the person in some small mannerism or intonation, and then you gradually expand the likeness until you have a characterization."

Leslie Howard is another player who relies on the fusing of player and part. He calls it cheating when the actor neglects to think himself into his rôle. That kind of thought costs effort, however—and so the performer is sometimes tempted to go through the appearance of impersonation without making that outlay. "But if you are a cheat, how the camera shows you up," he says of motion picture acting.

Living the feelings of another person is not a wholly subjective process, though. It is also based on noticing how people behave. Peggy Wood says you can seldom get nearer to any human being than his shirt-front. That shirt-front is his shield and buckler against the world; but his mannerisms betray him. Watch Caspar Milquetoast, and you know how he feels. If you are an actor, you can make yourself feel like him. That is what the player does when he takes his examples from life.

Noel Coward and Gertrude Lawrence demonstrated the effectiveness of this process in "Red Peppers." The Peppers were a seedy vaudeville couple playing in a third-rate music hall—quarreling with each other, but putting up united resistance to the local manager. Each of these portraits was done in mosaic. It consisted of innumerable fragments supplied by memory, for the early stage experience of both portrayers had brought them into contact with performers of this sort.

Another instance of dramatic observation was the central figure in "Personal Appearance." The rôle, played with ironic humor by Gladys George, was that of a cinema star, based on the vanity and shallow emotionalism traditionally attributed to players. Miss George took this somewhat conventional outline and infused it with vitality. She did so by copying from life, her performance being a composite of ten or twelve women. From one she borrowed touches of overdone elegance, from another the hint of a self-pity, from a third the garbled French phrases —and so on. Her procedure was not accidental. Beginning as a child actress, she had taught herself to weave into her rôles traits which she observed in all kinds of people. Parts so approached were especially convincing to audiences, she discovered.

Acting and stage directing have many things in common, for the player is the material which the director must manipulate. David Garrick was a master at rehearsing other people, according to Kitty Clive, one of his leading women. In her old age she wrote him:

> Wonderful Sir,—Who have been for these thirty years contradicting an old proverb—you cannot make bricks without straw; but you have done what is infinitely more difficult, for you have made actors and actresses without genius; that is, you have made them pass for such, which has answered your end, though it has given you infinite trouble . . .

Sir Charles Hawtrey, who died in 1923, is famous for the skill with which he trained people who acted with him. Noel Coward, one of these persons, declares that he never heard Hawtrey say an unkind word even to the most inept player. The insight that made him a superb actor taught him to understand the limitations which performers contend with.

One of the foremost producers in America at present is Guthrie McClintic. After a brief experience as an actor, he turned to staging plays—and his initiation in acting has proved invaluable in this work. At rehearsals, his first aim is to establish confidence between the cast and himself; he wants to do away with strain because individuals so beset are too rigid to think the thoughts of the *dramatis personæ*. This process of relaxation is only the first step in McClintic's rehearsing. He builds on that.

There are directors who never acted, but who understand how to evoke the best from their casts. This is true of Philip Moeller of the Theatre Guild. He confesses that he never played a part but once—and in that emergency he did everything a performer should avoid. What Moeller has used to good purpose in staging a long list of dramas, is a sympathetic understanding of the qualities behind acting. Intelligence and sensitivity are the two things he looks for in selecting players. He says he cannot induct them into the rudiments of their calling, but if they have a grounding in it he counts greatly on the new responses he can draw out of them.

Rachel Crothers, the dramatist, started out to be an actress. Taking entire charge of her own productions, she has long been adept at breathing the breath of life into them. "It doesn't sound to me as if you were talking to him," she will say at a rehearsal, when someone is inclined to speak lines instead of conversing. Acting is not a series of tricks, she states, but the total of the player's reaction to life.

David Belasco was an actor in his obscurer days, and this doubtless developed that miraculous understanding of the player which he used later as a director. Not long ago Frances Starr told me how he put the final touch on a scene in "The Easiest Way." It was close to the end of the play, when the heroine, pushed to the wall by her own weaknesses, tried to shoot herself. But she was too much of a coward to pull the trigger, and could only drop the gun with a scream of self-disgust. There was nothing left for her but the easiest way. In her own words, she was going out to supper and to hell afterwards.

There had been a successful dress rehearsal which had lasted all night. Belasco reassembled the cast at noon the next day, merely to run through a few places in the performance, he announced. Beginning with the last act, he wasted little time in reaching the scene of the heroine's ultimate defeat. The great manager, usually considerate of his actors, began to harry Frances Starr, to shout at her, to find fault with everything she did. The company watched with smothered resentment.

"He made me go over and over that moment with the revolver, from noon till eight o'clock at night. The scream never suited him. I was tired and desperate. I would stand there with that gun at my head and think, 'If this were loaded, I'd shoot!' After eight hours of that, he made me go back another time. He said in his most cutting tone, 'You can't do that scream. Bernhardt could do it, Duse could do it—but you can't. Oh, no!' All of a sudden I screamed. Where that cry came from, I don't know. Then I fainted.

"They sent me home. My sister put me to bed, and the doctor gave me a sedative. Late in the evening, Mr. Belasco came. 'How's the little girl?' he asked my sister. She was frigid. 'She's in bed and the doctor has been here,' she told him; but he insisted on coming in to see me. He was in a wonderful humor. 'Well, little girl,' he said, 'we accomplished something tonight. That was a great piece of work you did! Great.'

" 'But I'll never be able to do it again,' I said. He smiled. 'Don't you worry,' he told me. 'You can always do it, after this. That thing is *there*. It will always be there.' And," added Miss Starr, "it always was. For me, that was a surgical operation. I grew years in that day's work."

Here, then, is one of the ways in which characterizations are born. Often, painless thinking is not enough—a nerve has to be touched. Players generally say nothing about it.

From these scattered and incomplete instances, it might seem that there is a constant amid the variables of acting, some force which the craftsman uses and which accounts for his or her impact on audiences. But it would be ill-judged to jump to that conclusion on so small a basis of fact and without first making a more orderly survey of the progress of acting in the English-speaking theatre.

It will be necessary to look at this calling as it has developed from Shakespeare's day, to see it flowering in one generation, meeting set-backs in another, but always producing a few persons who could transcend the mechanisms which hampered the playing of people around them. These transcendent players are the acute cases, burning with a fever of creative energy.

Thus a study of acting resolves itself into a study of actors. How individuals have practiced acting, not what people have generalized about it, must be the object of this search. Under that scrutiny, dead and gone performers cease to be mere names, and become men and women once more. Seeing their struggles with circumstance and with themselves, one begins to perceive the intricate interlocking of personality and product. "Acting is not a series of tricks, but the total of the player's reaction to life."

That is why this art, like others, cannot be examined apart from the people who make it. "All theories are gray and dim," wrote Goethe, "but the tree of life is green."

LONG AGO

2.

Players of Shakespeare's Day

WHEN Shakespeare came to London young and unknown, in the late 1580's, the town was full of actors. Five well-recognized companies of men played engagements there from time to time, varying their seasons with road tours, and in addition two companies of boys were in high favor. There were also smaller organizations.

Each of these groups was licensed under the patronage of some peer of the realm. This the law required. Compliance was not difficult, for the English Renaissance was reaching its peak, and noblemen of Queen Elizabeth's court prided themselves on their sympathy with the arts. Then, as now, when a theatrical enterprise was being launched, the organizers went out and looked for backing. Their "angels" were not picture corporations or Wall Street men, but courtiers.

The courtier's investment was not heavy. He generally gave the glory of his illustrious name and a few odds and ends in the way of "liveries" and hospitality. The organizers ran the company on their own, and made it pay if they could.

At the start of Shakespeare's career, the best adult companies were the Queen's, the Earl of Leicester's, the Lord Admiral's, the Earl of Pembroke's and the Earl of Worcester's. Such organizations had their ups and downs, just as companies have today. When a patron died and a troupe had to find another backer, sometimes a rival group would get its best actors away from it. There were road or "strolling" companies, too. When city actors went on the road, they called it "going into the country."

Metropolitan theatres where Shakespeare worked in his earlier years—or rather, where the organization to which he belonged is known to have worked—were the Theatre and the Curtain, both in Shoreditch; the Rose, on the Bankside; and a playhouse in Newington Butts. The Globe was still in the future. (The name Curtain came from location near a "curtain" or outer wall of a disused fortification.) These theatres, unlike the courtyards of several inns where companies still played occasionally, were just outside the limits of the City of London.

There was reason for this. Not only was there a strong Puritan sentiment in the City, but its merchants also felt that plays interfered with business. They complained of theatres as resorts of "maisterless" men—in other words, of the unemployed. They feared that apprentices, sent on errands, would drop in at playhouses and waste time. So James Burbage, the member of Lord Leicester's company who built the first English theatre, had very wisely chosen a site under the jurisdiction of Middlesex, where the authorities were easier-going than in the City. He called his playhouse The Theatre. Other builders chose other favorable localities.

In 1571, when Shakespeare was seven years old, Parliament had taken steps to clear the highways of that era's thieves, gangsters, and panhandlers, and the legislation incidentally involved the licensing of players. Before then there had been actors, but their legal status shaded off into that of rogues and vagabonds. Thereafter they became members of a recognized craft, into which they could throw their energies with a fair hope of being undisturbed.

In 1572, Burbage and other members of Lord Leicester's men had written the Earl:

> We therefore, your humble servaunts and daylye orators, your players . . . are bold to trouble your Lordshippe with this our suite . . . that you will now vouchsafe to reteyne us at this present as your household servants and daylie wayters, not that we meane to crave any further stipend or benefite at your Lordshippe's hands, but our Lyveries as we have had, and also your Honour's License to certifye that we are your Household Servauntes, when we shall have occasion to traveyl amongst our frends, as we do usuallye once a yere, and as other noblemen's players do.

The license would protect them from village constables, who could otherwise arrest them as vagrants.

Two years later, the Earl obtained for these men a special patent of incorporation "to use, exercise & occupie the art & faculty of playeing Comedies, Tragedies, Enterludes & Stage playes." The persons to whom this charter was issued were "James Burbadge, John Perkyn, John Lanham, William Johnson & Robert Wylson."

With these documents to give him security, Burbage was able to make his dream come true. This dream was to erect a building especially arranged for presenting plays. By 1576 he had opened his Theatre.

Actors of Shakespeare's day—there were no actresses—were men of all sorts. A few of them possessed great skill, while more than a few had distinctly inferior gifts. Some of them turned their hands to playwriting as well as acting. Some made money at their calling and died rich, while others were always hard up. Some of them fought duels and got into tavern brawls.

They were all caught in the great rising surge of the English drama. Already Shakespeare's predecessors were pruning it of crudities, and shaping it for beauty and power. The tide moved swiftly. Plays were written, bought by rival companies, and produced in rapid succession. The theatre of that day was full of imagination and vigor, qualities that were epidemic. The contagion fed every artistic impulse, and yet there was nothing conscious or studied about the whole process. Like the boy's whistle, it whistled itself. It could not be held back.

The style of acting that matured under these conditions was probably more exuberant and less carefully executed than that in our own theatres. These performers put on plays at top speed, and never had time for finishing touches. Their stage and their audiences, moreover, demanded a breadth of manner which is not needed today.

Perhaps a hint of their spirit, tempered to the modern theatre, may be caught in the work of the present Abbey company, of Dublin, for it is said that the Irish possess Elizabethan traits. Maureen Delaney, of the Abbey players, is a unique character-actress. Her gestures are larger, her emotions more unabashed than is usual now in the English-speaking drama. She blends broad humor with the bitterest tragedy. She does not shrink from doing things that are sublime, but that might easily slip over into being ridiculous.

Some such abounding richness must have imbued the best players of Shakespeare's day. For them, a rolling poetic phrase was not a thing to be approached with misgivings—it was very nearly their native speech. Within Shakespeare's lifetime, men of the Globe-Blackfriars company were to bring acting to so high a state that their tradition would be carried on by their apprentices and followers for years after them. (The Blackfriars was the winter playhouse of the Globe troupe, beginning in 1610.)

Many performers who were part of that magical epoch have left scant traces of themselves. But this is no excuse for fancying them to have been as bloodless as the bits of parchment on which their names are recorded. They were actors busy with rehearsals and performances. They knew the miseries of stage fright, and they understood, too, the reactions of audiences.

Some of these players resorted to obvious tricks and gags to get laughs, or split the ears of groundlings with their ranting. "The twelve labours of Hercules have I terribly thundered on the stage," confessed Robert Greene. But other actors were capable of keen and pitying insight. In his "Apology for Actors," Thomas Heywood wrote of the joy of seeing a part convincingly played, "as if the personator were the man personated."

Into that world of the theatre with its vitality and rapid pace came a young man from Stratford-on-Avon. Things had not gone well for him in his home village. For several years his father's business had been slipping downhill. And then there was his own marriage.

It had been the Elizabethan equivalent of a shotgun wedding. When the boy was eighteen, two friends of the Hathaway family had filed a bond in the consistorial court of the Bishop of Worcester, in order to expedite the youth's marriage to Anne Hathaway, who was eight years his senior. This was arranged in November 1582. Six months later, his daughter Susanna was baptized in the parish church of Stratford.

When this child was about a year and a half old, twins, Hamnet and Judith, were also baptized there. That was on February 2, 1585. Shakespeare presumably left his wife and children sometime that year. There was also a poaching incident in which he seems to have been concerned and which was perhaps a contributing cause for his departure.

What drew young Shakespeare, the son of a glover, butcher and dealer in farm commodities, into the theatre? Direct evidence is lacking. But there are people connected with the stage today who will tell you that they grew up in small towns, knowing the theatre only as outsiders, yet always longing to be part of it. He seems to have been like them.

When he was about five his father, as High Bailiff of Stratford, welcomed two companies of players to the town, and performances were given at the Guildhall. It is possible that the child of five may have been present with his father on one of those occasions. Plenty of people can remember being taken to the theatre at as tender an age. After the licensing of companies began in 1572, many of them paid visits to the town, and the boy Shakespeare had ample opportunities to see plays acted.

Among the troupes which came was the Earl of Leicester's, and its manager or leader was James Burbage. Leicester's men visited Stratford when Shakespeare was nine, and again when he was about thirteen. Years later, it was this group, or a branch of it, which he joined.

The company changed patrons, and therefore names, many times during its rise to pre-eminence, but its personnel stayed fairly constant, save for expansions. After Leicester's death in 1588 it merged with Lord Strange's men, and when Lord Strange succeeded to his father's title it became the Earl of Derby's. It was later known as Lord Hunsdon's, and as the Lord Chamberlain's. On the accession of James I, it was taken under the King's patronage and styled "His Majesty's" or "the King's" players. This was the path that lay ahead of it.

Whether some remembered encounter at Stratford led Shakespeare, in his early twenties, to apply to Burbage, is a question that cannot be answered. But the association, once made, was never broken. James Burbage was, himself, a man of uncommon calibre, and so was his son Richard. When Shakespeare came to know them, something must have told him that these were his people.

He began his career, according to traceable tradition, by taking care of gentlemen's horses outside the playhouse. In modern terms, he helped them park. His first biographer said only that he entered the theatre in "a very mean rank."

By the Christmas season of 1594, William Shakespeare had advanced so far as an actor that he, Richard Burbage, and William Kemp were the principal players in two command performances given by their company before Queen Elizabeth. Not bad for a man who had left Stratford a few years earlier because of poverty and a difficulty over deer-stealing.

He had also emerged as a dramatist in his own right. Several of his plays had already been produced—among them, "Love's Labour's Lost," "The Comedy of Errors," "Romeo and Juliet" and "Richard III."

In being both actor and playwright, he was merely doing what a number of other players did. An early actor-dramatist was Robert Wilson, author of "Three Ladies of London." Ben Jonson was a member of the Lord Admiral's men, as was also Thomas Heywood, the writer of some two hundred plays. William Rowley was another author-actor.

It might be suspected that Shakespeare acted only at the outset of his career, but this seems not to have been the case. In the First Folio of his works, collected by his associates after his death "to keep the memory of so worthy a Friend and Fellow alive, as was our Shakespeare," his name stood next to Richard Burbage's at the top of the list of "the principall actors in all these playes."

His name heads the cast of the original production of Ben Jonson's "Every Man in his Humour," in 1598, and when Jonson's "Sejanus" was put on at the Globe in 1603, Shakespeare was again in the cast. By this time his distinction as a dramatist was at its height; he was growing rich, and he could have given up acting if he had wanted to.

He was "exelent in the qualitie he professes," according to Chettle, a contemporary publisher. ("Quality" was the word applied at that time to acting as a profession. "Give us a taste of your quality," says Hamlet to the First Player.) He "did act exceedingly well," was what William Beeston said years later. Beeston's father was a minor member of the company in which Shakespeare worked.

The dramatist seems to have been an actor of character parts. In "Every Man in his Humour," he is said to have played "Kno'well, an old gentleman." He did the Ghost in "Hamlet," perhaps choosing that role because he wanted to be sure what kind of Ghost he would have in his play. His work in the part is reported to have been "the top of his performance."

For many years the company to which Shakespeare belonged, and the Lord's Admiral's company, were the foremost troupes in England, and they were rivals.

The Lord Admiral's men were under the management of Philip Henslowe, not an actor but a shrewd business man. He had married the widow of his prosperous employer, and the money she brought him went into pushing his various ventures. He was enterprising and longheaded. His first playhouse was the Rose, on the Bankside.

Henslowe kept a diary which has been preserved. It is not a chatty comment on current events, but a daily tally of receipts and expenditures running from 1592 to 1609. His "takings" at each performance are set down. So are the sums he paid authors for their plays, and the terms on which he engaged actors.

For instance, Thomas Heywood bound himself "to play only at this house for 2 years," and a Thomas Hearne agreed to serve for two years "in the qualatie of playinge." If you want to know the price of sixpenny nails at that period, you will find it in the diary. If you want to see which theatrical people were pressed for cash, their names are there, too. It is an unvarnished record. Henslowe lent at ruinous rates, sometimes as much as three-and-a-third per cent per month. He gave bribes, and entered them in his book.

Henslowe showed no lack of energy in buying plays

by popular authors. He doubtless left their presentation to his son-in-law, Edward Alleyn, one of the most famous actors of the day. However, the attractions put on under Henslowe's management have been mostly forgotten, while those done by the Burbage company are still glorious. Henslowe and Alleyn amassed fortunes, but records indicate that the Burbages were never more than comfortably off.

That there was scant fraternizing between the two organizations, is apparent in the diary. Few of the Burbage contingent appear in it. Thomas Pope is mentioned, but only as someone on the opposing side of a lawsuit with one of the Henslowe followers.

However, Burbage's sons, Cuthbert and Richard, could learn from the rival management. The Bankside, where Henslowe had started, was showing itself to be the coming theatrical district. It was south of the Thames. Shoreditch was north of it. James Burbage died in 1597. His two sons, together with Shakespeare, Augustine Phillips, John Heminges, Thomas Pope and William Kemp—all members of the company—had the Theatre torn down at the end of 1598, and used the building material for the erection of a playhouse which they called the Globe, on the Bankside. From the start, and right under Philip Henslowe's nose, the new theatre was a success. It was at this juncture that Shakespeare became a "sharer," receiving part of the profits, along with the other players just mentioned.

Before this, he had begun to restore the fallen fortunes of his family in Stratford. His only son had died, but there were his father and mother, his wife, and two young daughters to provide for. This he did. He brought his youngest brother, Edmund, to London and made a player

WILLIAM KEMPE.

the original Performer of Dogberry in Much ado about Nothing.

From a Wooden cut Prefixed to Kemps Nine Daies Wonder. 4to. 1600.

WILLIAM KEMP
In 1600, the comedian published "Kemps Nine Daies Wonder," an account of how he danced his way from London to Norwich. This woodcut, prefixed to the quarto, shows him and his "taberer."

of him, but Edmund died at twenty-eight. There are indications that little sympathy existed between the dramatist and Anne Hathaway. Although he purchased the second largest house in Stratford and had it renovated, he delayed many years before he moved into it. London held him.

Shakespeare's ideas about acting throw the best light now available on the stage technique of his day. This is because he speaks as a person whose standards in other things we know so well. His plays have not shriveled into mere period pieces. His characters are not quaint figures, but great studies of human nature. Could a man who portrayed life so truly, have had only a shallow taste in the acting of his creations? That seems unlikely.

An actor himself, he used the plainest terms when he talked about his calling. The poor player who struts his little hour was a commonplace to him, and so was the "without-book prologue, faintly spoke after the prompter." But he had also seen better things than these in the theatre—he knew what genuine dramatic imagination could do. His views can only be learned from his writings.

In the Induction of "The Taming of the Shrew," an itinerant theatrical troupe encounters a lord on his way home from hunting. The nobleman, it appears from his remarks, is a frequenter of playhouses and an interested observer of the actor's art:

> Lord—Do you intend to stay with me tonight?
> 2nd Player—So please your lordship to accept our
> duty.

> *Lord*—With all my heart. This fellow I remember
> Since first he played a farmer's eldest son:—
> 'Twas where you woo'd the gentlewoman so
>   well;
> I have forgot your name; but, sure that part
> Was aptly fitted and naturally performed.
> *1st Player*—I think 'twas Soto that your honor means.
> *Lord*—'Tis very true: thou didst it excellent.

In the theatre of that time "fitting" a play meant casting it. (For in "A Midsummer Night's Dream," after Quince assigns all the parts for the interlude, he says, "and I hope here is a play fitted.") Aptly fitted and naturally performed, Shakespeare's way of judging acting has nothing strange or antique about it.

There is evidence, too, that he was acquainted with that merging of the player in his part which Salvini called transmigration, the process behind Duse's blush and Garrick's sudden pallor. An incident in "Hamlet" makes this clear. The First Player recites a long speech about the Trojan War and Hecuba's grief. When it is over, one of the spectators glances at the actor and observes, "Look, whether he has not turned colour and has tears in's eyes."

This, Hamlet is aware of. For afterward he bitterly contrasts his own inability to be stirred by his father's murder, with the performer's emotion for an imaginary event. He says,

> Oh, what a rogue and peasant slave am I!
> Is it not monstrous that this player here,
> But in a fiction, in a dream of passion,
> Could force his soul so to his own conceit
> That from her working all his visage wann'd;

. . . . and all for nothing!
For Hecuba!
What's Hecuba to him, or he to Hecuba,
That he should weep for her?

At some time Shakespeare must have seen an actor thus wholly imbued with the character he portrayed.

To doubt it simply because we fancy the Elizabethan stage to have been crude, is needless. For the heights a player's imagination can reach, depend on the individual —not on the acting conventions which surround him. The English theatre of that day flamed with imagination. It was young and daring, the people in it thought all things possible to them. It was the very atmosphere to develop lightning strokes in its artists.

But it was also plentifully supplied with bad acting; we have Shakespeare's word for that:

> Oh, there be players I have seen play, and heard others praise, and that highly [cries Hamlet] that neither having the accent of Christians, nor the gait of Christian, Pagan, nor man, have so strutted and bellowed, that I have thought some of nature's journeymen had made men and not made them well, they imitated humanity so abominably.

To this, the First Player answers, "I hope we have reformed that indifferently with us, sir." The Player's comment leads one to infer that the practice of strutting and bellowing had been pretty thoroughly discussed by some groups of London actors, perhaps by members of the Burbage company.

The man who wrote "Hamlet" knew the upper reaches and the lower depths of the player's craft. He had seen an onion hidden in a handkerchief, to induce tears. Was that done in Stratford by some performer in a strolling troupe? He had heard lines spoken in the manner of Quince in "A Midsummer Night's Dream." But such crudities as these could scarcely have been committed by London players.

Their faults grew partly out of conditions in the theatres. The Globe accommodated about 1200 people in the audience, and to be heard by so large a crowd in an unroofed structure required volume of voice. Since the "groundlings" stood, there must have been a good deal of moving about while the performance was in progress. Nor was this the only kind of distraction:

> In our assemblies at playes in London [wrote Gosson] you shall see such heaving and shooving, such ytching and shouldering to sytte by women; such care of their garments that they be not trode on; . . . such ticking, such toying, such smiling, such winking . . . that it is a right comedie to mark their behaviour.

With these competing interests among onlookers, it is small wonder that players were tempted to introduce a little bellowing. Having found that it caught people's attention, they probably indulged in a great deal more of it.

The company dressed for the performance directly behind the stage in a building called the tiring-house. It formed the permanent rear wall of the scenes, and had doors for entrances and exits. This was not only a place to dress, but also a storage space for costumes and properties. For although there was no scenery, all kinds of rocks, caves, thrones, chairs, draperies, beds, and tombs were used to enhance illusion.

Amid a clutter of wigs, beards, handsome costumes, and minor paraphernalia, actors at the Globe doubtless crowded together, making up for the afternoon's play. Very likely they had devoted the morning to a rehearsal, and two or three of them might be going over lines and "business" in nervous haste.

Performers of first rank are known to have had theatrical servants, and so some of the actors would be waited on by attendants. Presumably, too, these notable players occupied the best locations—that is, the places most accessible to the stage.

As the hour for the play drew near, a trumpet sounded to summon the audience, and when the last blast was heard, the actors knew that the opening moment had come. Then the poor, quaking boy who had to say the prologue drew aside the arras from one of the doors and stepped before the spectators. The performance had begun. In this close association of the tiring-house, Shakespeare, Burbage, Augustine Phillips and other members of the Globe company spent day after day, and it is not difficult to see how intimacy of work, life, and ambitions welded most of them into a group of friends whose solidarity was broken only by death.

Who were some of the actors of that day, and what sort of work did they do? Among the earliest whose talents are recorded are two comedians, Richard Tarleton and Robert Wilson. In 1583, the year Shakespeare's first child was born in Stratford, these "rare men" were selected to head the Queen's players, a company assembled for her by the Master of the Revels. "Richard Tarleton, for a wondrous plentifull pleasant extemporall

wit, he was the wonder of his tyme." Wilson was com-
mended for "a quick, delicate, refined, extemporall wit."

These performers improvised scenes as they went along,
a feat requiring nimble thinking and smoothness of execution. It was a practice mentioned by Shakespeare. "The
quick comedians extemporally will stage us," says his
Cleopatra. (Improvisation is at present in high favor as
a method of training young actors, students being given
scenes to improvise before their instructors.)

Tarleton, dying in 1588, could never have played any
Shakespearean rôle. In his will, which bequeathed silver
plate, money, and jewels, he described himself as a groom
of the Queen's chamber. He had a reputation for being
able to "undumpish" the great Elizabeth when she was
in a bad humor.

Robert Wilson's career was already under way in 1572,
for he was a member of the Burbage group which applied
to the Earl of Leicester at that time. His "extemporall"
skill very naturally led him into playwriting.

William Kemp, creator of Peter in "Romeo and Juliet,"
of Dogberry, and of other comic parts, was a picturesque
figure. He possessed a fund of humor, plenty of egotism,
and an unfortunate temper. His contemporary fame was
great.

Besides being a comedian he was a notable dancer, creating his own jigs. He called them "A pleasant new Jig
of the Broom Man," "Master Kemp's new Jig of the
Kitchen Stuff Woman," "Kemp's new Jig betwixt a Soldier and a Miser and Sym the clown," and so on. He
also danced a Morris all the way from London to Norwich, "attended by Thomas Slye, my Taberer." Persons
of importance entertained him along the route. He arrived in Norwich, and hung up his buskins in the Guild-

hall there, his whole progress being a publicity stunt worthy of a later age. He finished by publishing his own account of the affair.

A slightly bitter comment on acting at about that time says, "Clowns have been thrust into plays by head and shoulders, ever since Kemp could make a scurvy face. . . . Why, if thou canst but draw thy mouth a-wry, lay thy leg over thy staff, saw a piece of cheese asunder with thy dagger, or lap up drink on the earth, I warrant thee they'll laugh mightily." It is likely that the writer had seen this foremost of clowns do those very things.

When the Globe Theatre opened on the Bankside in 1599, Kemp was one of the actors taken into partnership by the Burbages. His share was one-tenth, the same as Shakespeare's. At this juncture the dancer and comedian was at his zenith.

But within six months he sold his share, and presumably left the company. His was the only defection in many years among the original shareholders. It is said that he was angry over being reproved for introducing "gags" into his parts. Shakespeare may have had this controversy in mind when he made Hamlet insist that the clowns "speak no more than is set down for them," for the drama must have been in composition soon afterward.

In March 1602, when the new "Hamlet" was what everybody talked about at supper parties, Kemp, instead of being in the cast, was borrowing twenty shillings of Philip Henslowe. Later that year, he connected himself with the Earl of Worcester's men. He died in obscurity sometime before 1609. The funny man's epilogue was tragic.

Little is known about the rôles played by several of Shakespeare's closest associates. John Heminges is reputed to have been the original Falstaff. He stuttered, and this probably restricted his work to comic parts. Serving as the "book-keeper" of the company, which may have meant that he was the stage manager, his name appears often on the records of those concerned in performances at Court. He was a partner, or "householder," in both the Globe and the Blackfriars theatres. Henry Condell joined him in collecting the First Folio of Shakespeare's plays.

Augustine Phillips' standing as an actor brought him articled pupils. (New players got their training by apprenticing themselves to established performers.) Phillips died in 1605, and in his will he remembered all the members of the company, leaving Shakespeare a thirty-shilling gold-piece and various sums to others.

Besides its small group of sharers, the company had hired members. One of them, Richard Cowley, is said to have been the first Verges. John Lowen played Henry VIII, but he may not have been the original portrayer.

Who did the women and girls? Presumably, younger members of the troupe. They began with children's rôles. Then, as they grew to be ten, twelve or fourteen, they were graduated into girls' parts. Later still, those who were too big and clumsy were soon playing men. Thus, in the routine training of Burbage and other distinguished players, they served their turns as heroines. Heroines being important, it is probable that a good deal of pains was taken long ago, in training talented boys for this work. Their characterizations, though they had drawbacks, could not have been as wooden and insensitive as we smugly suppose.

There were performers of note outside the Globe organization. First among them was Edward Alleyn, actor-

manager of the Lord Admiral's men. Of about the same
age as Shakespeare and Richard Burbage, he was born in
London and "bred an actor." His fame in heroic parts
began early, his style seeming to have been of the robust
sort. He created the title role in Marlowe's "Tambur-
laine," and Orlando Furioso was another of his characters.
Some of his prompt books and property plots are extant,
including at least one part from which he studied. The
stage directions are set down in Latin.

Alleyn acquired a big country estate at Dulwich. He
retired from playing in 1604. In 1614, being childless,
he founded the College of God's Gift, at Dulwich. It
has since been reorganized as Dulwich College, and its
graduates are proud to call themselves "old Alleynians."
One of them is Leslie Howard.

But greatest of all actors in the days of Elizabeth and
James I, was Richard Burbage. There are various reasons for believing him to have had rare gifts, but the most
convincing is this: he played Shakespeare's transcendent
parts, Hamlet, Othello, Richard III, Macbeth, and others,
and he played them with the author looking on.

If he had been wretched in them Shakespeare would
have contrived to shift those rôles to someone else, for
authors are authors. That never happened, however.
From the time when Burbage first electrified his hearers
with Richard III's cry, "A horse, a horse! My kingdom
for a horse," it was for this player that Shakespeare wrote
his most powerful delineations.

This might, to be sure, have been simply because nobody better was available. Still, if the playwright had
merely gritted his teeth and endured the things Burbage
did, would he have stayed a life-long friend of Burbage?
Dramatists scarcely show such regard for actors who dis-

tort their creations. So there must have been artistic
sympathy between the two men.

Richard Burbage was three years younger than Shakespeare, but his connection with the theatre started sooner.
He was already acting as a youth when the outsider from
Stratford came to London. Their acquaintance must
have begun early. The only extant anecdote involving
the two men states that once, while Burbage was playing
Richard III, he had accepted the invitation of a lady in
the audience to come to her house after the performance.
Shakespeare, getting wind of it, contrived to be there in
advance. When Burbage arrived, the dramatist welcomed him with the jest that William the Conqueror came
before Richard III. The last few years of Shakespeare's
life were spent mostly in Stratford, but this friend was
one of those he remembered in his will. A few months
later, Burbage named an infant son for him.

In Burbage, environment and heredity converged to
the making of a great actor. His father was not only a
player of standing, but a person of vision, energy, and
originality. His mother's people were said to have been
performers, also.

The boy grew up in the theatre at the time of its
awakening vitality. He was the child of his era. Then,
just as his talents for the stage were maturing, he came into
close touch with a man who was writing parts that needed
great acting, parts far richer in reality and humanity than
any Burbage had known hitherto.

How could he have failed to be stirred by them?
"What a piece of work is man! how noble in reason! how
infinite in faculty! in form and moving how express and
admirable! in action how like an angel! in apprehension
how like a god! the beauty of the world! the paragon of

animals!   And yet, to me, what is this quintessence of dust?"   Lines like these come to us worn with usage, but when Burbage first looked at them, they were new. They had never been said until he said them.   As time went on, there must have been a growing confidence between author and player, each calling out powers in the other.

It was Burbage's habit, wrote an early chronicler, to transform himself into his part, "so putting off himself with his Cloathes, as he never (not so much as in the Tyring-house) assum'd himself again until the play was done."   In a scene where he might be a mere listener, he did not lose the illusion of reality.   "Even then, he was an excellent Actor still, never falling in his part when he had done speaking, but with his looks and gestures maintaining it still to the heighth."

Richard Burbage died of a stroke in 1619, at the height of his fame, having given "35 years paines" to his calling.

Expressions of grief at his loss were plentiful in the verse of the day.   Thomas Middleton wrote lines "On the death of that great Master in his art and quality, painting and playing, R. Burbage."   (Besides being an actor, he was a painter of considerable ability.)

The Earl of Pembroke penned a letter one evening, and in it he said, "My Lord of Lenox made a great supper to the French Embassador this night here, and even now all the company are at the play, which I being tender-hearted, could not endure to see so soon after the loss of my old acquaintance Burbadge."

With Burbage's passing, a twilight of the gods began to fall upon the English theatre, although its shadow was not at once apparent to contemporaries.   Shakespeare had died three years before, but not until his work was finished. That triumphant, rushing impetus which had made his era was spent.

> . . . the bright day is done,
> And we are for the dark.

England's spirit was changing. Young eager men were caught up in the Puritan movement, just as their predecessors had been swept into the playhouses. Four years after Shakespeare's death and a year after Burbage's, the Pilgrims sailed on the *Mayflower*.

At the Globe and Blackfriars theatres able players succeeded to the rôles that had been created by the original members of the Burbage company. But in 1642, with the Civil War, all theatres were closed by decree, and in 1644 the Globe was torn down. The actors' tragic protest at losing both art and livelihood went unheeded.

They scattered, many of them serving in the King's army. No plays were acted in England for a space of eighteen years, save for occasional surreptitious performances. The dark had come.

3.

The Ways of Betterton and Others

"HOW shall I show you Betterton?" wrote Colley Cibber. Thomas Betterton began his career in 1660, the year in which London playhouses reopened after long disuse, and he was still at the height of his fame in 1690 when young Cibber entered the theatre.

"You have seen a *Hamlet*, perhaps, who, on the first Appearance of his Father's Spirit, has thrown himself into all the straining Vociferation requisite to express Rage and Fury, and the House has thunder'd applause; though the mis-guided Actor was all the while (as Shakespeare terms it) tearing a passion into Rags." Betterton's playing of the scene was not done in that florid style. It began with a breathless silence. "Then, rising slowly to a solemn, trembling Voice, he made the Ghost equally terrible to the Spectator as to himself! and the boldness of his Expostulation was still govern'd by Decency, manly, but not braving."

Samuel Pepys saw Betterton in "Hamlet" as early as August 1661, and commented in his diary, "Above all, Betterton did the Prince's part beyond imagination." The actor, then twenty-six, had been on the stage little more than a year. Seven years later, Pepys was still impressed. He wrote, "To the Duke of York's Playhouse, and saw *Hamlet*, which we have not seen this year before, or more; and mightily pleased with it; but, above all, with Betterton, the best part, I believe, that ever man acted."

The Prince of Denmark was only one of a long list of rôles played by this man in the fifty years he gave to the theatre. In "Romeo and Juliet" he did Mercutio; he was Sir Toby Belch in "Twelfth Night," and Brutus in "Julius Caesar." He did King Lear, Macbeth, Othello, Henry VIII, and Falstaff. He was also an actor of contemporary plays, originating many famous characters in Restoration comedies, among them Lord Bellamy in Shadwell's "Bury Fair," Sir John Brute in Vanbrugh's "The Provok'd Wife," Valentine in Congreve's "Love for Love," and Mirabell in that author's "The Way of the World."

"He never prostituted his power to the low ambition of a false applause," said Cibber. That was a temptation to which many players yielded, for audiences were given to resounding handclaps. A trick of voice or gesture would set them off.

> I have heard him say, he never thought any kind of it [applause] equal to an attentive silence; that there were many ways of deceiving an audience into a loud one, but to keep them hush'd and quiet, was an applause that only truth and merit could arrive at . . .

Yet if Betterton were to appear in one of our theatres, his playing would scarcely be to the taste of a modern audience. There would be too much facial expression, and a trend toward recitation, though he was by no means a recitationist. He was first of all a portrayer of character. He "kept his Passion under, and shewed it most (as Fume smoaks most, when stifled)," observed

Anthony Aston. Betterton used restraint, but he used less of it than modern actors do.

That was because he had to meet the requirements of playhouses of his time. Stages had deep platforms built out in front of the proscenium arch and were lighted with candles, very badly. A flicker of expression, the slight reaching out of a hand—which can tell so much on the screen or in the theatre now—would have been lost to Betterton's spectators. Sound carried poorly in those theatres—often remodeled from indoor tennis courts, and thus having long narrow auditoriums. So voices had to be resonant.

Besides, Restoration audiences bestowed only about half of their attention on the drama. They came to gossip, to push their love affairs, and to quarrel, all of which they did while the play went on. They were also privileged to sit on the stage. Despite these distractions, "Betterton, from the Time he was dress'd, to the End of the Play, kept his Mind in the same Temperament and Adaptness, as the present Character requir'd," stated Aston.

This witness was himself a player and a minute observer. Highly as he thought of Betterton, it was not for his looks:

> Mr. Betterton . . . laboured under an ill figure, being clumsily made, having a great head, a short thick neck, stooped shoulders, and bad fat short arms, which he rarely lifted higher than his stomach . . .

For all that, Betterton could seize and hold attention from the instant he entered a scene. He was "a superlative good actor," according to Aston. "If I was to write of him all Day, I should still remember fresh Matter in his Behalf."

Betterton's performances were not without imperfections. He was among the players who were uncertain of their lines in March 1662, when Pepys saw "Romeo and Juliet." "I am resolved to go no more to see the first time of acting, for they were all of them out more or less," he set down. On another occasion, he was annoyed at Betterton and Harris for laughing uncontrollably at a mistake in a scene.

Forgetting lines was excusable in these actors, who knew nothing of the careful rehearsing a company is put through today. They changed their bills frequently. Three successive presentations of a drama meant approval; ten or twelve, an exceptional hit.

The life of this greatest of Restoration players centered in his work. He might have been a jolly good fellow, attending parties at the artists' studios—like Harris, who played Romeo—but he was apparently too busy. Besides acting steadily, he wrote several comedies; and as he grew older he directed productions in which he had the leading rôles.

His last appearance was on April 25, 1710, in "The Maid's Tragedy." He was then seventy-five. For several days, he had suffered severely with gout, but he managed to go on for the performance by wearing slippers. Across the stage in those slippers, limped the man who had been Valentine in "Love for Love," Hamlet, Othello, and Solyman the Magnificent. There was an indignity in his plight that his fellows, who were fond of old Thomas, conspired not to notice.

But the exertion he made drove the gout to his head, according to medical ideas of the time. He died three

THOMAS BETTERTON

The greatest actor of the Restoration played from
1660 to 1710. The engraving was made from a painting by Sir Godfrey Kneller.

days later, and was buried in the cloisters of Westminster Abbey.

Sir Richard Steele, attending the interment, thought of the rôles he had seen played by his old friend—Othello, in particular. Steele remembered Othello's agony as he questioned Desdemona about the handkerchief, his wrenching struggle between jealousy and tenderness. "Whoever reads in his closet this admirable scene, will find that he cannot, except he have as warm an imagination as Shakespeare himself, find any but dry, incoherent, and broken sentences." Dry, broken sentences were out of fashion in 1710. "But a reader that has seen Betterton act it, observes there could not be a word added; that longer speech had been unnatural, nay impossible, in Othello's circumstances."

To see how Betterton became an actor, it is necessary to look at certain events which began in 1660, when the Commonwealth ended. For something happened then in England that has never happened since. Acting had to commence all over again.

If every theatre, every motion picture house, and every film studio in the United States had been closed in 1920 and were only now on the point of reopening, our situation would be somewhat parallel. Where would our actors come from? We would have to turn to those who played before 1920 and to a generation of young folk who had never seen any acting. That was what theatrical companies did in 1660.

Early that February, General Monck entered London, and this was a step toward the return of Charles II. Oliver Cromwell was dead. Having lived under a dictator, the English were in the mood to prefer a King.

So London was in immense excitement. Within a month, Pepys was drinking the King's health, although Cromwell's son remained nominally Lord Protector.

And the ferment must have seethed mightily among the handful of former actors in town. After eighteen years, none of them was as young as he had once been, and they had had to skulk around shabbily enough in the long interval. It was these men who, before the Merry Monarch was yet back from the Continent, were applying for licenses to put on plays. The theatre does not die easily.

First to get a company together was John Rhodes, a printer and bookseller, long ago wardrobe keeper at the Blackfriars, the winter playhouse of the Globe company. The Blackfriars theatre had been demolished, and Rhodes' performances were given at the Cockpit in Drury Lane.

Among his actors was Thomas Betterton, then twenty-five and new to the stage. Betterton was the son of an under-cook to Charles I. The boy was seven when playhouses were closed, and it is not unlikely that young Thomas had seen plays in his childhood, for the King had been patron of the Globe-Blackfriars company, and interest in it probably seeped all through the royal household. But if any such early impress was left on Betterton, he never said so. He seems to have spent little time talking about himself.

His family had given him the rudiments of a genteel education, intending to place him well in life. But owing to the Civil War, the best the father could do was to apprentice his son to a bookseller. This brought the studious youth into touch with John Rhodes.

Rhodes is a picturesque figure, emerging for a few months' activity in London in 1660 and thereafter returning to obscurity. He served as a focus of theatrical reinfection, for germs of ideas incubate and are passed along as unobtrusively as are other germs.

He must have talked often with Tom Betterton about old days at the Blackfriars, perhaps discovering a latent enthusiasm in his listener. At any rate, here is the probable source of whatever the young man knew about acting.

If Betterton were Rhodes' only protégé destined to make a record in the Restoration theatre, this theory would be merely a fancy. But Edward Kynaston was Betterton's fellow apprentice, and he, too, became famous. Together they speak for Rhodes. Perhaps he read plays with them in secret, firing their imaginations with accounts of old actors. Rhodes drew about him other youths of like tastes, for two more men who served long and creditably on the stage, James Nokes and Cave Underhill, started in his company. As soon as it was possible to get a license, Rhodes came forward with a whole group of young men ready to act.

His was not the only theatrical organization. Two more were quickly formed. One at the Red Bull in St. John's Street was made up of men who had been young players before the Civil War and who were now anywhere from thirty-five to forty-five years old.

Among them was Charles Hart, said to be Shakespeare's grand-nephew, grandson of the poet's sister, Joan. Hart's acting career had begun in his boyhood, when he was apprentice to Richard Robinson at the Blackfriars and Robinson was one of Shakespeare's associates listed in the First Folio.

Nicholas Burt was another player at the Red Bull. He had been trained by John Shancke, also on the First Folio list. Still another was Major Michael Mohun who, before he won his military title, had played at the Cockpit. One more was Walter Clun, reputedly the natural son of Ben Jonson, and formerly an actor of girls' parts.

The third of these pioneer companies was under the direction of William Beeston. He was the son of Christopher Beeston, who had had a minor connection with the Globe company while Shakespeare was in it.

Thus the Restoration stage drew on the past. Each of these early organizations was linked in some way to the great days of the theatre, which were now scarcely more than a fable.

Charles II entered London on May 29, 1660—"all things very gallant and joyful." Soon he was living at the Palace of Whitehall, supping late, being most affable, and beginning to notice Lady Castlemaine who was then merely Mrs. Palmer.

With the monarchy re-established, theatrical affairs looked up. Men of far more influence than Rhodes or Beeston were about to launch themselves as managers. Before long there was a realignment into two groups which were to remain notable and opposing forces for many a year.

These two companies were the King's and the Duke of York's, and they both started in November, 1660. Two men with standing at Court became the respective managers.

The organizer of the King's players was Thomas Killigrew, whom Pepys met on board the ship which brought the new monarch back from exile. "A merry droll, but a gentleman of great esteem with the King, who told us many merry stories." He came of good family, was page of honor to Charles I, and had remained loyal to Charles II.

Killigrew picked his company chiefly from players trained before the Commonwealth. Being close to the King, he probably had first choice and felt that he was getting better people because they were more experienced. Among them were Mohun, Hart, Burt, and Clun. There was also John Lacy, a comedian and dancing master. To them Killigrew added young Edward Kynaston, Rhodes' discovery.

The Duke's company was formed by Sir William Davenant who soon proved himself the Belasco of that time. He drew on Rhodes' group of new actors. At the head of his list stood Thomas Betterton. An addition was Harris, a painter as well as an actor, afterward praised for his Cardinal Wolsey, Romeo and Sir Andrew Aguecheek. Others included James Nokes and Cave Underhill.

Davenant was Shakespeare's godson. In his childhood he had known his godfather, and this contact with so great a personality seems to have shaped his life.

The boy was ten when Shakespeare died. At eleven he wrote "an ode in remembrance of Master William Shakespeare." His admiration carried him so far that in later years he encouraged rumors, probably untrue, that he was the famous man's illegitimate son. Sir William lacked neither vanity nor a sense of advertising.

His father was John Davenant, an Oxford innkeeper, under whose roof Shakespeare often lodged on trips between London and Stratford. John Davenant was "a lover of plays and play makers." He and his wife had five sons whom they educated well. William was the second.

Young William could scarcely have attended performances at the Globe or Blackfriars while his godfather was living. But as a youth he went to those playhouses, where dramas were still done as they were when Shakespeare appeared in them. If the young man never beheld Burbage's Hamlet, he saw Burbage's immediate successor, Taylor, and Taylor, it is recorded, "acted Hamlet incomparably well." Davenant also saw Henry VIII done by John Lowen, who "had his instructions from Mr. Shakespeare himself."

Davenant turned early to playwriting, became a dramatist of standing, and was made poet laureate in 1637, after the death of Ben Jonson. In 1639 he was given a patent to direct a playhouse, but the Civil War seemingly put an end to his theatrical ambitions.

Going into the King's army, he was knighted for bravery. Shortly after 1650, he was a political prisoner and might not have got out alive if the poet Milton had not interceded for him.

By 1656 he had come to the surface again, and he was far from relinquishing his passion for the theatre. He hit upon a device which did excellent service in the United States in the nineteenth century, and which survives in the opera house still standing in many a small town. The words "play" and "theatre" being frowned on under Cromwell, Davenant decided to present entertainment in the guise of "opera." (The famous Boston Museum, Wood's Museum in New York, and Barnum's Museum in New York were similar arrangements for getting people inside a theatre without their having to acknowledge it.)

So Sir William wrote, published, and produced a play set to music, in 1656. The authorities offering no interference, he continued to present similar attractions.

He entitled his earliest English opera "The Siege of

Rhodes. Made a Representation by the Art of Prospective in Scenes, and the Story sung in Recitative Musick." This is generally agreed to have been the first use of movable scenery in England, outside of performances at Court. The heroine's part was sung by a Mrs. Coleman, and she was thus the first woman to appear in a professional production on the English stage. However, her lines were sung, not spoken. Actresses were introduced in drama very early in the Restoration.

This, then, outlines Sir William Davenant's life up to his inauguration of the Duke's company. Under patronage of the Duke of York—later, James II—the impressario steered his enterprise straight to success.

He had a showman's instinct. Besides his resourcefulness in supplying opera, there are other signs. When his own play, "Love and Honour," was put on, he achieved a stroke that modern publicity men might envy. For the King lent his coronation suit to Betterton who wore it in the part of Prince Alvaro, and Henry Harris, as Prince Prospero, appeared in the Duke of York's costume. Davenant introduced many mechanical contrivances to the stage and he fostered a craze for transformation scenes. He re-wrote the "Macbeth" in which Betterton acted, to accommodate a ballet and flying witches.

The theatre which this manager helped to re-establish differed greatly from Shakespeare's theatre; no longer was it a roofless enclosure where apprentices and "maisterless men" could drop in. It became a luxury business patronized largely by the Court, the smart set, and the disreputable riff-raff that hung on the edges of these circles.

Davenant lived only eight years after the rebirth of the stage, but that was long enough for him to transmit his touch with the past to actors of this new age. His recollections of the old players, Taylor and Lowen, were helpful to Betterton when the latter did "Hamlet" and "Henry VIII." It was Davenant's influence that made Betterton a student of Shakespeare.

What sort of acting was done by women of the Restoration theatre?

On December 8, 1660, when Killigrew's company presented "Othello," a woman was cast as Desdemona. She is said to have been Mrs. Hughes, Prince Rupert's mistress. A special prologue was recited, prophesying that, as men between forty and fifty had been playing young girls, this innovation would prove welcome. It did. Women quickly became popular in plays.

In the short interval before they had completely superseded men, Charles II went to the theatre to see "Hamlet," but the performance was late in starting. So the monarch sent the Earl of Rochester behind the scenes to ask the reason. "The Queen has not quite shaved," Rochester reported. "Odsfish!" said King Charles. "I beg her Majesty's pardon."

But within a year or two, the English stage was abundantly provided with actresses. Some of them had natural facility, youth, and charm—and most of them were not reputable. They often left the theatre as rapidly as they had entered it, retiring under the protection of various noblemen. When Pepys jotted down the fact that a certain actress had quit the stage "to be kept by somebody," he added, "which I am glad of, she being a very bad actor." On the average, these women probably bothered their heads very little about skill at playing.

There was one notable exception. This was Mary

Saunderson, who married Betterton. She was the first great English actress, and a person of the highest character.

From the start, she must have been in love with her work and presumably with Betterton. These two pre-occupations, so fortunately linked, enriched her life. She had some thirty years of distinction in her profession, and forty-seven years of happy marriage. Here is a tale of mutual constancy that scarcely seems to fit the playhouses of the Merry Monarch's era; yet they were its setting.

Mary Saunderson was one of four young women whom Davenant engaged when he decided to take actresses into his company, presumably in the spring of 1661. She and Thomas Betterton may have met first at rehearsals of "The Siege of Rhodes," which the author-manager expanded and used as his initial attraction when he opened the Duke's Theatre in Lincoln's Inn Fields.

Betterton played Solyman the Magnificent, and the young actress, Ianthe. They were married at Christmas time, 1662. From then on, she appeared in casts as Mrs. Betterton. Pepys thought highly of her as a player but he never mentioned her looks. The presumption is that she was not strikingly pretty.

She was the first woman to do Juliet, Ophelia, Queen Katharine in "Henry VIII," and Lady Macbeth. She had to play them with inadequate rehearsals, and in the midst of appearing in other attractions. All this might have made her a dramatic hack, but apparently the heavy demands fed her talent. Colley Cibber considered her an "original master," taking her lights and shades from life.

That she put imaginative power into her work is shown by what he wrote of her, having seen her when she was on the verge of retirement:

Mrs. Betterton, though far advanced in years, was so great a mistress of nature that even Mrs. Barry, who acted Lady Macbeth after her, could not in that Part, with all her superior strength and melody of her voice, throw out those quick and careless strokes of terror from the disorder of a guilty mind. . . . Time could not impair her skill, though he had brought her person to decay.

This suggests extreme decrepitude, and probably Mrs. Betterton looked decrepit to young Master Colley in 1690. However, she was then about fifty-three, and she lived more than twenty years longer. After she had withdrawn from the stage she coached younger actresses.

Nell Gywnn was one of Mrs. Betterton's contemporaries. In 1665, when Nell was fifteen or sixteen, she made her appearance with his Majesty's company at Drury Lane, where she was introduced by one of its leading members. This was Charles Hart, her lover.

Nell had a gift for comedy. Hart saw it and he trained her. She did him credit in hoydenish parts, giving them a captivating zest; but she had her limitations. In serious rôles, she was hopeless.

Pepys was carried away by her comedy. After seeing her in "The Maiden Queen," he observed:

So great performance of a comical part was never, I believe, in the world before as Nell do this, both as a mad girle, then most of all when she comes in like a young gallant; and hath the motions and carriage of a spark the most that ever I saw any man have. It makes me, I confess, admire her.

Yet his good sense told him that she played tragedy "most basely." This puzzled him. Once having enjoyed a merry impersonation, he wrote, "which makes it a miracle to me to think how ill she do any serious part . . . like a fool or a changeling."

Like a fool or a changeling—the phrase brings Nell before one's eyes, stiff and dazed. Tragedy was a department of life which she could not, and would not, comprehend. She was no longer anything real, but just an inept person, trying to conform to an outward pattern.

Within two years of her début, she angered Hart by going off to Epsom for the summer with Lord Buckhurst. But Buckhurst left her, and she returned to Drury Lane where she continued to act with Hart. A few months later she was attracting the attention of the King. Her devotion to him was sincere until her death at thirty-seven, three years after his demise. "Let not poor Nelly starve," he begged in his last hours. She had two sons by him, the older being the Duke of St. Albans.

Mrs. Barry, the successor to Mrs. Betterton as Lady Macbeth, began her career in the theatre at about the time Nell Gwynn was ending hers. That was in 1673. A far greater actress, Elizabeth Barry had none of that quick, ready assurance.

She was dismissed at the end of her first year's work. But Lady Davenant, who had brought her up, had her reinstated in the company. Several of its members thought she would never make an actress—so why bother with her? She couldn't dance and she hadn't a very good ear. That meant that she could not readily imitate a spoken intonation at rehearsals.

But what Mrs. Barry did possess, said Cibber, was "a good understanding," and this eventually carried her far beyond the range of individuals who were more facile. Her power of pathos was great. In the flowery language

of John Downes, the prompter, she could draw tears from
the auditory.

> Her Face somewhat preceded her Actions, as the
> latter did her Words [Anthony Aston recalled]
> . . . her Face ever expressing the Passions; not like
> Actresses of late Times, who are afraid less they
> should crack the Cerum, White-Wash or other
> Cosmetic trowl'd on.
> And yet this fine Creature was not handsome, her
> Mouth op'ning most on the Right Side, which she
> strove to draw t'other Way. . . . Mrs. Barry was
> middle-siz'd, had darkish Hair, light Eyes and was
> indifferently plump.

Betterton and Mrs. Barry liked to act together. He
said she often saved a very dull play.

In private life, so some of her disgruntled suitors
insisted, the money she made by her charms was of para-
mount importance to her. But there must have been
integrity somewhere in her character, for her acting had
it. She died in 1713 of the bite of her lap dog. In her
delirium, she recited blank verse.

Nance Oldfield was sixteen in 1699, when she entered
the Theatre Royal. Colley Cibber, who was then one
of the managers, thought little of her. In 1703, an older
actress being ill, her part fell to the girl. Cibber did not
like that, for the rôle was opposite his.

He made himself as unhelpful as possible at the rehearsal (there seems to have been only one), thinking
that the young woman's performance would be bad,
anyway. But when the time for the play came, he recorded the "amazement that her unexpected performance
awaked me to; so forward and sudden a step into nature
I had never seen; and what made her performance more

valuable was, that I knew it proceeded from her own understanding, untaught, unassisted by any more experienced actor."

An old kindergarten device for drawing pictures was a piece of cardboard with slits cut in it. The child laid it down on a sheet of paper and made marks through these openings. Then he removed the cardboard and beheld on the paper a fairly recognizable representation of a dog or a tree.

Among records of the Restoration theatre there are only slits through which one may catch glimpses, now and then, of some performer's methods. By penciling them in, however unrelated they seem, we must hope to get outlines of what acting then was.

Edward Kynaston was a new, young actor when Betterton was new and young. Like Betterton, he was John Rhodes' find. Like Betterton, also, Kynaston was still playing many decades later.

There was something special about him, too. He adapted himself to one of the greatest changes that ever came about on the English stage—the introduction of women. He was at first a player of young girls, making his start as "the loveliest lady that ever I saw," according to Pepys. Kynaston's popularity was nicely under way when women stepped in; and if he had possessed nothing beyond a knack for female impersonation, that would have been the end of him as a performer. But he began at once to astound audiences with protean feats, appearing in several women's and men's rôles in a single piece.

Soon he left that behind, also, and emerged as a delineator of character. In his maturity, he was notable for his power of saying lines as though he had just thought of them. As Henry IV, "every sentiment came from him as if it had been his own, as if he had himself, that instant, conceived it, as if he had lost the player and were the real king impersonated."

In those witty, if indecent, comedies of high life which epitomize the Restoration, Kynaston could repeat bon mots as if he were extemporizing, and he never laughed at his own jokes. Moreover, he always treated other characters as if they were real people. At that time, it was not unusual for important actors to elbow humbler members of the cast out of the way, even though the minor player might be impersonating a duke while the elbower enacted a mere commoner. Kynaston scorned such tactics, and was content to surpass "in true and masterly touches of nature."

Charles Hart's work was excellent in comedy. Among many such performances, he spoke the prologue and had a leading part, in 1672, in "The Country Wife," a play which was revived in New York, with Ruth Gordon, in 1936-37. Hart was also considered to do fine heroic acting; people referred to the luster and dignity of his manner. There is little evidence, though, that he could stir any deep feeling in his audience. He seems to have been finished and adept, rather than inspired.

The Restoration stage owed much to him, however. For before the Commonwealth he had gone through an exacting school of the theatre in the company of the King's players, and he was never content with slovenly execution. In care and deftness, he could serve as a model to young men and women who knew nothing of the old-time training. Nell Gwynn's instant success was due, at least in part, to him.

In all the Comedies and Tragedies he was concerned [wrote John Downes] he Perform'd with
that Exactness and Perfection, that not any of his
Successors have Equall'd him.

Hart's life off the stage was a period piece. After he
had been deserted by Nell Gwynn successively for Lord
Buckhurst and King Charles, he became the consoler of
Lady Castlemain whom the sovereign had discarded.
Though Hart had the background which might have
made him a very great player—for his middle years of
ill fortune must have acquainted him with bitter struggle
and defeat—he remained to the last a technician, and a
ladies' man.

James Nokes, the comedian, had a transparent simplicity. The louder the house screamed with mirth at
some tangle he was supposed to be in, the more distressed
Nokes looked. Yet while spectators were laughing themselves weak, they were sorry for him, too. People feel
like that about Charlie Chaplin.

Cave Underhill, another comedian, was fuller of animal
spirits. "His Nose was flattish and short, and his Upper
Lip very long and thick, with a wide Mouth and short
Chin, a churlish Voice, and awkward Action (leaping
often up with both Legs at a Time, when he conceived
any Thing waggish, and afterwards hugging himself at
the Thought.)"

But old age overtook the man who would jump up and
hug himself when he felt waggish. He became a pen-
sioner of Drury Lane, for by this time the King's and
the Duke's companies had united. Emerging from retirement, he played the gravedigger in "Hamlet" at his
benefit, looking worn and disabled "as if he himself was

to have lain in the grave he was digging." That was very nearly true. He died soon after.

The pencil marks are made. What picture of Restoration acting do they form when one looks at them as a whole?

Here was a calling that had its vanities, its emotions turned on at the spigot. Some of its practicers were lazy, like a certain player who never worried about learning his lines. When he slipped up he would murmur, "Odso! I believe I am a little wrong here." And the audience would forgive him.

Rehearsals being hasty, handy methods for getting effects were often resorted to, and performers were prone to use all the reliable tricks. "Claptrap" was one of their slang terms, meaning literally any procedure to trap applause.

Yet in a profession so conducted, there were individuals who could not be satisfied with tricks and dodges. They took their examples from life. And these people generally had long careers, holding their own for many years against newcomers. Time winnowed out the indolent, the over-sensitive, the accidental successes. Those who remained did not stay through luck, but because of qualities in themselves.

Against this background, Betterton and Mrs. Bettterton stand out for the intensity of attention they fixed on their work. They had plenty of friends, but the racy doings of London allured them only mildly. They lived in a playhouse that lacked all order and discipline, yet they managed to invest their rôles with a force that came of concentration.

The Restoration rescued plays and playing from

oblivion; it introduced women performers; it made use of a curtain and changeable settings. Dim and dusty now, the theatre Betterton knew was distinctly modern. And the acting in Restoration comedies, wherein every-day manners were minutely copied, was the forerunner of playing on Broadway today.

4.

Much Ado About Declamation

BY THE time of Betterton's death in 1710, acting had begun to slip down the incline of an artistic slump, for the English stage was getting away from life. Players adopted what they called an elevation of the voice, a practice borrowed from France where, under Louis XIV, the grand manner had long been cultivated. This alternate elevation and depression of the voice produced a sort of theatrical intoning, considered the acme of elegance in tragedy and heroic verse.

The new style was in high vogue in the 1720's and 1730's, a change which Anthony Aston noted with regret. Jotting down his recollections of Betterton's contemporaries, he said of Mrs. Barry, "Neither she nor any other Actors of those Times, had any Tone in their speaking (too much, lately, in Use)."

It would be delightfully simple if, in glancing back through centuries, it were possible to trace a slow but steady progress in the skill of performers—if each generation could be seen to be a bit ahead of the preceding one. But that is not how acting has developed. It has gone through cycles, accompanied by back-washes and eddies. At one period or another, some way of playing is used by an actor of great gifts, or by a group of such actors. But they have copyists who gradually get a dimmer view of what they meant to copy; and so what started at a white heat in some individual, peters out in habits and rules. But decay fertilizes the soil for fresh growth. Somewhere another originator springs up, and that is the beginning of a new cycle.

In the thirty-one years that intervened between Betterton and Garrick, English playing was increasingly uninspired. Declamation roared while passion slept, observed Dr. Johnson. But comparatively few theatregoers of the era could detect the snores of passion because the center of the stage was so resoundingly occupied by hard-working elocutionists.

The earliest actor to gain pre-eminence in this interval was Barton Booth, who established himself by creating the title rôle of Addison's "Cato," in 1713. His acting was mannered and painstaking. Well-mouthed Booth, Alexander Pope called him, and the phrase was considered a commendation. (Barton Booth, 1681-1733, was not an ancestor of Edwin.)

"Though in the customary rounds of his business, he would condescend to some parts in comedy, he seldom appeared in any of them with much advantage," wrote Aaron Hill. Naturally, the actor was not called on to condescend very often. His skill consisted in "an adaption of his looks to his voice, by which artful imitation of nature, the variations in the sounds of his words gave propriety to every change in his countenance."

Theophilus Cibber, Colley's blackleg of a son, was so fatuous an admirer of Booth that he even liked his comedy. But no one shared this opinion. Booth's tragic manner, Theophilus described thus: "His Voice was raised or sunk, extended or contracted, swelled or softened, rapid or slow, as the Sense and Spirit of the Author . . . required; and his articulation was so excellent he was heard to the farthest Part of the Theatre when he almost whispered." Nevertheless, this player's taste set limits beyond which he would not let his elocution carry him. "He despised a Ranter, and scorned to purchase Applause at the Expence of his Lungs. . . . When he wept, his tears broke from him perforce;—He never whindled, whined, or blubbered."

"Cato," in which Booth scored so heavily, was a stilted tragedy in verse, but all the political speeches in it were applied by the hearers to the struggle then going on between Whigs and Tories. So the drama caused a sensation, packing Drury Lane for thirty-five successive nights.

From the moment he was shown the manuscript, Booth wanted to play Cato. He had had an excellent grounding in Latin, and Roman history meant something to him. More than two hundred years later, when Philip Merivale was cast for Hannibal in "The Road to Rome," it happened that the Carthaginian general had been his special hero at school. Whether or not Cato was Booth's favorite Roman, the background of the story and its opportunities for effective declamation all appealed to him. But he concealed his eagerness, lest some other member of the company insist on taking the rôle away from him. Apparently no one saw the possibilities in it that Booth did, and when he played it he made an immense impression.

With "Cato" to his credit, he was on the crest of the wave. He was well-connected, being related to an earl, and he had a host of fashionable friends. Each evening some nobleman's chariot-and-six would be waiting at the stage door to "whip him twenty miles in three hours" to Windsor, where he would spend the next day in exalted social circles and return in time for the play that night. For fifteen years he was the most illustrious member of his profession in England.

He was Betterton's pupil, but even Booth's ardent partisans agreed that he never equalled his teacher. Perhaps this was not so much the fault of the pupil as of the time in which he lived. How could any young person avoid succumbing, just then, to the pseudo-classical spirit that had been creeping into the theatre? Everybody said it was so refined. If you didn't like it, you weren't "modern." The newer people of the stage were a bit ashamed of Shakespeare's crudities.

Prim and trim, and delicate and chaste,
A hash from Greece and France, came Modern Taste.

Barton Booth got his first enthusiasm for acting by taking part in a Latin play at Westminster School, where he was being prepared to enter one of the universities. His family had meant him for the Church, and indeed, his earliest instructions in histrionics were given him by his schoolmaster, a doctor of divinity famous for his oratory in the pulpit.

Instead of going to college, young Barton ran away and joined a strolling theatrical troupe. Before long he was appearing in Dublin. He returned to London in 1701 and presented himself to Betterton, who took an interest in the beginner, gave him lessons, and arranged for his London début. The veteran was then sixty-six. Doubtless Booth learned a good deal from him but it is likely that the pupil considered his teacher old-fashioned, for Betterton used none of that "tone" which was the latest thing in elegance. Booth must have been pretty sure that he was improving on his tutor.

At the height of his fame, Booth was best in majestic parts. He "thought it depreciated the dignity of a Tragedy to raise a Smile in any part of it," his reason being that he feared some of the audience might laugh in the wrong places. He was given to reciting long speeches with illustrative gestures.

> I'll bend the Bow, I'll launch the whizzing Spear,
> Bound o'er the Mountain, rush into the stream,

he would begin, and would continue for twenty lines or so, accompanying each phrase with action, while his admirers sat enraptured. They knew this was Art because they had been told so. Of course they were aware that if a person said, "I am going to walk," he did not think it necessary to act out a pantomime of donning his cloak and sword. But in the theatre, these people believed, things were different; drama was one thing and life was something else.

Another of the player's famous speeches was one which started, "When through the woods we chased the foaming Boar." It is not difficult to guess that this was a description of a hunt, leading up to a climax which brought a deafening outburst of applause. Such narratives were popular in the theatre for many generations. To acting, they were what a cadenza is to a violin concerto. Everything stopped while the performer showed what he could do.

Anyone who wants to know what they sounded like need only listen to current sports on the radio. "Zansky's got the ball, folks! No, he . . . Yes, he's got it! He's off. Watch him, folks! The twenty yard line!

The fifteen! The ten! Oh boy, what a runner *that* baby is!" While the vocabulary may not be classic, the intention is the same as was Barton Booth's when he chased the foaming boar—to give listeners a sense of excitement.

Booth was a meticulous worker who loved his calling and said a whole lifetime was not long enough to practice it. He studied the poses of classic sculpture, and incorporated them in his acting. After 1728 he ceased to play, for he was a sick man beset with an incurable jaundice. He died within a few years.

Booth's successor was James Quin, a heavy tragedian, a wonderfully good Falstaff, and a picturesque figure in private life. Fond of good eating and drinking, he would wake in the morning to inquire whether his favorite fish were in the market that day. If his servant said no, he turned over and went back to sleep. It was Quin who wished that his throat were the arch of Westminster Bridge, with the Thames running claret.

In tragic ability, he ranked further below Booth than the latter did below Betterton—which shows the downward trend of the period. Immense dignity and strong lungs were Quin's stand-bys. He had a way of "heaving up his words" and would stamp as he spoke, to give added emphasis. He was twelve years Booth's junior.

Playing Cato after Booth, Quin made a less powerful effect. Where Booth got "from forty-eight to fifty thundering claps," Quin could raise only a half a dozen. Still, it is recorded that his first appearance in the rôle won hearty approval. After his line, "Thanks to the gods, my boy has done his duty!" the audience shouted, "Booth outdone!"

Here is Quin on another occasion:

Quin presented himself, upon the rising of the curtain, in a green velvet coat, embroidered down the seams, an enormous full-bottomed periwig, rolled stockings, and high-heeled, square-toed shoes. . . . With a deep, full tone, accompanied by a sawing kind of gesture, which had more of the senate than of the stage in it, he rolled out his heroics with an air of dignified indifference . . .

But this manner fell away from him when he played Falstaff. At once he turned human. He *was* Sir John, glowing and swaggering with gusto, for Quin had a rich vein of humor. Who could take more pride than he in Falstaff's round belly with fat capon lined? They two were brothers under the padding.

While he was still a struggling young actor, he had asked the manager to let him play this rôle. He was sure he could do it. The manager needed someone, but he preferred to abandon his plan of putting on "The Merry Wives of Windsor," so convinced was he that he could not find anyone to impersonate the fat knight. Two years later, however, Quin got his chance in the part, and made a hit. Falstaff was not the only comedy success of his career, but it was his greatest. The convincingness of it must have sprung from the intensity of interest he felt for the part. He and Falstaff understood each other.

The tree of life is green. Quin's work in comedy seems to have been his own product, while his tragic manner was a pattern that he superimposed upon himself. In everyday affairs, he was witty and endowed with stout common sense. But he never turned his humor or his good judgment on the heroic conventions of the stage; those accepted methods he took for granted.

His repartee was famous. Once when he was seriously

ill, the doctors stood by, wondering how they could make the patient sweat. He looked up at them and remarked, "Only send in your bills, and it's done."

Although he was hot tempered, overbearing, and far from strait-laced, he was honorable in every business dealing, and most generous to members of his profession. A young actor who was out of work and scarcely had a shirt to his back, was surprised to receive a call one morning from James Quin. The latter came bringing him a new suit of clothes, and word to report at once for rehearsal, for the old player had been using his influence. Grateful but not beyond asking for more, the youth suggested that he would need a little cash till his first pay day. Quin grew gruff. "Nay, I have done all I can for you; but as for money, Dick, you must put your hand in your own pocket." He had slipped a ten-pound note into it.

With Garrick's rise came Quin's downfall, for little David undermined the grandiloquent technique that Quin believed in. At first the established actor regarded Garrick with contempt. "If the young fellow is right, I and the rest of the players have been all wrong," he said— and he felt that he had put the newcomer in his place. But after a fight of ten years against innovations, Quin saw that he had lost. This was in 1751, and he was nearing sixty. Without complaint he retired to his home in Bath, where he lived comfortably on his income. He and Garrick grew to be very good friends.

Quin emerged twice from private life to play Falstaff. The third such invitation he declined, for he had lost two front teeth. "I will whistle Falstaff for no man," he insisted.

When he withdrew from the stage, everyone said that

the school of Betterton had been conquered by the school of Garrick. That opinion was passed along, and is still accepted as implying that Betterton and Quin acted in the same style. But this seems hard on Betterton, who had then been dead forty years. Would he have claimed Quin—and the ruck of whindlers, whiners and blubberers —as his pupils? It is doubtful. People of 1740 and 1750 knew Betterton's ideas only in debased form, just as Betterton had seen only the thinned-out second generation of descendants from the Burbage tradition.

Charles Macklin got his early impressions of the theatre during the same years when Quin was receiving his, but he turned out to be a wholly different sort of player. Temperamentally a rebel, he never accepted the rules which Quin and everybody else believed in. He was a large ungainly Irishman, possessed of originality, vitality, and unceasing restlessness. He lived to be ninety-eight— according to some calculations, still older—and when he was over eighty, he created the rôle of Sir Pertinax Mc-Sycophant in "The Man of the World," a comedy which he himself had written. Both his performance and the play were successful.

But it is best to concentrate on the first fifty years of his life, since they had a definite influence on acting in England. There have been disputes as to whether he was born in 1690 or in 1699. However, it seems reasonable to accept the later date. He did not retire from the stage till 1789, and he died in 1797.

Macklin's education was sketchy. As a child, he had shown talent for acting. He was apprenticed to a saddler in Dublin when he was fourteen but, the trade being uncongenial to him, he became a servant to students at Trinity College. Before long, he attached himself to strolling theatrical troupes, playing shabbily through Ireland and England. By 1725, he appeared in London, at the theatre in Lincoln's Inn Fields.

Already, he had his own ideas about acting, for long afterward, when he was recalling this first metropolitan attempt, he said, "I spoke so *familiar*, sir, and so little in the *hoity-toity* tone of the tragedy of that day, that the Manager told me I had better go to grass for another year or two." Which meant that poor Macklin went back to the provinces.

The hoity-toity tone of tragedy was being upheld at that time by Barton Booth, with his seemly oratory and his poses copied from Greek and Roman statues. What chance did an outsider stand, particularly an outsider who was an iconoclast, and a rough, awkward fellow? Booth was a scholar and a gentleman. Macklin was neither—but he was a genius.

So he disappeared from notice, taking his unsatisfactory acting with him. In poor companies or small towns, people had to put up with it. Continued practice doubtless wore off some of his crudities, but it never altered his notion that characters on the stage ought to behave as they do in life. Coming back to Lincoln's Inn Fields in 1730, he made a favorable impression in one of Henry Fielding's plays, and he continued for some time to do small parts. In 1733 the Drury Lane management, in a quarrel with members of the company, went out into the highways and byways to look for new talent. That brought Macklin a Drury Lane engagement which lasted, with breaks now and then, for many seasons. He was regarded merely as a dependable player.

Macklin became known all over theatrical London, and

everywhere he went he talked about his views of acting, for he never lacked assertiveness. He took pupils. He married a Miss Purvor, trained her, and made her an excellent character actress. He became acquainted with a youth named David Garrick, who longed to be a player. To him Macklin confided all his theories. The older and the younger man were often seen in long discussions, and it was through Garrick that Macklin's ideas later gained general acceptance. He himself was too harsh and pugnacious to have won people.

The instructions he gave his students reveal some of his methods. Beginners would be told to start by saying a speech as if it were a commonplace remark in everyday life. After that, force was to be added, but the casual inflections retained. The startling thing about this was that anyone, at that period, should think of uttering anything on the stage as if it were commonplace. Macklin's garden had three parallel paths a moderate distance apart. Up and down the middle one he would tramp, with a pupil walking in each of the others. Every few paces, the teacher would order them to stop and improvise conversations with each other, while he listened and commented freely. This was very different from declaiming well-memorized orations.

His criticisms were blunt, often bitter. Frequently, he would advise an aspirant to take up bricklaying. He was tender of nobody, but those who could endure his insults learned much. Those who could not, soon ceased to be pupils—and so Macklin's teaching was not very profitable.

At rehearsals he would command anybody who played a scene with him, "Look at me, sir, look at me! Keep your eyes fixed on me when I am speaking to you. Attention is always fixed." To this day, directors struggle with inexperienced players to get them to pay actual attention to what another character is saying. Preoccupied with their own lines, they are merely waiting for cues. Giving oneself up to listening is not so easy as it seems. Even in life people do not always do it.

For years in his earlier career he mulled over a daring plan to play Shylock as a serious character. It had long been accepted as comic, and Shakespeare's "Merchant of Venice" had not been presented for more than a generation. A shoddy adaptation called "The Jew of Venice" was used instead. Macklin wanted to restore Shakespeare's drama to the stage, and to break completely with prevailing impersonations of the money lender. No longer was he to be the butt of slap-stick humor, but an individual with human traits. Hath not a Jew eyes? Hath not a Jew hands? If you prick us, do we not bleed?

Macklin had acted many a season at Drury Lane before he could induce the manager to try this departure. Finally, in 1741, the project was launched and rehearsals commenced. Everybody predicted failure, but Macklin said he would stake his life on the outcome.

On the opening night, he made his entrance in something approximating Jewish dress—a long black coat, over long loose trousers. He also wore a red hat, which he understood to have been required of Hebrews in Italy. His first scenes set the key of his whole performance,

> Hath a dog money? is it possible
> A cur can lend three thousand ducats?

He had his audience with him from the start, but as the power of his impersonation grew, spectators were overwhelmed. The tragic figure of Shylock emerged, and stood before them. Macklin was terrific in the scene where the usurer, tortured by the loss of his daughter and his ducats, gets comfort out of news of Antonio's misfortunes. "What, what, what? Ill luck, ill luck?" He ran his fingers through his hair. It stood up. His heavy, seamed features were drawn with malign anguish. Every Shylock since then has owed something to the portrait Macklin outlined that night.

The manager told him, "Macklin, you were right at last." When the play was over, the actor found the greenroom crowded with critics and members of the nobility, come to congratulate him. This was the most satisfying moment of his whole life. He had waited long to taste such success, and he found it sweet. Now, more than fifteen years since he had been sent to grass because he spoke "so familiar," his ability won ungrudging recognition. He said that, though he was not worth fifty pounds that evening, he felt like a king.

Macklin's triumph as Shylock and Garrick's début as Richard III came within a few months of each other. Together, they marked the close of this age of declamation, though it would still be a few years a-dying.

How far the stage had veered away from representing life may be judged from an essay on the art of acting published by Aaron Hill at about this time. Hill, a gentleman who wrote plays and was so sincerely interested in the theatre that he lavished his private fortune on it, advocated a new and "natural" system, in contrast to the methods then prevailing. He complained bitterly of the brash volubility he heard in playhouses. He was all against the "glib, round, rolling emptiness . . . pouring out its over-measure with no meaning, from a Voice that neither touches, nor is touched by, character."

Seeing these faults, he was confident that he had worked out a technique of acting which would cure them. Of course, he conceded, a player *might* study his rôle by imagining himself to be the character—it would, indeed, be the ideal way. But Hill thought that obviously too slow and difficult. Right here he showed that he was not an actor, for he was unaware that the born actor's delight is to get himself inside the skin of his part. Aaron Hill believed his theories provided a short-cut to impersonation.

He had observed that emotions react on the muscles. There is the clenched fist, for instance, or the grin, or the dragging step. He had also noticed that it is easier to put oneself in a given state of mind, if one can assume its outward signs—the dragging feet inducing the despondent mood, and so on. From this sound psychological basis, Hill reasoned all too fast.

If every feeling has its attitude, learn what those attitudes are and apply them when necessary, he counseled. He recognized ten dramatic passions—joy, grief, fear, anger, pity, scorn, hatred, jealousy, wonder and love. They were definite, detached—not John Jones' pity or anger about something in particular, colored by the kind of person John is. They were just pity, by itself, and anger, by itself. Each of these passions had its clear characteristics, and Mr. Hill's system thus provided the actor with ten "applications" of emotion.

Application 3, for example, told how to express the passion of fear. "It is an apprehensive but unsinewed struggle, betwixt caution and despair," said the definition. The muscles were to be tense, the eyes "widely stretched, but unfixed," the mouth still and open. In Application 7, it was announced that "there is no other difference but the turn of an eye in the expression of *hatred* and *pity*."

Warming to his subject, Aaron Hill yielded to the horrid fascinations of analysis. He labeled and defined at a great rate. Jealousy had precisely two stages—first, doubtful suspicion; and second, "where jealousy extracts confirmation from appearances." Joy was to be expressed by muscles intense and a smile in the eye; anger, by muscles intense and a frown in the eye; wonder, by muscles intense and an awful alarm in the eye.

Application 10 read, "How the Passion of Love is to be express'd, by the Actor. Love is Desire kept temperate by Reverence. It is expanded softness in the heart . . . and can never be represented without a look of apprehensive Tenderness. . . . This passion cannot bear a cold, formal Emptiness, a big broad mellow Troll of smooth unanimated wordiness." Many a declaration of love in heroic verse must Hill have seen played in that manner. Therefore he admonished the actor seeking to express love elegantly, to use "an inclining look divided gracefully betwixt a tender *Fear* and a triumphant *Pleasure*." Thus, he assured his readers, every accent would confess the Passion.

No trace of this technique is visible in love scenes on the stage or screen at present. Where is the director who would dream of requesting Leslie Howard or Brian Aherne to divide an inclining look betwixt tender fear and triumphant pleasure? Such a suggestion would be like the photographer's metal brace, concealed yet clutching a sitter behind the ears. Mr. Howard and Mr. Aherne deal in character. They want to put a living human creature before the audience, and they know that this person will have his own way about expressing the Passion of Love. Whatever the way, it will follow Aaron Hill's pattern only in eschewing a cold formal Emptiness, or a big broad mellow Troll of smooth unanimated wordiness.

Hill knew the work of Booth, Quin and Macklin. It was he who counted Booth's forty-eight or fifty thundering claps in "Cato." But for all his observations, Hill never noticed that Booth's Cato, Quin's Falstaff and Macklin's Shylock were their best parts because, in each case, the actor saw something in the rôle that touched him on the quick. There was a relationship between the depth of the player's interest in the character, and his power of projecting it.

Thus a live force in acting could cut its own channels, occasionally, across all the rules of three dull decades. But this did not happen often, for it is always difficult for people to escape the ideas that surround them. Not to go down in the welter, requires uncommon keenness of vision and immense courage. Macklin had those qualities.

5.

Garrick and Siddons: Opposites

SARAH SIDDONS and David Garrick differed in background, in style, in temperament. She was staunch, but he was likeable. The daughter of strolling players and trained to the stage from childhood, she took years to reach her full stature as an artist. Garrick, who had no theatrical blood in his veins, was a born actor. He was brought up in the conservative little cathedral town of Lichfield, and yet he learned in flashes things that many performers acquire only with pain. There is no one recipe for genius.

When Garrick burst upon London in "Richard III" in October 1741, he came as a young insurgent, breaking down rigid elocutionary standards. His playing was impetuous and full of sudden shifts of feeling. He thought his speeches as he said them, making his characters living creatures:

> When three or four are on the stage with him, [said an early account] he is attentive ·to whatever is spoke, and never drops his character when he has finished a speech, by either looking contemptuously on an inferior performer, unnecessary spitting, or

84

suffering his eyes to wander through the whole circle
of spectators. . . .

He played in a style that was "easy and familiar, yet
forcible," said Thomas Davies. At first there were a few
objectors to this manner. Dry-as-dust correspondents
wrote to the new actor, pointing out what they believed
to be his errors. Garrick courteously acknowledged
these letters and filed them, but he pursued his own
course.

The part of Richard had been shrewdly selected for his
London début by the young man of twenty-five. He
was sensitive about being small, and he felt that, as the
humpbacked Gloucester, his lack of size would not be
held against him. Besides, the swift changes in Richard
—schemer, lover, hypocrite, soldier, and fallen monarch
—suited his talents.

There was the scene in which Richard, pretending to
have been interrupted at his devotions, entered with open
prayer book in hand. After the fraud had served its purpose, Garrick tossed the book aside—and the audience
broke into handclaps. This bit of "business," since used
by many performers, was his invention. It was only one
of many original touches with which he delighted spectators that evening. Next day, the *Daily Post* contained
this item:

> Last night was performed gratis the tragedy of
> "King Richard the Third," at the late theatre in
> Goodman's Fields, when the character of *Richard*
> was performed by a gentleman who never appeared
> before, whose reception was the most extraordinary
> and great that was ever known on such an occasion.

(The playhouse where this happened was unlicensed. It operated by the subterfuge of presenting a "concert" for which admissions were charged, followed with dramatic entertainment "gratis.")

Within a week or two, traffic jams were caused by the crush of coaches bringing patrons to see Garrick. His first season closed in April 1742, he having played about 160 nights and introduced himself in eighteen or nineteen parts. Some were comic, some tragic. One of the rôles was King Lear. From the start, he showed amazing truth and versatility.

His Hamlet, always among his best parts, also dated from his early career. He did it first in Dublin in the summer of 1742, after having studied it carefully. An account of his way of acting has been preserved in the correspondence of a German, Georg Christoph Lichtenberg, who visited London and was captivated by the portrayal. He wrote about it with a detail that is cinematographic.

Take the scene where Hamlet comes to meet the Ghost. The stage is dim. The hour is midnight. Horatio and Marcellus are "in uniform," while Hamlet folds his black cloak around him against the nipping air. As his companions are talking, Hamlet walks up-stage on the left, and is standing there with his back to the audience. Just then Horatio catches sight of the Ghost, at the right. "Look, my lord, it comes."

Hamlet turns, and as he does so, his arms no longer wrap around him for warmth. They loosen inadvertently, and are thrown up, wide apart and limp, as high as his head. He staggers back a few steps, his two friends catching hold of him. There is a long silence. The audi-

DAVID GARRICK

Garrick conducted the Shakespeare Jubilee at Stratford-on-Avon in 1769, and this portrait commemo-
rates the occasion.

ence is as still and breathless as Hamlet himself, sitting "as if they had been painted on the walls of the house."

Now the Ghost beckons. Without taking his eyes away from the apparition, Hamlet frees himself from Marcellus and Horatio. The Ghost begins to move and gets out of sight before Hamlet stirs. Then, a few steps at a time, with pauses between—as if the phantom, off-stage, were also moving and halting—Hamlet follows. His eyes are fixed on the Ghost, and his fear and wonder never leave him as he passes out of sight of beholders in the audience. Even then, he seems to carry them with him.

Garrick was born in 1716. His father was an impecunious captain in the British army, and his mother the daughter of a vicar choral at Lichfield cathedral. David, one of their large family, was reared in genteel penury, in proximity to the cathedral. The Garricks were shabby, but their standing admitted them to Lichfield's best society. (Samuel Johnson, a struggling young schoolmaster in town, did not move in those circles.) Letters written by the boy, Davy, to his father reveal the atmosphere of affection and humor in which he was brought up. Here were parents who dealt tenderly in an age of harsh discipline. Perhaps it was this early influence that developed Garrick's easy charm, his uncombative nature, and his life-long dependence on the liking of people around him.

When he was eleven, he got together a group of children and gave a performance of Farquhar's "The Recruiting Officer." His family tradition was against the stage; there was a vague intent to educate David for the law.

By 1738, three things had happened which determined his future. He was now living in London. An uncle of his who was an importer of wines had left him a modest legacy. Thus David and his brother Peter set themselves up as wine merchants, dealing with coffee houses patronized by theatrical people. While he hung around to get orders, David would entertain diners with imitations. He was an extraordinary mimic, and stage-struck.

However, he had too sensitive an affection for his mother to hurt her feelings by going on the stage. Before the end of 1737, Captain Garrick had died. His wife, who never ceased to grieve for him, quietly followed where he had gone in little more than a year.

David was now free to do as he chose. He became a pupil and friend of Macklin—and here is the undoubted cause of the young man's swift success. Those naturalistic ideas about acting which Macklin had developed, Garrick seized upon with an understanding that was genius. He saw the rightness of them. Like a high-speed engine, once primed, there was expansive force in his own cylinders.

Among persons whom Garrick liked to visit behind the scenes was that excellent comedian, Yates, at Goodman's Fields. One evening when Yates was to do Harlequin, he was taken ill, and Garrick substituted for him. The young man decided to test his talents further—for all his life he combined daring with caution.

In London of that day—as in New York now—as soon as hot weather came, some of the players used to migrate to summer theatres in the provinces. The proprietor of the Goodman's Fields playhouse organized a small company to go to Ipswich in the summer of 1741—and David Garrick got himself accepted as a member of the troupe. Calling himself Mr. Lyddal, he played fairly important parts throughout the Ipswich season and made a considerable stir in the town.

So the statement on the program on the night of his

London début, to the effect that he had never acted before, was just the customary announcement on such occasions. His "Richard III" was not without preparation. Before he "commenced actor" he had studied many parts and had had advice from Macklin. He had also given himself practice before audiences.

While Garrick's reputation was still new, he went through his famous love affair with Peg Woffington. She had arrived in London from Ireland in 1738—a comedienne and all-round actress of great charm, who played in an unaffected style that David liked. She was Ophelia to his Hamlet, in Dublin in the summer of 1742.

Woffington had delightful qualities—but loyalty to one lover was not in her. She would promise Garrick to discard Lord Darnley, and she would promise Darnley to see no more of David. In such matters, though, she was forgetful. Garrick asked her to name the day and marry him. They exchanged gifts and vows—but the marriage never came off.

Returning to London from Dublin, David and Peg set up housekeeping along with Macklin. Each of them paid the household bills every third week. Macklin, having a bitter quarrel with Garrick over business shortly thereafter, took cruel delight in telling of David's anguish when Peg brewed the tea too strong, in the weeks David was paying for it. The anecdote was damaging to Garrick at the time, and even to this day. Here was the first of all those little tales anent the great actor's stinginess. His boyhood had been spent in the pinch of refined poverty, and it was still close behind him when he saw Woffington's free hand with the tea. In later years his many large generosities were never reported with the gusto that kept these other stories current. People whose I. O. U.'s he tore up, generally told nobody.

When the final break came between him and Woffington, he returned all her gifts except a pair of shoe buckles which he begged to keep for remembrance. Macklin would have it that they were precious to David because they were expensive.

A few years later—in 1749—he married a jewel of a wife. She was Eva-Maria Violette, young and lovely, a ballerina who had come to England from Vienna and was a protégée of Lady Burlington. She retired from the stage, and devoted the rest of her life to being Mrs. Garrick. A charming hostess to their fashionable friends, she was also her husband's confidante in his work—understanding her Davy, and giving him that unswerving faith and affection that his temperament fed on. They had no children. He boasted that from the time of their marriage they were never separated for twenty-four hours.

Garrick's domestic tranquillity was a balm in the midst of his irritations as manager and chief actor of Drury Lane. Every author whose play he rejected, every disgruntled performer, wrote an angry letter or said cutting things. Persons who were not worth his little finger, could wound him—for he had a thin skin and a kind heart.

As the same time, he grew egregiously fond of flattery—"of praise a mere glutton." One of his contemporaries—more discerning than most—insisted that Garrick craved approval because he was never quite sure of himself.

But in spite of everything, he steered a steady course as a manager. He had not only his leading women's jealousies to contend with, but their husbands', as well. "I shall engage the best company in England if I can," he wrote Mr. Pritchard, when Mrs. Pritchard feared that Mrs. Cibber might be in the ascendant. "I shall, to the best of my ability, do justice to all. . . ." The same sort of professional plots and counterplots that are supposed to thrive in Hollywood, went on in the greenroom of Drury Lane.

Mrs. Abington gave Garrick endless annoyance, but she was unexcelled in high comedy. So, when he filed away one of her irate letters, he jotted on it, "From the worst of women"—and kept her in the company.

For Kitty Clive's comedy, the manager had high regard. She was a character actress of first rank. Quick of mind and tongue, she often gave David high words. As both of them grew older, the words grew softer, and they became good friends.

Besides bringing in natural acting, Garrick achieved another advance for the theatre. It was he who banished audiences from the stage. From Shakespeare's time onward, spectators had had seats there, often crowding the players. The battle of Bosworth Field was sometimes fought "in less space than that which is commonly allotted to a cock-match," and death scenes were acted with men-about-town grouped close to the expiring performer. In 1762, however, Garrick remodeled Drury Lane, increasing the seating capacity and limiting the audience to the front of the house. He also introduced order and strict discipline at rehearsals. Every modern company owes him a vote of thanks for making the playhouse a fit place to work in.

But with all his reforms, he never dared play Macbeth in other than the traditional uniform of a British army officer. Historically accurate costuming was still unknown.

His large, dark, piercing eyes with their darting glance, were Garrick's salient feature. A cast made from his face in later life shows these eyes drooping at the outer ends. There are also deep lines from the nose to the corners of the mouth, and the whole effect is that of a tragic mask. As a young man, he was handsome and had a neat figure. Once a lady asked Foote if the puppets at a certain exhibit were to be as large as life. "Oh no, madam. Only about the size of Garrick," answered the venomous Foote.

It flattered Garrick to be told that he could not help acting well, and never needed to take pains. But the fact is that he bestowed care on his work. During performances, to be sure, he did everything with such ease that the enraged Mrs. Clive declared, "That man could act a gridiron." However, on the days he was to play, he shut himself up at home, ate lightly, and saw no one. It was then that he thought his way into his parts, and got his attention so fixed upon them that minor distractions at the theatre made no difference.

> Garrick, Madam, was no declaimer, [said Dr. Johnson]. There was not one of his scene-shifters who could not have spoken "To be, or not to be," better than he did. . . . A true conception of character, and natural expression of it, were his distinguished excellencies.

There was a deaf-mute miniature painter named Shireff who took peculiar pleasure in going to the theatre to see Garrick, for he explained that this actor's face was "language."

> The great art of David Garrick consists in . . . putting himself in the situation of the person he is

to represent, [wrote Friedrich Grimm]. He ceases
to be Garrick, and becomes the person he is concerned with. . . . All the changes that are seen
working in him proceed from the way he is affected
within himself; he never passes beyond truth, and he
knows that strange secret of making himself effective
without any other help than that of passion.

The man who understood these mysteries was frequently kind to the rawest beginner. A youth, Jack Bannister, supplied a racy account of a scene in Garrick's
dressing room. Its distinguished occupant was shaving:

> *Garrick:* Eh! Well—what, young man, so, eh?
> So you are still for the stage? Well, how—what
> character do you—should you like to—eh?
> *Bannister:* I should like to attempt Hamlet, sir.
> *Garrick:* Eh! What? Hamlet, the Dane! Zounds,
> that's bold. Have you studied the part?

Garrick then suggested that his visitor give him a
speech, and added, "Don't mind my shaving." Holding
himself by the nose to facilitate the operation, he nevertheless listened critically, until he could endure the recital
no longer. Brandishing his razor, and with his face half
lathered, he rushed at the aspirant crying, "Yaw, waw,
waw!" Then, when he had finished shaving and put on
his wig, he remarked, "Come, young man, let's see now
what we can do." Whereupon he spoke the speech that
Bannister had done so badly, and showed him why he was
wrong. "By the death of Garrick this young man lost
a good friend and an excellent instructor," said Davies.

Garrick aged rapidly. Gout and the stone afflicted
him. In June 1776, at sixty, he took his leave of the stage.
It is no exaggeration to say that when he died two years

and a half later, he left hundreds of friends—for friend-ship was another of his talents. England gave him a stu-pendous funeral in Westminster Abbey, with a duke, two earls and a viscount among his pallbearers.

In turning from this man to Sarah Kemble Siddons, one feels oneself handling a tougher, grittier clay. Hers was in name only, the weaker sex. For three-quarters of a century these two great people influenced the English-speaking stage, yet their paths crossed only briefly. She was nearly forty years his junior. He began acting in 1741, and she closed her professional career in 1812.

Contrasted with the sheltered childhood of Garrick, Sarah Kemble's was rigorous. The eldest of twelve off-spring born to the strolling theatrical manager, Roger Kemble, the child was never neglected or slatternly. Her mother taught her to sing and play the harpsichord, and sent her to school whenever the family stayed long enough in one town. Her maternal grandfather had done chil-dren's parts under Betterton, and both her parents had—alas—played with Quin. There was always a touch of Quin in what the Kembles later called their "family manner."

Sarah, who was born in 1755, began to act when she was scarcely more than a baby. Barns were her nurseries —for itinerant companies often used these quarters, with-out all the refurbishings that our summer theatres now bestow upon them. She was trained to a careful diction, and to many of the stage practices which Garrick, in London, had long since brushed aside.

In her early 'teens, Sarah was already beautiful—with great eyes and classic features, including the large Kemble nose. "Damn it, madam, there is no end to your nose,"

MRS. SIDDONS—from a portrait by Sir Thomas Lawrence.

said Gainsborough when he was painting her, in after years. This girl played young heroines, going through what was expected of her with no particul. élan. She was busy falling in love.

A personable William Siddons had joined the company. He was eleven years older than she, and at sixteen she promised to marry him. Her parents were against the match, for William was not much of an actor. But she was loyal to her "Sid," and in time the opposition relented. The wedding took place in November 1773, some months after Sarah's eighteenth birthday.

This was her one romance. She was never swept away by any other man, although years with "Sid" somewhat rubbed off his glamour. When she grew famous, the Kembles made him stop acting because they said his inferiority reflected on her and the rest of them. So he lived on his wife's earnings, in the midst of his in-laws. The worst he ever did was to get grumpy and die of rheumatism. But all that was many years ahead for this bride and bridegroom.

They were soon playing in a company in Cheltenham Wells. Already, the young actress was doing Belvidera in "Venice Preserved." It was always one of her best rôles. Her first child, Henry, was born in the fall of that year—but the event seems to have been a mere incident in her workaday life. In the spring of 1775, she was acting in Liverpool.

Garrick, in London—nearing the close of his career— had already heard of her. As the powerful manager of Drury Lane, he always had an ear to the ground—and several people had brought him news of an obscure actress in the provinces, who gave unusual promise.

Sarah Siddons' work at that time was not the thing it later became, but it must have had touches of the qualities that afterward made it unique. She was now a barnstormer, remarkable as a "most extraordinary quick study," playing leads with the routine confidence of one bred to the stage. We have her own word for it, in recollections which she jotted down in her old age. She tells of her first attempt at Lady Macbeth:

> On the night preceding that on which I was to appear in this part for the first time, I shut myself up as usual, when all the family were retired, and commenced my study of Lady Macbeth. As the character is very short, I thought I should soon accomplish it. Being then only twenty years of age, I believed that little more was necessary than to get the words into my head, for the necessity of discrimination, and the development of character, at that time of my life, had scarcely entered into my imagination.

There could be no more straightforward account of how she then looked at acting. It makes what follows the more illuminating:

> But to proceed. I went on with tolerable composure, in the silence of the night (a night I can never forget), till I came to the assassination scene, when the horrors of the scene rose to a degree that made it impossible for me to get farther. I snatched up my candle, and hurried out of the room in a paroxysm of terror. My dress was of silk, and the rustling of it, as I ascended the stairs to go to bed, seemed to my panic-struck fancy like the movement of a spectre pursuing me. At last I reached my chamber, where I found my husband fast asleep. I clapt my candlestick down upon the table, without the power of

putting the candle out, and threw myself on my bed, without daring to stay even to take off my clothes. . . .

Here is a glimpse of that underlying imaginative power which the actress later learned to call on, at will. In the dark, still house it takes her by surprise; and its first effect is merely to disrupt her accepted procedure. For the next evening she did not even know her lines, and gave a performance that she was thoroughly ashamed of. But she never forgot the horror of that night—and some vestige of it emerged long after in the hypnotic force of her Lady Macbeth.

Mrs. Siddons' everyday manner was one of great calm. Her personality seems to have had two levels—like those stretches of the subway where express trains run farther down in the earth than the locals. Most of her early acting was done on the local level. Later, she learned her way to the one beneath it, where an unslackening impetus carried her straight to her destination.

In August 1775, she received an offer from Garrick to come to Drury Lane. There was, however, a slight obstacle, for she was soon to have another child. This must have been a bit annoying to Garrick, beset as usual with leading-woman trouble. He would have liked to discipline Mrs. Abington, Mrs. Yates, and Miss Younge, by introducing an outsider in his autumn season. Still, he could wait.

So he wrote, insisting that Mrs. Siddons should not come to London till she felt thoroughly able to travel, and meantime he offered to advance funds to the Siddonses. Sally, their second child, was born in Gloucester on November 5, the mother having played up to within a few hours of the birth.

On December 29, Sarah Siddons made her London début as Portia, then one of her favorite rôles. The occasion was a fiasco—and her whole season with Garrick the bitterest experience she had known. She afterward blamed him plentifully. But records show that he did not do badly by her, keeping her through to the end of the spring and giving her good parts.

She was not, in truth, quite ready for London. On her opening night she showed "a painful timidity"—and no audience likes that. It suffers embarrassment for the player. Years later when she was mistress of her art, she said she had often noticed that if she tried to play a part better than ever, she always did worse. That probably happened to her Portia. All through the winter, her acting was good one evening and bad the next. Then, too, she rated herself a comedienne. It was tragedy that released her powers, but she did not know it yet.

Coming from the country, where her dressing room had often been partitioned off with a blanket, she found herself in the best-run theatre in England, among players of high skill. (The leading ladies let her feel as gauche as possible.) Till now, she had never seen finished acting or a well-directed performance—for there were no films then to carry the work of the finest actors everywhere.

And so that winter at Drury Lane must have taught her more than she was willing to admit. She heard Garrick improve on many a stagey inflection that she had been brought up to accept. He took a world of pains at rehearsals—and here was a woman of the keenest instinct, watching everything. She was no copyist, but the things she saw and listened to must have sunk into her. This, then, was Garrick's uncredited influence on Mrs. Siddons' work. She was always different, after that season.

He cast her for Lady Anne opposite his Richard III, on May 27, 1776, and in June they gave a command performance before George III. When the actor-manager was rehearsing her, he criticised the way she used her arms—and it is likely that she then inclined toward stiff Quin-like gesturing. However, she resented his correction, and persuaded herself that he feared lest her hand hide "the tip of his nose." She had many complaints against him.

After she was sovereign of the stage, someone said to her that Garrick's Richard III had not been terrible enough. "Good God, what could be more terrible?" she returned with the bluntness that left her little small-talk.

Then she told about playing Lady Anne with him. There was a scene where Richard, married to Anne, was already planning her death. In this, he was so much more sinister than she had expected, that he unnerved her, and she neglected to follow one of his directions. Thereupon, he shot her a glance over his shoulder, and his look was so dreadful that she always recalled it with terror. Oh, she could never forget Garrick, she said.

The end of the season came, and with it Garrick's farewell to the stage, on June 10, 1776. Mrs. Siddons sat in a box.

Then she and her husband packed up and went off to play for the summer in Birmingham, assuming that Sarah would be re-engaged next season at Drury Lane. Even though she had not made a sensation, they believed she was on a sure footing as a London actress. But Garrick was no longer patentee of the theatre, and from the new management there soon came a letter stating that Mrs. Siddons' services would not be needed.

This was a very nearly killing blow to the actress. She had been banished as worthless—that was the way she put it. For six years, she never saw London again.

In those years she came to herself and to the sure use of her talents. She had looked upon disaster. After that, the inner struggles, the bitter regrets, the ceaseless loyalties of life became clear and familiar things to her.

With two young children to support, she could not afford the luxury of despair—and so she kept working wherever she and her husband could get engagements. They were better engagements, though, than she had before her London venture. The best provincial managers began, as we say, to "feature" her.

One of the finest actors with whom she worked in this period was John Henderson—a man of originality, whom she called "the soul and life of feeling." (When he did Iago and recited the verses to Desdemona, he spoke as if he were inventing them as he went along. Other Iagos always seemed to have memorized them.) It was Henderson who recommended Sarah Siddons to the manager at Bath.

There she appeared in October 1778, as leading woman of the Orchard Street Theatre; and there she stayed most happily until her return to Drury Lane in 1782. Next to being the rage in London, came being the rage in Bath —and Mrs. Siddons soon had that sort of following. In four years her fame gathered so much momentum that Drury Lane had to get her back.

On October 10, 1782, her London reappearance was a whirlwind of success. She had chosen the title rôle in Southerne's tragedy, "Isabella; or the Fatal Marriage," and her rehearsals made a profound impression on the actors. She had become a thorough artist. Her little boy, Henry, now eight and cast for Isabella's child, broke into sobs as she went through her death scene—for, although he was used to the make-believe of plays, he thought that this time his mother was really dying.

She was soon exercising that same power on all her London audiences. They came and wept—sometimes people fainted. Every part she played had a unity and simplicity about it that came from her own personality. Garrick had been many-sided. She was not. She gradually gave up comedy. Her playing was like a gorge with a dark river running through it ceaselessly.

But with this immense capacity for feeling, she created no scenes in ordinary life, went through no outbursts. Her usual manner was so impassive that people found her dull. In conversation, Garrick made the individual he was talking with, feel interesting to himself. Sarah Siddons lacked that knack. Her attention was concentrated on her work, her children, and her close friends.

She was a devoted mother. When she came to London in 1782, she had three beautiful children—Henry, Sally and Maria—and three years later her second son was born. In 1794, she finished off her family with one more girl. Her maternal attitude was one of her best strokes of publicity—but, like every scene she played, it sprang from genuine emotion in her.

The style of acting which came into vogue with Mrs. Siddons was quite different from Garrick's. He had been an impressionist, and she was a modified classicist. It was now forty years since he had burst upon London with his fresh, natural method—but that was an old story now. The time was ripe for a new cycle.

The new one was not so much an advance, as a reaction. Sarah Siddons had simply found a way of acting that fitted her. She transfused the classic idea with intense and true emotion. Her parents had never been converts to the new-fangled naturalism; but their oldest child, Sarah, could draw what she needed from opposing sources. Garrick's spontaneity had not been lost on her. (Her brother, John Philip Kemble, never got beyond a splendid elegance. His great contribution to the theatre was his scholarly taste in the correct historic costuming of his productions. In this, he was an innovator.)

Mrs. Siddons always depended on filling her consciousness with the mood of her part. "Abstraction" was what she called this process. When she first did Constance in "King John," she saw that the misfortunes which beset Constance happen off-stage—and yet the actress must show mounting rage and despair. (Lynn Fontanne told me that in "Design for Living" she had to begin the play in a high state of emotion—and it was one of the hardest things she had ever done.)

Mrs. Siddons' way of keeping herself at that high pitch was this:

> I never, from the beginning of the play to the end of my part in it, once suffered my dressing-room door to be closed, in order that my attention might be constantly fixed on those distressing events which, by this means, I could plainly hear going on upon the stage. . . . In short, the spirit of the whole drama took possession of my mind and frame.
> . . . The quality of abstraction has always appeared to me to be so necessary in the art of acting that . . . I wish my opinion were of sufficient weight to impress the importance of this power on the minds of all candidates for dramatic fame. . . .

In thirty years of acting Lady Macbeth, she made it her practice to spend the morning before each performance in reading over the whole play. Doing so, she generally found some new hint in it, "something which had not struck me as much as it *ought* to have struck me."

Lady Macbeth was the most famous of all her impersonations, and she made her first London appearance in it in February, 1785. Someone who saw her in the part at Drury Lane said that, all through the play, her words were like an accompaniment to her thoughts. The thought was always apparent, always powerful. "Her eyes never wandering—never for a moment idle—passion and sentiment continually betraying themselves."

In the assassination scene her phrase, "My hands are of your color," was horrifying in all its suggestion. It was, of course, the forerunner of Lady Macbeth's obsession with her hands in the sleepwalking scene. There, the actress rose to her greatest heights. A portrait of her in the costume of the scene shows her with her hands folded into each other and held close against her, as if to keep the spot on them from being seen. Her "Oh, oh, oh!" was "a convulsive shudder—very horrible."

In all her rôles—many of which were sympathetic—her interpolated gestures and her silences were most telling. She was always "in character." Persons who acted with her agreed that her eyes were often terrifying, just as she herself had found Garrick's in "Richard III." Hers had a strange light in them when she was greatly moved.

She had a way of saying the simplest phrases that struck directly through to the hidden emotion in her audiences. "I hardly breathe while she is on the stage," Washington Irving put it. "She works up my feelings till I am a mere child." Drawing on deep levels in her own consciousness, she got response from those levels in other people.

With Garrick, the sensitive layer that must be part of every artist was close beneath the surface—but in Siddons it had been buried deep, and was not readily accessible. This was the source of the difference in their work and their lives. They were both born for the things they did, and their successes came of finding their paths to those things.

Their styles of acting might not fit our present stage. But the ideas behind their playing are eternally true and fruitful in the theatre.

MIDDLE DISTANCE

6.

Three Men of Genius and Failings

SCENE—New York.

Time—November 1810.

As the curtain rises, an imaginary orchestra plays "Yankee Doodle," for this is a new world and a new century. Following Garrick and Siddons, who combined genius with level heads and admirable conduct, the stage has now entered upon a Byronic cycle. Three of its giants in this era are drunkards touched with madness. The first of the three—George Frederick Cooke—has been in his glory since 1800. The other two—Edmund Kean and Junius Brutus Booth—will soon come forward.

Cooke, Kean, and Booth bring acting of the highest rank to the United States. Not that the theatre is new in America; but Cooke, whose arrival now impends, is the first great London star to cross the Atlantic. He comes with the cachet of Covent Garden, where he has played on an equal footing with Mrs. Siddons, the Tragic Muse. He speaks of her irreverently as Sarah.

In view of his unquestioned position in England, some New Yorkers doubt the rumor that he is already on the high seas. There must be some hoax about it. But the *Evening Post* publishes reassurances:

The Mr. Cooke who is coming out on the *Columbia*, is the great tragic actor of that name. Too much credit cannot be given to the managers of our theatre, for their enterprise and liberality in venturing upon so bold a speculation. . . .

The United States has three circuits for players, in the year 1810. The northern one comprises New York, Boston, Newport, and Providence; the central circuit has its headquarters in Philadelphia, and includes Baltimore and Annapolis; in the South, the chief seat of the drama is Charleston, the company from there occasionally journeying northward to Richmond.

That is about all the "road" that exists; nobody dreams of playing in the new capital of Washington, or in the smoky little settlement of Pittsburgh. When actors venture to Maine, Saratoga, Albany, or towns along the Delaware, they give lectures and readings.

"His arrival may be hourly expected, and indeed we understand that several sharp sighted pilots have been employed at the Hook, two or three days past, groping about with lanthornes on the end of poles, to find the great Cooke in the late fogs. . . ." Thus reads part of a column in the *Evening Post* of Friday, November 16, 1810. On Saturday appears an announcement that Cooke has reached New York aboard the "Columbia."

This is followed on Monday with a paragraph describing the rush of people to buy tickets for the London star's first performance. There is also an open letter, signed Enquirer, stating that Enquirer understands Cooke to be the rival of John Philip Kemble, and suggesting that the readers be given information on this point. (It is plain that the art of advance publicity is not unknown in 1810.)

On November 20, comes an advertisement:

> The Managers feel extremely grateful by having it in their power to announce the Engagement of MR. COOKE of the Covent-Garden Theatre for TWELVE NIGHTS.
>
> First night of Mr. Cooke's Engagement—On Wednesday Evening, Nov. 21, will be presented Shakespeare's Tragedy of Richard III, Or The Battle of Bosworth Field. Richard, Mr. Cooke.

Neither the *Evening Post's* pages nor those of the *Columbian*—another daily journal—reveal the whole truth about how George Frederick Cooke has reached America. On this twentieth day of November, it is not yet generally known that he had to be smuggled aboard the "Columbia" to escape his creditors. For in spite of his handsome earnings, he literally throws his money away when he is in alcoholic moods.

According to greenroom gossip he is, at intervals, a monster of inebriety—quarrelsome, coarse, sodden. He says it is an insanity that seizes him. New York actors have heard all about him.

They can scarcely believe their eyes when they behold the man who has landed. He is a suave, courteous gentleman, impeccably dressed in gray. His hair is white, and he looks old for his fifty-four years, but there are no marks of dissipation on him. His eyes, set far apart, have a sidelong glance full of sardonic humor. This is Cooke sober.

The New York in which he finds himself is a bustling little metropolis with a population of 96,000. Its theatrical district comprises exactly one playhouse, which stands on the east side of Park Row facing City Hall Park, the fashionable new promenade.

The theatre, named the Park, is a well-designed structure accommodating 1200 people. But those 1200 seats are not enough for the crowd that struggles to attend George Frederick Cooke's first night in "Richard III." The curtain is to rise at half past six in the evening, and long before that hour patrons have been jostling their way to the entrances.

Excitement is not confined to the front of the house. Behind the scenes, Cooke trembles like a beginner; but once he faces his audience, he is its master.

> The greatest proof of the deep interest taken in the acting of Mr. Cooke . . . was the profound stillness which prevailed during his performance, in spite of overcrowding, disputes for places, etc. Every private concern was instantaneously given up and silenced at the sight of Richard [says a review in the *Columbian* next day]. . . . He gives the character a sneering, contemptuous and sarcastical turn beyond anything we had imagined; and to some of his reflections . . . he imparted a pathos and effect new and astonishing to an American audience.

Besides this reporter, the *Columbian* has another dramatic critic—THESPIS, a most perspicacious observer. He publishes a long article on the second day after Cooke's appearance. "Mr. Cooke's style is vivid, original, and impressive," states THESPIS. He goes on to admit that the actor's physique and walk are not superlative:

> In what, then, it may be asked, does the wonderful superiority of Cooke consist? We answer in the

force and comprehension of his genius, the boldness and originality of his manner . . . and the quick and piercing expression of his eye, united to his thorough knowledge, not only of the text, but the meaning of its author. . . . He not only enters on the threshold of the character, but is absolutely lost in its mazes. . . .

The supporting rôles, adds this reviewer, "were most unmercifully butchered."
Of Cooke's Shylock, THESPIS writes a week later:

Mr. Cooke, beyond all other players that have appeared on the American boards . . . adheres to the text and spirit of his author. He is less solicitous to attract admiration by polished gestures and striking attitudes . . . than to fix and enchain attention by never losing sight of the prevailing tone of mind and peculiar genius of the character he personates. . . . No actor appears less inclined to gain applause at the sacrifice of nature.

In another issue of the *Columbian*, there is an anecdote about a sailor who saw Cooke and said, "Damn the fellow! He doesn't mind being on the stage any more than if he wasn't acting."
Such playing as this is new to New York, which has suffered much from high-tragedy walk and high-tragedy voice. Another theatregoer, after an evening at the Park, calls the star from Covent Garden "the first natural actor we ever saw."

Cooke was born in 1756, and was brought up in the town of Berwick-on-Tweed, in the north of England. He had no theatrical connections, but very early he fell in love with plays and acting:

The first play I ever read was "Venice Preserved."
I also remember that from some prints I had seen of
theatrical characters . . . and from the representation of a puppet show, I formed my first, strange and
incoherent idea of a stage, [Cooke wrote in a brief
chronicle of his career which he once set himself to
compose during an imprisonment for debt]. The
first play I ever saw acted, was "The Provoked Husband, or a Journey to London," by a part of the
Edinburgh Company, in the town of Berwick upon
Tweed, where I was then at school. This must have
been about the year 1766 or 1767. . . .

He was then ten or eleven. When he was about fifteen, he managed to get to London and go to the theatres.
That was in 1771.

He was there again in 1774. "Now I began to see
acting," his chronicle states exultantly. He first saw Garrick—whom he called "the great master of the stage"—in
1775. He also saw Macklin. Years afterward, he said
his recollections of London players of that period were as
clear as though he had watched them yesterday. He
listed the rôles he had seen Garrick play: "Lear, Hamlet
twice, Benedick twice, Don Felix twice, and Kitely.
Alas! no more!" For the actor-manager soon retired.

All the rest of Cooke's life, Garrick was his idol, and
next he ranked Macklin. He was their disciple; he believed that the player should speak and behave as nearly
as possible like a real person. But by the time Cooke got
to the top, Garrick's influence had been pushed aside by
that of Mrs. Siddons and John Philip Kemble, who sub-
scribed to the "recitative" style.

But this is anticipating. The youthful Cooke—his head
full of the glories of London acting—lost little time in

joining strolling companies. For many years, he never lacked provincial engagements. The public liked him, and among players he was known to be "very correct"— which meant that he took pains to speak the author's lines, instead of floundering through half-learned speeches. In his diaries he was honest with himself about his work, making such comments as, "This evening I acted Kitely. I believe I never acted it worse." "Acted in the evening with good effect." "In the evening acted Richard; the house good but I was indisposed, and could not give that effect to the character which I have often done, though the applause was very much the same."

On October 31, 1800, Cooke appeared for the first time at Covent Garden, and made an immense impression as Richard III. He followed this success with many others that season.

Cooke's acting was at its best in villains—not blood-and-thunder villains, but hypocrites. He had the gift of letting spectators feel the shifty undercurrent beneath the surface, and he did it with a sly, bitter humor. Sometimes his voice would fade to a whisper, in the delight the villain seemed to take in his own wickedness.

The mind of the individual he depicted was what he always sought to know. "He not only enters on the threshold of the character, but is absolutely lost in its mazes." That phrase written about Cooke, applies equally well to Helen Hayes' Queen Victoria, to Maurice Evans' Richard II, or to Noel Coward in the "Astonished Heart."

"It is common for many on the stage to say they have *studied* a character," Cooke wrote in his diary, "when they even know not what the expression means; their *utmost* idea of studying being to obtain a knowledge of the author's words."

In those days a star's prompt-books were tools of his trade. This was because the actor had a large repertory —forty or fifty parts, perhaps—and he might need to refresh his memory, if some play were billed in which he had not lately appeared. One of Cooke's rôles was Octavian in "The Mountaineers," a now obsolete drama by George Colman, the younger.

It was in verse, but when Cooke wrote out the lines of his part he set them down as though they were prose. This is evidence of his method of study. He also interpolated notes to indicate the thought behind the speeches. Thus, "Oh, Octavian, where are the times thy ardent nature painted? (A pause—recollection strikes forcibly, and the tender passions are aroused.)"

Again, "Prosperity's a cheat! Despair is honest and will stick by me steadily. (The rage of despair *under*.)" "The remembrance of all his former happiness," was another of his directions to himself; as was also, "Recollection of his loss, and despairing grief and rage mingled."

In the season of 1810-11 he acted not only in New York, but also in Boston, Philadelphia, and Baltimore—the journeys to those cities taking days by coach or by steamboat. Wherever he went, he drew crowds. "Why, this beats Sarah," he exclaimed when he saw the street full of people waiting to attend his opening in Philadelphia. He was always sober at the start of a new engagement, but his good beginnings never lasted. Nevertheless, the box-office reports of his tour read well, even today.

"I don't want to die in America. John Kemble will laugh at me," said Cooke. Yet he never took decisive steps about returning to England. Both his health and his power of will were undermined.

As late as July 1812, he was playing in Providence; and there he made his last stage appearance, on July 29. He died in New York on September 26, 1812, of hardening of the liver induced by alcoholism. His body was interred in the strangers' vault in St. Paul's churchyard.

Nine years later Edmund Kean, on his first visit to New York, had the ashes reinterred in the same churchyard, and erected a monument to Cooke. But even in his grave, that strange, wild genius could not rest quietly. At the reinterment, his skull was claimed by an admirer, and was afterward used in a performance of "Hamlet." Kean took a toe joint. The Players Club, of New York, has among its memorabilia a tooth that was once George Frederick Cooke's.

Edmund Kean, like Cooke, was an adherent of Garrick; but unlike Cooke, Kean never saw him. For Kean was born in 1787, eight years after Garrick's death. Despite the gap, the influence of Garrick's acting touched him in his childhood.

Kean's birth was shabby and clouded. He was illegitimate; and he used to wonder whether his mother, Ann Carey, really was his mother. She had miscellaneous other children, and her only interest in him was for what he earned. The evidence seems to show, though, that he was her son by Edmund Kean, sometimes referred to as an architect. He was in the employ of the Royalty Theatre, in London. The Royalty was a minor playhouse, and Miss Carey was a minor actress there.

She was the vagabond daughter of George Saville Carey, an impecunious lecturer on mimicry. Her grandfather, Henry Carey, had written ballads, operas, and "God Save the King." However, the Careys had been running downhill for three generations. Ann Carey played in humble theatrical troupes, told fortunes, or went from house to house selling perfumes and face powders. On these rounds she generally took along her handsome little boy, Edmund, because people were attracted by him and lost their sales resistance. He would dance or recite, and they would give him pennies—which Nancy pocketed. He had begun to act almost as soon as he could walk, having appeared as Cupid in a spectacle at the age of two.

There was a Miss Tidswell, an actress at Drury Lane, who took more care of him than Miss Carey did, and who gave him his first training in acting. Through Miss Tidswell, he sometimes played children's parts on the sacred boards of Drury Lane. She was a slightly passée player with leanings toward the Garrick, or naturalistic, style.

It was this approach to acting that she instilled into the child when she taught him his parts. She used to place him before a portrait and tell him to talk to it, in saying his speeches. He was never to recite; he was to speak to someone. Such a record as this shows the very first notions of his calling that Edmund Kean could have had.

The boy could do amazing things. With utmost earnestness, he would give whole scenes from plays; he would fight, bleed, and die; he would impersonate Garrick as Richard III, or give imitations of actors he himself had seen. Miss Tidswell must have been proud of her pupil, but she was not tender. He said she used to beat him and tie him to the bedpost, to keep him from running away. Perhaps she was at her wit's end—for he was always rebellious.

This child grew into a slender, small youth, agile in mind and body, possessed of dark curls and glinting black eyes. He joined crude theatrical troupes, performing at fairs and turning somersaults as Harlequin. But he had an unquenchable ambition to be a great tragedian.

His whole life was the dramatic school in which he trained himself, its instructions being far more cruelly administered than any that are now given in college courses. In 1806, (he was nineteen) he filled small parts at the Haymarket Theatre, London, without attracting the least notice. Thereafter small cities, poor audiences, and poorer salaries were his fate—a fate which doubtless had some connection with his drinking and wild conduct. There was an unbalanced strain in him.

He was a hard worker, nevertheless. He turned his hand to anything; in pantomimes he was not only Harlequin, but trainer of the ballet and scene designer, as well.

But besides versatility, he had incredible artistic courage. Acting often to a handful of spectators, during these years he shaped his fiery, tragic impersonations; he tested his ideas, expanding some and casting others aside. He never sank under the thought that nobody cared whether he played well or badly. *He* cared, he cared!

"He used to mope about for hours, walking miles and miles alone, with his hands in his pockets, thinking intensely on his characters," somebody remembered after he was famous. "No one could get a word out of him. He studied and *slaved* beyond any actor I ever knew."

In 1808, he married Maria Chambers, and life with him turned her into a thoroughgoing trouper. The superb thing about her was her unflinching belief in him. She went hungry with him. With him, she walked a hundred and fifty miles to the town of Swansea about a month before her first child was born, and played at the theatre when they reached there.

She grew used to his coming home drunk. Perhaps she excused him because he was overworked, for to play Richard III and follow it with Harlequin in the afterpiece, required brandy-and-water. She grew used to never having quite enough money to move to the next town. Yet for all she endured, he requited her poorly later on.

How could a man bursting with gifts and energy spend years wandering through England without recognition? It was not merely aberrations that kept him back. His acting was not bombastic enough to be popular. A critic in Guernsey wrote of Kean's "impudence and incompetency," and thought it fortunate that the actor could not get a London hearing. Why, he showed no proper respect for his audience! He seemed unconscious of its existence; at moments he even turned his back on the public.

In November 1813, Edmund Kean received an offer from Drury Lane Theatre. When he found that Mr. Arnold, the manager, had come to Dorchester to engage him, Kean said he staggered as if he had been shot. He was to have six trial parts. The poor fellow told his wife that, if he succeeded, he thought he would go mad.

But difficulties intervened, giving him ample time to emerge from that state of anticipation. As usual, the Keans were without funds. Their elder child, Howard—four years old, and already initiated into giving little entertainments in inn yards—had sickened of brain fever. He died at Dorchester on November 23.

"Howard, sir, died on Monday morning last. You

may conceive my feelings and pardon the brevity of my letter," wrote the father.

There were funeral expenses to be met, which Kean did with the proceeds of a benefit performance. Then he borrowed five pounds from the local manager, and went to London.

What happened to him there through the months of December and January while he waited for the opportunity that had seemed so near, is a tale of hope deferred that makes the heart bleed. Drury Lane officials turned cold to him; for the manager of a second-rate theatre suddenly insisted that Kean was under prior contract to his playhouse. Months earlier this impressario had appeared to hold out an engagement, but had neglected to complete the arrangement. Now he chose to feel injured.

All this put the threadbare player from the country in very bad odor at Drury Lane. Even the candle-snuffers were admitted to see manager Arnold ahead of him. The actor was haughtily informed that he must get a signed release from the opposing manager. Kean wore himself out trying to do so. His hopes rose and fell.

On a small advance, he had got his wife and little son, Charles, to London. But what were they living on? How could they eat? Only God, and two kindly maiden ladies who were their landlords, knew. Once a week came salary day, when Kean would present himself in agony to learn whether his name had been put on the list. It was never there.

After some eight weeks of suspense and undernourishment, he was finally informed that he might open on January 26 as Richard III. But he was afraid to risk this rôle for a début, for the public expected kings to look majestic—and he was a small man. "Shylock or nothing," he said. This was the very last ditch. So Shylock it was.

On the morning of the opening date he had his only rehearsal. Members of the company were contemptuous. They said he ought to sit out in front and learn what good acting was.

"This will *never* do, Mr. Kean," protested Raymond, the stage manager. "It is totally different from anything that has ever been done on these boards."

"Sir, I *wish* it to be so."

"It will not do, Mr. Kean. Be assured of it."

"Well, sir, perhaps I may be wrong; but if so, the public will set me right."

At home in the evening, as he was leaving for the theatre, he told his wife, "I wish I was going to be shot." (Burgess Meredith's account of his opening night in "Winterset," which appeared in *Stage Magazine*, described the sinking of heart with which he started to the theatre. It is to the everlasting credit of actors, he added, that they never do run away from a first performance.)

At Drury Lane, Edmund Kean made up, dressed, and avoided the greenroom where it was customary for the performers to assemble. He knew what they thought of him. So he prowled about in dark corners of the stage, waiting for his scenes. No one spoke to him, except when the call-boy—vastly upset at having hunted high and low for him—found him in the entrance for his first scene and said, "You are called, sir." In his isolation, Kean must have been drawing all his forces together, filling himself with that deeply-rooted concentration that can carry a trained, sure player over obstacles.

From his first entrance before the half-filled house, his triumph grew and grew through the play. His face was like a Titian portrait; his Shylock was a man stung by

wrongs. Here was acting quite different from the polished, scholarly declamation for which Kemble and
Young set the fashion.

When Kean realized that the audience "was going with
him," as he later told his wife, he was filled with such
immense excitement that he "could not feel the stage
under him." It was a creative excitement, and it conveyed itself to the whole theatre. In the end there was
shouting and cheering; his success was a sensation.

Thereafter, Edmund Kean was never poor or neglected.
His playing soon got the account books of Drury Lane
out of the red, and began making a fortune for him. Raymond, the stage manager, licked Kean's boots. Sum-
moned to the star's dressing room one evening, he felt
flattered to see a bowl of steaming punch in readiness.
Ah, he was to partake!

But the tragedian had something to say first. "Look
you, sir. Now that I'm drawing money to your treasury,
you find that I'm a fine actor. You told me, when I rehearsed Shylock, that it would be a failure. . . . Now
you smother me with compliments. . . . There, sir, to
the devil with your fine speeches. Take that!" And the
hot punch went splashing into Raymond's face.

Kean's second rôle in London was Richard III, which
he dreaded to play because he knew he must now satisfy
great expectations. On the morning of the day he was
to appear he said, "I am so frightened, that my acting will
be almost dumb-show tonight." It was not, though; it
was overpowering—all originality, life, and rapid fluctua-
tions. But after the performance he was ill for a week.

(Neither then nor now can a player make an audience
yield itself up to him without an outlay of vitality. Lynn
Fontanne once confessed that she always spent the day in

bed after an opening night. Following the première of "Strange Interlude," she slept fifteen hours. Katharine Cornell told me that she had to save herself in every way to get through six nights and two matinees a week of "The Wingless Victory"; and John Gielgud admitted to Lucius Beebe that eight weekly performances of "Hamlet" were too much to ask of anybody.)

Years of success did not improve Edmund Kean. He grew spoiled, more unbalanced, more dissipated than ever. He who had traveled afoot, could not tour the provinces without his own coach-and-four; he had a secretary and a valet. Yet he grudged money to his wife and son. His love affairs were heartless; he had a form-letter which initiated all of them.

But he still worked hard at his calling. He would wait till his household had gone to bed, and then—by the light of many candles in his drawing room—would rehearse a part through the night. In the morning, he would act it for Mrs. Kean, asking her, "Do you think that will do?"

Aside from this audience of one, he took little advice about his playing. Once he let Garrick's widow rehearse him in her husband's manner in the closet scene of "Hamlet." Docilely, he tried to do what she said. But later he was indignant; for he could neither capture Garrick's effect nor return to his own. He was always dissatisfied with his Hamlet after that.

It was the spoiled, successful Kean who came to America at the end of the year 1820, making his first appearance in the United States at the Anthony Street Theatre, New York, on December 29. He became so much the rage that tickets for his performances were put up at auction, bringing far above the box-office prices. His tour of the country—the "road" had expanded rapidly since Cooke's day—coined money both for him and for the playhouses.

The acting which Americans paid so roundly to see was well worth what it cost. Kean always showed them a real person—generally a person driven by anguish—for he was extraordinarily sensitized to suffering and terror. There was a swift, sultry quality in him, and he used it to clarify the character he was presenting. In Hamlet's scene with Ophelia, after his, "Get thee to a nunnery. . . . To a nunnery, go," he had a sudden instant of relenting. He followed her, caught her hand as she was leaving him, and kissed it in spite of himself. The effect of this on the audience was electric, said Hazlitt. It was no mere trick; it demonstrated Hamlet's divided, wavering mind.

Kean's acting was full of contrasts and colloquial touches. But the greatest thing about it was its dynamic quality. His Othello was a tremendous portrait of grief, rage, and inward torture; Kean was small, but nobody thought so when he was Othello. His Richard III on Bosworth Field fought like someone "drunk with wounds."

In this season of 1820-21 and again in 1825-26, Kean left an influence on American actors with whom he played; for a luminous personality in the theatre is a tonic. During his first engagement in Boston he was supported by Mrs. Duff, leading woman of the local company. She was an excellent actress then; but after she worked with Kean she was a great actress.

In Albany in 1825, the Iago to the English star's Othello was a youth named Edwin Forrest. When the visitor saw something Forrest did in the part, he asked, "My God, who told you to do that?" "It is my own idea," was the answer. "Everyone who plays Iago after you will do it, too," the star told him. Forrest never ceased to admire Kean, although his own style of acting was different.

Between his two visits to America, Edmund Kean went through the scandal that wrecked him. It was the dragging into court of his relations with Mrs. Cox—an alderman's wife—who seems to have been a lady not above reproach. (The love letters in the case are now among the treasures of Harvard University.) After this damaging notoriety, Kean was never the same. His features grew bloated; he could not learn the lines of new parts. Only thumping drinks of hot brandy could give him power in his old impersonations. He died, old and broken at forty-six, in 1833.

Kean was a man of the theatre, who neither knew nor cared about anything else. He measured people in private life by their ability to judge acting. It was his only standard. Lord and dukes, he said, talked *such* nonsense on the subject; but lawyers, doctors, and literary men showed discrimination. Even when he went to his country place, he left his secretary in town and plied him with orders. "Write and send me play-bills *every day*. How was the box-plan for the 17th?"

Junius Brutus Booth—the father of Edwin—was so like Kean in physique and in unaccountable behavior, that people often said he was Kean's imitator. This was not true, for Booth followed the Kemble method of "recitative." He was not a realist, like Cooke and Kean, but a classicist or "idealist."

Like Mrs. Siddons, however, Booth could infuse warmth and feeling into his method. So he was a more compelling exemplar of it than John Philip Kemble. It is probable that the elder Booth never realized what he absorbed from Kean.   He was a beginner on the stage in the very season when Kean made his conquest of London—when Kean pervaded the atmosphere of the whole theatre like heat lightning. So the younger man must have felt the superiority of fire to elegance. At all events, there was always fire aplenty in his acting.

Walt Whitman saw him play "Richard III" at the Bowery Theatre, New York, in 1834 or 1835:

> Though Booth père, then in his prime . . . was the loyal continuer of the traditions of orthodox English play-acting, he stood out "himself alone" in many respects beyond any of his kind on record, and with effects and ways that broke through all rules and all traditions. . . .
>
> I happened to see what has been reckoned by experts one of the most marvelous pieces of acting ever known. . . . I can (from my good seat in the pit pretty well front) see again Booth's quiet entrance from the side, as with head bent he slowly walks down the stage to the footlights with that peculiar and abstracted gesture, musingly kicking his sword, which he holds off from him by its sash. Though fifty years have passed since then, I can hear the clank and feel the perfect hush of perhaps three thousand people waiting. (I never saw an actor who could make more of the said hush, or wait, and hold the audience in an indescribable half-delicious, half-irritating suspense.) . . .
>
> As in all art utterance it was the subtle and powerful something *special to the individual* that really conquered. . . . Yes; although Booth must be classed in that antique, almost extinct school, inflated,

stagey . . . his genius was to me one of the grandest revelations of my life, a lesson in artistic expression. The words fire, energy, *abandon*, found in him unprecedented meanings. . . .

An audience might be ever so languid, yet Booth could rouse it to something close to frenzy. He was a very uneven player—not in the least like Kean, who appeared to act spontaneously but planned everything beforehand. Booth varied with his moods, and thus supporting performers could only pray that the star would not be inspired to drag them by the hair.

When James E. Murdock was a young actor, he was cast as Wilford to Booth's Sir Edward Mortimer in "The Iron Chest." This chest, always locked, contained papers recording a disgraceful secret in the past of Sir Edward. Wilford was his secretary, and there was a telling scene when Wilford managed to unlock the receptacle and get his hands on the papers—only to be discovered by his employer.

Booth's instructions were to take plenty of time, and—kneeling in front of the chest—to hold its lid open with one hand, while the other reached in and hunted among the documents. No matter how long the interval might seem, Wilford was to busy himself with the papers until he felt Sir Edward's hand on his shoulder. Then, in alarm, he was to let go of the lid, which would fall shut with a clang. He would turn and meet Eir Edward's gaze.

That evening Murdock, very nervous, hunted through the contents of the chest. After an eternity of waiting, he felt a heavy grip on his shoulder, let the lid fall, and turned to find Booth holding a pistol at his head and glar-

ing like a demon. "Then for the first time I comprehended the reality of acting."

This happened when Junius Brutus Booth was an old
stager. What of his beginnings in the theatre?

Born in London in 1796, he was well educated in the
classics, but became stage-struck and left home for the
town of Deptford where he made his début at seventeen.
This was in December 1813. Soon Booth was filling leading rôles in the provinces, and it took him only three
years to get a trial night at Covent Garden, as Richard
III. On that evening when he won praise from the London critics—it was February 12, 1817—he was not quite
twenty-one.

As to the enmity between him and Edmund Kean which
promptly developed, Kean does not figure well in the
story. He arranged for a joint performance of "Othello"
—he to play Othello and Booth, Iago. It looked like a
handsome compliment; but when the night came, Kean
called up all his powers and overwhelmed the new man.
Othello grew gigantic as the tragedy unrolled, and Iago
shriveled. Booth suffered horribly. He refused to play
again with Kean. So all the theatregoers took sides, with
Drury Lane and Covent Garden ranged against each
other. There were riots in the pit every time Booth appeared. But he rode out the storm.

Early in 1821 he married Mary Anne Holmes. He
was not free to marry; for he had run away from a previous wife, his objection being that he didn't like her.
This time he knew his own mind, and he never swerved
from his choice. However, thirty years later his first
spouse came to America and sued for divorce—to the surprise and horror of his grown children.

His bigamous marriage in London probably had something to do with his quitting England shortly thereafter. In the spring of 1821, he booked passage to the United States for himself, his new young wife, and his pony. No publicity preceded him; through his whole life he never cared for publicity. But he could not help doing things that attracted attention, and so he got along very well.

Mr. and Mrs. Booth and the pony landed at Norfolk, Virginia, at the end of June. Going to Richmond, he presented himself to the manager of the theatre, who must have been astonished to find a celebrity on his doorstep at a time of year when box-office receipts needed stimulation. They got it; Booth made his American début at Richmond on July 6, 1821, in "Richard III." From then until his death in 1852, on his way from an engagement in New Orleans to another in Cincinnati, he was an American star, save for two seasons when he made reappearances at Drury Lane.

His power over audiences seems to have come, even at the start, from an instinct for entering into the mind of his character. How he did so, his son Edwin described:

> Whatever the part he had to personate, he was from the time of rehearsal until he slept at night, imbued with its very essence. If *Othello* was billed for the evening he would, perhaps, wear a crescent pin on his breast that day; or, disregarding the fact that Shakespeare's Moor was a Christian, he would mumble maxims from the Koran. . . .
>
> If *Shylock* was to be his part at night, he was a Jew all day; and if in Baltimore at the time, he would pass hours with a learned Israelite, who lived nearby, discussing Hebrew history in the vernacular and insisting that, although he was of Welsh descent, that nation is of Hebraic origin. . . .

As years went by, Booth's eccentricities and his fits of drink increased. Many times he seemed insane. In his case, as in Cooke's and Kean's, there is no way of telling just how much was madness and how much alcohol. One suspects Booth, at times, of pretending to be crazy for the fun of seeing what would happen.

Nevertheless, he had many tender qualities. His letters to his wife were signed, "Your husband and worshipper." He possessed no vanity—and when he was himself, he showed a childlike trust in everybody and a genuine sympathy for man and beast. No animals on his farm might be butchered, nor could there be any hunting.

In reminiscences, Barton Hill told of being a member of the company at Pittsburgh in 1849, when the elder Booth played "Hamlet" there. Hill had been ill and could scarcely stand. However, he was to do Horatio. When he came to Booth's dressing room in the evening, to get instructions, the star saw how weak he was. "Never mind, my boy; I'll tell you as we proceed." Booth gave no further directions, but in every scene with Horatio he put his arm around him—the friendship of Hamlet and Horatio made this natural enough—and thus led and helped him through the whole performance.

A silent, shy lad of sixteen was waiting in the entrance each time Hamlet came off, ready to hand him the sword or cape or "property" he might need. This was Edwin Booth.

Do Cooke, Kean, and Booth prove the old argument that genius is close to madness? No; for there were Garrick and Siddons—as great, or greater, than they—who led lives that ran to no excess. Then why devote attention to

these three men? Because in them we see the acting temperament exaggerated—enlarged till it becomes easily visible to the naked eye. They conceal nothing of the
enthusiasm and pain, the passion for the work and in the
work, which are lavished on acting whenever it rises to
heights.

The Old

EDMUND KEAN as Richard III
This shows the monarch on Bosworth Field.

7.

Teapot Acting in the Palmy Days

THIS chapter is an entr' acte affording time for a glance at the seamy side of playing in the palmy days. Such men as Cooke, Kean and Booth might be giants, but the stage of the period was by no means peopled with giants. It had its teapot actors.

If you want to know how the term "teapot acting" originated, just stand in front of a mirror placing, say, the left hand on the left hip and extending the right arm sidewise and upward in a graceful curve. You are now a human teapot, with your left arm for the handle and your right for the spout. To attain variety, you may go into reverse—handle on right, spout on left. As you alternate, recite something; even the alphabet will do, if repeated with authority. Here you have the rudiments of teapot acting. It was a name applied in contempt, as "ham acting" is now; and it always referred to the other fellow. The teapot never saw himself or herself as such.

Teapots were the routine actors of that long era when mutilated versions of Shakespeare and second- or third-rate poetic dramas were mainstays of the playhouse. The glories of this era were effulgent during the first half of the nineteenth century, and its waning influence continued much later.

Its outstanding figures were not teapots—nor were they limited to the three men of the preceding chapter. There were also Fanny Kemble, Mary Ann Duff, Edwin Forrest, Charlotte Cushman, William Charles Macready, John Drew (progenitor of all the Drews and Barrymores), Tyrone Power (great-grandfather of the present cinema actor), Anna Cora Mowatt, E. L. Davenport (father of Fanny), Henry Placide, J. W. Wallack, and others—all exceptional personalities.

But what about run-of-the-mill performers? What was their playing like, and what was the theatrical system that bred it?

It was a wholly different system from that which prevails today. New York did not then control the production of plays. This process went on in many cities and was run on a standardized basis, like the automobile industry at present. Filling stations and spare parts were available over a wide area. When stars toured, they carried no casts or scenery with them, but depended in each town on the support of a local stock company.

Every playhouse was thus the notable actor's filling station. He brought only his own impersonations and the local manager supplied all accessories. These included an Ophelia, a King, a Queen, a Polonius, for the star's Hamlet; a Romeo, a Mercutio and a whole outfit of Montagues and Capulets for Juliet; a Claude Melnotte for the Lady of Lyons; and all the characters needed for such standard plays as Massinger's "A New Way to Pay Old Debts," Otway's "Venice Preserved," Sheridan Knowles'

"The Hunchback," Home's "Douglas," Bulwer-Lytton's "Richelieu," and a long list of others.

This spare-parts system had its drawbacks, for there could be very little team work in acting. But the great stars knew how to offset that. Each of them was a lone wolf, able to depend on himself or herself for the fate of an evening's performance. By bitter experience he learned to put no trust in casts which changed with every town. For while some excellent performers were nurtured in the old stock company, it also harbored many incompetents.

From the moment the curtain rolled up, anything might happen. Laertes or Ophelia might "dry up" in their lines; cues might be missed; Juliet's balcony railing might collapse—for there were never any rehearsals with scenery. So Hamlet, Juliet, the Lady of Lyons, and the rest of them grew adept at facing emergencies. Their only comfortable moments were probably their soliloquies.

Edmund Kean's directions to the nineteen-year-old Forrest, were of the simplest. "Keep in front of me, and don't let your mind wander," said Kean. That was all. If he could get that much co-operation, he would be responsible for everything.

Most of the "business" in standard plays was traditional. The visitor merely said, "Kindly take the left in this scene. I take the right." He or she was also privileged to indicate whether he intended to look off-stage toward right or left for some invisible event like the struggle of a mob or the peaceful sleep of King Duncan. Members of the cast must then conform, despite mutterings if a star were so brash as to see a mob on the right that Macready or Forrest looked for on the left.

Present stage practice lacks all these ready-made contrivances. In getting ready for the American presentation of "Tovarich," Marta Abba and John Halliday rehearsed for three weeks in England and gave a number of performances before sailing for New York. Here, they had another three weeks of preparation with the Broadway company. Modern ensemble playing is smooth because time is lavished on making it so.

Plays in the palmy days, however, did not run long enough to warrant the expense of many rehearsals. This was why stars became lone wolves.

But what did the average player become, under these same conditions? The stock company in which he or she worked had grooves for its scenery and more grooves for its performers. It was all a matter of slapping a production through in a hurry.

Those grooves for the settings were tracks, or racks, running parallel to the proscenium line, and numbered one, two, three, and four. A scene was set by pushing flat wings of canvas out from the grooves at either side of the stage, and letting down back-drop and borders. First and second grooves took care of front scenes; fourth groove called for the full depth of the stage. Each playhouse had a standard outfit of scenery. There were interiors and exteriors—a cottage, a mansion, a palace, a garden, a street, a woodland, and so on. While special sets were sometimes painted, it was a poor stage manager who could not contrive a scenic investiture out of the supply on hand. It never fitted perfectly, but nobody expected it to.

The cast of characters was knocked together with equal readiness—for ladies and gentlemen of the company were also kept in grooves, theirs being designated "lines of business."

> In those days the old system of lines of business was strictly adhered to, [wrote Frederick Warde, concerning the company in the north of England where he got his start in the 1860's].
> So we had our leading man and leading lady; the juvenile or second lady; the first and second chambermaids, as the soubrettes were then called; the first and second old women; and several utility ladies. In addition to our leading man we had a juvenile and light comedian, a heavy man, first and second low comedians, first and second old men, two walking gentlemen, and several responsible utility men. . . . We also had a stage manager who sometimes acted; a prompter, a call boy and a dancing master. . . .

Here was the personnel sufficient for a whole season's attractions. This happened to be an English organization; but Clara Morris gave a similar description of the company in Cleveland, Ohio, where she played as a girl.

Everywhere, the "line of business" was inflexible. The leading woman—often the manager's wife and a bit matronly—was entitled to play Ophelia. There might be a walking lady who would at least look the part. But would the leading woman relinquish it? Not while there was a breath in her body. Others of the company would not budge from their rights, either. So if the scenery was rarely a fit for any one drama, neither were the actors.

(Today the theatre has gone to the opposite extreme. If a character is supposed to have a wart on his face, someone with a real wart is likely to be engaged. When "You Can't Take It With You" was in preparation, theatrical agencies had to search their lists for a man who

could both act and play the xylophone. They found
one.)

The "line of business" made for economy of effort.
Performers were "up" in the rôles that belonged to their
"lines"—and that saved a deal of memorizing. With
a drama and a farce in every evening's bill, one man in
his time played many parts. In his second season as a
utility, Frederick Warde appeared in eighty rôles.

The ordinary acting fostered by this system was not
inspiring. There was, for example, the Hamlet of whom
a Scotch woman said, "I lik-ed the play verra weel, with
the seengle exception of the gentleman in black, who went
aboot preachin' ower muckle." An actor named Duff
was accustomed to make a strong impression in a combat
in "The Lady of the Lake." As he fell, wounded, it was
his habit to roll over with his face away from the footlights. He contrived to do it so that he lay over a trap,
beneath which a property man was stationed with a brush-
ful of stage blood—the brush being thrust up to smear
the actor's face. Then, when he struggled to his feet to
resume the fray, he appeared to be bleeding desperately.
But one night he fell over the wrong trap, and the audience saw the paintbrush come up through the floor a few
feet away.

Obscure tragedians and tragediennes were the most horrible examples of teapot acting. They loved speeches
that they could "get their teeth into," according to "Trelawny of the Wells." Lofty manner and standardized
emotion were all they had to offer.

Comedians and character actors, never so oppressed
with dignity, sought to give their acting a resemblance to
life. Still, there were those among them who merely
copied other players—like a certain comedian whom John

Bernard described. "Lewis was his model, but he had unluckily caught only that great actor's legs."

When Anna Cora Mowatt's comedy "Fashion" was presented at the Park Theatre, New York, for the first time, in March 1845, it made a great hit. Edgar Allan Poe was among the critics who reviewed it, and from his comments it is possible to get an idea of how it was acted. He did not care for the stage conventions then in use:

> . . . In the category—total deficiency in verisimilitude—we must include the rectangular crossings and recrossings of the dramatis personae on the stage; the coming forward to the footlights when anything of interest is to be told; the reading of private letters in a loud rhetorical tone; the preposterous "asides." . . .
>
> Some of the author's intended points were lost through the inevitable inadvertences of a first representing, but on the whole went off exceedingly well. . . . Trueman and Tiffany were represented with all possible effect by Chippendale and Barry—and Mrs. Barry as Mrs. Tiffany was the life of the play. Zeke was caricatured. Prudence was well exaggerated by Mrs. Knight—and the character in her hands elicited more applause than any one other of the dramatis personae. . . .

It is clear that the two old men and the two old women of the company at the Park Theatre were among its most valuable assets. They were Chippendale and Barry, Mrs. Barry and Mrs. Knight. Besides acting, Barry served as stage manager. Mrs. Knight had been a star in her younger days, and Mrs. Barry had played Juliet at the Park in 1827. All of the quartet apparently overshadowed the leading man and the leading woman.

This was one of the foremost companies in America. While its resources were much above the average, its presentation of "Fashion" shows the general workings of the stock system at that time. From Anna Cora Mowatt we get a still closer view, for she attended a rehearsal on the day before her play opened:

> The stage was lighted by a single branch of gas, shooting up to the height of several feet in the center of the footlights. It sent forth a dim, blue, spectral light. On the right of the stage was the prompter's table—on the left, the manager's table. Beneath the spectral light sat a palefaced prompter, with the manuscript of Fashion in his hand. At his side stood the "call boy," a child of about ten years of age. He held a long strip of paper, somewhat resembling the tailor's bills of young spendthrifts as they are represented on the stage. This was the "call" for the actors, and directed him which to summon from the green room.
>
> . . . It was singular to see these kings and queens of the stage, whom I had been accustomed to behold decked in gold-embroidered robes and jeweled crowns . . . now moving about in this "visible darkness." . . . Every actor held his part, to which he constantly referred.

Although it was the day before the première, these players had scarcely had time to learn their lines. They knew no more leisurely way of putting on a new piece.

Following the success of "Fashion," Anna Cora Mowatt went on the stage herself, making her début at the Park Theatre in June 1845, supported by the company that had played her comedy. She was twenty-six—a writer for popular magazines, a novelist, and an amateur actress. In

Paris she had seen Rachel. Without taking herself too seriously, she had her own ideas about acting—and she was never a teapot. Pauline in "The Lady of Lyons" was her first professional rôle. She trained herself for it in private.

> The day before my début, it was necessary that I should rehearse with the company. . . . The actors crowded around the wings, eager to pass judgment on the trembling débutante. The stage manager, seated at his table, scanned her with cold and scrutinizing eyes. The pale prompter laid his book on his knee, that he might stare at her the more deliberately.

Next evening, when the call boy knocked at the door of the shabby star dressing room and said, "Pauline, you are called," she thought he was being "singularly familiar." However, she proceeded to the stage and seated herself on a sofa across from the actress who was to play her mother. Someone arranged the folds of her train. Then the intrepid Anna Cora heard the tinkle of a little bell, which meant that the curtain was going up, and she was frightened.

> I could only gasp out, "Not yet—I cannot!" . . . Managers, actors, prompter, all rushed on the stage; some offered water, some scent bottles, some fanned me . . . I was arguing with myself against this ungovernable emotion—this humiliating exhibition.

She pulled herself together and the curtain ascended. From that moment the performance went well for the new star. It ended with an ovation.

She was soon booked for a season's tour, and in her first year on the stage she played two hundred nights.

This meant learning many new parts. Among those she tossed off were Juliet, Mrs. Haller in "The Stranger," Lady Teazle, and the heroine in her own "Fashion." One rehearsal for each play was the usual quota.

Edgar Allan Poe thought Mrs. Mowatt a delightful actress:

> The greatest charm of her manner is its natural-ness. She speaks and moves with a well-controlled impulsiveness as different as can be conceived from the customary rant and cant, the hack conventional-ism, of the stage.

That hack conventionalism grew out of the routine of the theatre in that period. Old prompt-books and "sides" for parts are now evidence of what this routine was; for each prompt-book is a complete guide to the presentation of a play according to practice at the time the book was marked.

The pages may be annotated in several different hand-writings—witness to the care with which these documents were passed along by people who are mere shadows to present playgoers. A copy of "Cato" reads, "Marked from Vandenhoff's book, which he marked from J. P. Kemble's book—March 1838." J. W. Wallack's prompt copy of "The Will," printed in London in 1815, is in-scribed, "Henry B. Phillips, Prompter, Wallack's Lyceum, 1852." A Schiller's "Mary Stuart" bears information, "First and second acts can be transposed, and a better last act is appended from Fanny Kemble's version."

The striking brevity of stage directions in such books explains how a drama could be put on with only one or two rehearsals. "Enter R. U. E." (right upper entrance) the old directions may read, or "Enter D. F." (D. F.

means door in flat—a "practicable" door being cut in the flat canvas.   Otherwise, actors walked on through spaces between the wings.)   No time was wasted in going over these details at rehearsals; every player had been instructed early in his career in making entrances and exits.   To suggest his stopping to practice such trifles would have implied that he didn't know his calling.   He had also been schooled in an accepted drawing room manner, and in the conduct of stage struggles and arrests.   The teapots were sticklers for all the rules.   They knew how to faint, to fall, to stab themselves.

Those "rectangular crossings and recrossings" to which Poe took exception are plentiful in old 'scripts.   A modern director tries to have characters move about as though they were doing so of their own volition; but his forerunner just told players to cross from right to left or left to right.   That settled it—they crossed.   When Clara Morris entered Daly's company in 1870, she was surprised to find him stopping to think out plausible reasons for all those changes of position.

Speed being essential at rehearsals long ago, it was considered bad form to attempt any acting.   The thing to do was to "walk through," muttering lines.   Sometimes the visiting star attended a rehearsal.   Once in a while he would give advice to some young player, but most stars had tired of trying to get the results they wanted from any cast.   They were content if casts contrived not to get in the way.

Thus most of the training given to novices did not come from masters of acting, but from overworked prompters and stage managers serving as drill sergeants.   If walking ladies and gentlemen memorized their lines and "business,"

nobody pestered them with the psychology of their parts.
Though players of exceptional capacity went through this
apprenticeship without being denatured, the mediocre
grasped at rules and got no further. Never thereafter
were they able to see the forest for the trees.

A manual of acting published about 1850 tells the beginner how to behave at rehearsals:

> On hearing your *cue* . . . if it should be a letter
> or message you are to deliver, move quickly and
> gracefully on in a business-like manner, with your
> eyes fixed directly upon the person to whom it is to
> be given; present it in an easy and direct manner;
> keep your position firmly, with your arms hanging
> easily, and wait till you receive your reply or *cue*
> to retire. Turn easily round and make your exit in
> the same style with which you entered, assuming an
> easy, graceful carriage. . . .

All this sounds a good deal like a talk from a golf instructor. How, alas, was the flustered messenger to "move
quickly and gracefully on"? "Make your exit in the same
style with which you entered," would take care of itself,
however.

After a few ignominious efforts, the aspirant would
acquire a certain coolness about delivering missives. One
night he might be garbed as a Roman soldier, the next as
a hearty English yeoman, and the third as a Louis XIV
footman; but the procedure would be practically identi-
cal. He was by now persuaded that walking and talking
on the stage were quite set apart from walking and talking
in real life. Soon he found out that all entrances were to
be made with the up-stage foot, and that he was always
to kneel on the down-stage knee. "When a speech is

followed by an exit, always end at the wing," he also learned.

He received injunctions to memorize his lines accurately, and to give roundness to each word when speaking. He was to be prompt in arriving at the theatre, prompt in answering the call boy, and he was to comport himself in a "gentlemanly manner" in the greenroom. But as for looking into the mind of the character he played, that was an afterthought in his instructions.

Under such tutelage, the routine utility man developed in time into a conventionalized Romeo or a third-rate scowling tragedian. He grew proficient in externals, and at last settled into a happy confidence that wrecked him. He thought he knew all about acting.

There was no definite date at which the palmy days ended—but they and the stock-and-star system began petering out together in the 1870's.

Two New York managers, Augustin Daly and A. M. Palmer, were putting on new comedies and melodramas. They were not great plays, but they were well done. Both men selected their casts to suit each production, and rehearsed them painstakingly. It was Daly who first took a stand against the tyranny of the "line of business." Actors and actresses who signed contracts with him had to agree to let him cast them as he thought best.

This was revolutionary. Actors felt injured when rôles "out of their line" were given them. Still, it freed them of an incubus; and it greatly enhanced the effect of each drama.

The public had no objection at all to the innovation. It delighted audiences to see a production with costuming and scenery that really fitted the story. They enjoyed watching well-rehearsed players who knew all their lines and had practiced their scenes together. Meanwhile, the same sort of revolution was accomplished in England. (Robertson, Bancroft, and others helped it along.) Thus the length of runs in New York and London increased, and plays began to be sent on tour complete with actors, settings, and costumes.

When these attractions came into competition with old-fashioned stock companies in towns on the road, the stock companies suffered. Their local patrons had been getting pretty tired of the old round of garbled Shakespeare and standard dramas, done with little co-operation between star and support.

So it was decay from within, as well as assault from without, that destroyed the hardy old stock-and-star system. Slowly, there came to be less and less demand for players who were "up" in all the standard rôles. Actors and actresses who could adapt themselves to the newer tendencies did not fare badly. But those who could not forget that they had once had "lines of business" and had spouted their way through the classics, lost their usefulness. Sad as it was for them, the teapots were on the shelf.

8.

A Camille, A Hamlet, and A Rip Van Winkle

SCENE 1—Wallack's Lyceum, on Broadway near Broome Street, New York.

Time—Evening of January 22, 1857.

It is a bitter, snowy night and the theatre is little more than half full, but everybody in it is cheering. The curtain has just fallen on the first act of Matilda Heron's "Camille." Hers is not the conventional acting that these playgoers know by heart. It is even, some of them insist, quite shocking—but the shock is agreeable, tingling, like the feeling that runs up your arms when you put your hands on the knobs of those queer electric batteries. She *is* a battery; she exudes vitality. And no one who comes within range of this force can deny that a new and unique genius has appeared on Broadway.

Miss Heron affects no stagey air or voice. She looks, moves, speaks as she believes Marguerite Gauthier would; she seems "to be playing within herself, employed in the examination of her own heart, and forgetful of the presence of any auditor. . . . You lose sight of the actress entirely, and see only the woman."

Once in a while she walks across the stage with her

arms akimbo, or picks up her hoop skirts "as if she were getting into her coach." A critic in the audience dislikes that, for no lady would do it. But the lady of the camelias *is* no lady, and this is precisely what Matilda Heron wants to convey. At any rate, the critic forgives her because of the charms and beauties of her impersona-tion—chief among them, the truth of its emotion. "She is prodigal of touches of nature," says another observer.

One finds something most appealing in this Camille, as she sits turned negligently in a chair—her head slightly drooping, her hands in her lap, her hair parted in the middle and hanging in large soft ringlets that cover the lobes of her ears. Her eyes, under straight eyebrows, have a thoughtful, absorbed look. Her mouth, both sensi-tive and determined, is rather wide. There is "a halo of individuality about her."

The play proceeds. "Camille, or the Fate of a Co-quette," is its title. In various forms, the drama has been played all over the United States since it became the rage in Paris in 1852. Previous American presentations white-washed the heroine, but this is a more authentic version, adapted from the French by Miss Heron herself. She has worked over it for a long time.

With each act, the impression she makes on her audi-ence deepens. That is because "she never attempts to be grand before her subject warrants it; but when she has gathered sufficient warmth and vitality from her char-acter, she rises with the story of the piece, and reserves her intensest powers until it breaks into its climax." Her restraint is fifty times more moving than the wailing and tears of Camilles who have done the part before her. Her death scene "of measureless desolations and short-lived

JOSEPH JEFFERSON

MATILDA HERON

ecstacies" is "as noble a piece of acting as we desire to
see."

At the end, the house rises in a tumult of applause.
Matilda Heron is the Camille by whom all others will be
judged for years to come. The critics—among them Mr.
Wilkins of the *Herald*, Mr. Seymour of the *Times*, and
Mr. Fry of the *Tribune*—depart to write glowing ac-
counts.

There is one paper which can scarcely contain itself for
joy at Miss Heron's triumph. "We will take the liberty
to say that her present pre-eminent distinction was predicted by us three years ago," it states. This journal is
the *Spirit of the Times*, an excellent weekly devoted to
turf and stage.

> Decidedly the sensation of the week has been the
> debut of Matilda Heron. . . . Despite the common
> reluctance to endorse new merit . . . she overcame
> all obstacles, and won such a triumph as we have no
> recollection of in the annals of the stage. From a
> comparatively unknown and . . . quite obscure per-
> son, she rose to be the greatest woman of the stage;
> and the critics . . . balanced their enthusiasm by
> reflections upon those who had failed to discover as
> much as this before.

It seems that back in the autumn of '52—four years
ago—this Matilda Heron was at the Bowery Theatre. But
she attracted no attention beyond a few comments that
her playing was crude. However, George Wilkes, editor
of the *Spirit of the Times*, went to California late in '53
on some political errand, and there he saw Matilda Heron
playing in San Francisco. He pronounced her a genius,
and wrote an astute article about her which was published

in San Francisco. This article his own paper now re-
prints, with satisfaction.

What makes Miss Heron's playing individual? And
why, only a few years back, did it impress people as full
of crudities?

> The style of Miss Heron is a most peculiar one.
> When you first see her, it jars with all your pre-
> conceived notions of what you considered "acting,"
> [Wilkes puts it]. There is nothing of the actress
> about her, and your first impression is, that she has
> mistaken her vocation. . . . Generally in her earlier
> scenes there is an utter absence of effort. . . . In
> this gliding ease consists her deepest art. . . . To
> satisfy an audience, a performer must progress in
> merit from the first scene to the last. It will not do
> to begin well and continue only as well as he com-
> menced; he must end better than he began. . . .
> We admit, therefore, that the style of Miss Heron
> is fluctuating and uneven; but it is the unevenness of
> Nature, which takes repose between great ef-
> forts. . . . This was the unevenness that made Kean
> great; an unevenness that is described to us by one
> who saw him in Othello, as making him look in the
> first two acts like a little slip-shod tailor, but which,
> in the third, increased him to the measure of Jove,
> with the lightnings shooting through his fingers! . . .
> The chief peculiarity of Matilda Heron's style is
> its quiet intensity in the passages where others
> rave. . . . In ordinary passages, though always cor-
> rect, she is sometimes tame. . . . But give her a scene
> in which she can *create*,—some character in which
> her genius can step beyond the author's lines and
> have full scope to second him with her imagination,
> and she is truly great.

An oriental fable tells of two magnificent hunting dogs presented to Alexander the Great by a barbarian chieftain. Alexander tried them in the chase for a stag, found them useless, and had them killed. But the donor wrung his hands and said, "Oh, mighty king, had you but set those dogs to hunt lions, you would have seen what creatures they were!" Miss Heron's acting is like that; she must hunt lions.

This was Matilda Heron, at twenty-six. During that winter of 1857, her "Camille" ran a hundred nights at Wallack's. In later seasons she appeared in various plays, by herself and by other authors, but nothing else she ever did was so widely popular as her "Camille." Great-hearted, impulsive, improvident, to the American public she *was* Camille; and when she died, in 1877, "Camille" was engraved on her casket.

She was born near Londonderry, Ireland, on October 7, 1830, and was brought to the United States in her childhood. Studying for the stage under Peter Richings—an old actor and stage manager—she made her début at the Walnut Street Theatre, Philadelphia, in February 1851. She played Bianca in "Fazio," a standard star rôle of the period.

As she grew up in the palmy days, the bulk of the acting she must have seen was at variance from the ideas she afterward adopted. Edwin Forrest, then at his peak, was robustious—with rolling eyes, swelling muscles, and the roar of a splendid voice. So outlandish were some of his displays that Walt Whitman could not abide them. It was the greatness of Forrest's personality that his audiences felt; but certainly not truth to everyday life. Charlotte Cushman was a noble, brainy, magnetic woman. Her

Rosalind, said Lawrence Barrett, was "one steady flame of intelligence." But much of her work was in the declamatory style.

So from neither Cushman nor Forrest, nor from the many inferior copies of them, could Matilda Heron have got her naturalistic method. She must have thought it out for herself. In six years from her début, she was at the top of her profession.

Her first marriage was a melodramatic affair. In San Francisco, in June 1854, she secretly married a young lawyer. He wanted her to give up the stage; she temporized. They came to an understanding that she would go East to fill certain engagements and would take a trip to Europe which she had already planned. Then she would return to California and domesticity. So they parted after five days, "with loving words and bright hopes," says an account published in a Boston paper after her death.

At a men's dinner in San Francisco, someone spoke slightingly of Miss Heron to the man who was secretly her husband, and exhibited a daguerreotype which looked like her. This, said the snake of an informant, was the picture of a woman of doubtful repute in New York. The husband stopped writing to Matilda Heron, and waited for her return to ask for an explanation.

When they met, she was amazed at his question. Then she recalled that when she was seven or eight there had been some scandal about a young widowed sister of hers, whom she never saw again. The resemblance between them was striking. Thus the lawyer got his explanation, but lost his bride. Being a person of spirit, she told him to go back to San Francisco without her. A few years later he died.

It was while Matilda Heron waited for letters from the man who had been heels-over-head in love with her, that she saw "Camille" in Paris. The drama made a deep impression on her. Perhaps it called up her own unhappiness. Or perhaps Marguerite Gauthier, the social outcast, drew on the sympathy of Miss Heron, who was always vulnerable in her pity for unfortunates. Living in a conventional age, she was by temperament unconventional. From that time forward, her acting espoused the cause of the erring sister. "Give me any woman so long as she's lost," she used to say. Then and there, in Paris in 1855, she made her own translation of "La Dame aux Camélias."

So it is clear that her attention was deeply set on "Camille" nearly two years before her success in the play. As a human being, she warmed to the theme; as an actress, she knew that this was the part for her. Some strong attraction between player and rôle exists when the actor makes an enduring impression in the part.

But the performer's initial enthusiasm is not all. After that comes work, close intimacy with the character, and mutual adaptation. That is why actors say they grow in rôles by playing them.

Matilda Heron had done this before she brought her "Camille" to New York. In 1855-56 she acted it for eight weeks in New Orleans. "The success of the play was entirely due to the efforts of Miss Heron," wrote an actor who was there. Afterward she gave performances in St. Louis and Cincinnati.

All this explains her conquest at Wallack's in 1857. It was no happy accident, but the converging of forces that had been set in motion long before.

That engagement at Wallack's was fateful for her in another direction. Toward the end of 1857 she married

Robert Stoepel, who conducted the orchestra there. But she was not destined for fortune in matrimony. After much unhappiness, the alliance ended in divorce in 1869. The Stoepels had one daughter. Her stage name was Bijou Heron, and she afterward married Henry Miller.

Someone of Matilda Heron's blood is still working in the theatre. For Gilbert Miller—producer of "Victoria Regina," "Tovarich," "The Late Christopher Bean," and many other plays—is her grandson.

Scene 2—The Winter Garden, New York.   (It is not, however, the Winter Garden of the 1930's, but an earlier playhouse, on Broadway not far below Astor Place.)

Time—Monday evening, November 26, 1860.

Edwin Booth, a promising actor of twenty-seven, is playing "Hamlet" for the first time in this city. There are people in the audience who suspect that his performance will be a mere copy of his father's. They do not know that this young man has set himself to eradicate, as far as he can, everything in his work that he might have borrowed from Junius Brutus Booth.

The Hamlet this audience sees is a slender, graceful, princely figure in black. (Edwin Booth's height is about five feet seven, and he is far less ruggedly built than his father.) With his dark, waving hair—which he wears a little long—and his large, dark, brooding eyes, there is something moving and magnetic about him. Those eyes, even in repose, show a thin crescent of white below the iris.

When the final curtain falls, opinion is divided. The assemblage, by no means large, has shown considerable enthusiasm; but the older folk tell each other that this young fellow will scarcely set the river afire.

If you look in the papers next day to see what the critics say, you will find nothing. Last night's performance was not an important opening—for the opera, at the Academy of Music in Fourteenth Street, began its season with "La Juive."

Besides, theatrical news gets little space in the papers in these days of 1860. There are so many columns of alarming dispatches from the South; there is all this talk about secession. . . . And from Illinois, correspondents are telegraphing rumors as to the men whom the President-elect, Mr. Lincoln, is likely to chose for his Cabinet.

In the midst of such items, along about Thursday, you discover in the *Herald* several paragraphs in very small type about Monday's performance. You glance through them, and your eyes light on this: "Mr. Booth's Hamlet is, as we have said, a very clever performance, but does not call for minute criticism." Can it be that you applauded too heartily? You settle down to read the review:

> Mr. Edwin Booth commenced an engagement here on Monday, and has appeared three times as Hamlet to audiences more remarkable for enthusiasm than for numbers. . . . Mr. Booth's prime quality . . . is that he appears perfectly unconscious that there is an audience before him. He seems to us to possess this very important power of losing himself in the play to an eminent degree. We do not altogether fancy Mr. Booth's elocution. He reads the soliloquies intelligently and effectively, but has not yet mastered the art of speaking dialogue in a level, natural, offhand manner. . . .
>
> We should judge that he would appear to greater advantage in the French sensation dramas, where in his redundancy of gesture and action . . . he would

add to the effect of the performance. In Hamlet we naturally look for more repose than Mr. Booth is at present capable of giving us. . . .

In 1860, Edwin Booth's Prince of Denmark was, as we say of motorcars, an early model. As a creation it grew with time, acquiring greater restraint and new depths. But even at the start, his performance went straight to the heart of acting; he possessed "this very important power of losing himself in the play." It was that quality which would eventually modify all the others.

Doubtless it disappointed him to read—he had not yet given up reading his notices—that he failed to speak dialogue in an off-hand manner; for that was the very thing he wanted to do. He and his young wife had discussed this new method, and it appealed to them—within limits. Not that they quite approved of Matilda Heron!

> . . . The conversational, colloquial school you desire to adopt is the only true one, Edwin, for the present day, [Mary Devlin had written him before they were married] but, as you reasonably add, "too much is dangerous." For example, Miss Heron in the beginning of her career was praised for her "naturalness," and deservedly so. . . . But *now* . . . she endeavors, or labors rather, to be so very commonplace that it is simply ridiculous. . . .

Mary Devlin had married Edwin in the July preceding this New York engagement. She was twenty, and profoundly convinced that it was his destiny to be a very great actor. "If my love is selfish, you will never be great; part of you belongs to the world," she wrote him. "I *must* remember this. . . ."

Between him and the rôle of Hamlet, there was a temperamental bond. Not that he chose the part; it chose him. He could not escape it. His mind was introspective, gentle, shy, tragic—and the events of his life accentuated this. He had a quaint, quiet humor, but something akin to asthma gave him paroxysms of pain if he laughed loud or heartily.

Born in November 1833, on a night when there was an extraordinary display of meteors, he was the child of a problem-father. That relationship influenced his life and his Hamlet.

"My close acquaintance with so fantastic a temperament as was my father's," he confessed, "so accustomed me to that in him which appeared strange to others, that much of *Hamlet's* 'mystery' seems to me no more than idiosyncracy." Hamlet was no puzzle, after living side by side with a man who could put an antic disposition on before you could say knife. "And fools on fools still ask what 'Hamlet' means," was a quotation Edwin Booth inscribed in his prompt-book.

His childhood was spent at his birthplace—his father's farm, at Bel Air, Maryland. Under no circumstance was he to grow up an actor. But by the time the boy was fourteen, the habits of Junius Brutus had become extremely irregular; it was often touch-and-go whether he would be sober enough to get to the theatre. He needed someone to be with him constantly—and this was the responsibility put upon a diffident, sensitive lad.

Edwin was packed off to join his father on tour, serving as dresser, nurse, and watchdog. He would play the banjo and sing negro songs to amuse Junius Brutus and keep him out of taverns—but this was not always successful. There were all kinds of emergencies, in which a son who shrank from attention was chained to a father who drew a great deal of it.

Nevertheless, this brought the boy into the world of the playhouse. He never knew when he learned the lines of his father's rôles; he absorbed them from listening. In 1849, shortly before he was sixteen, he played his first small part. Something more than a year later, there came a night when Junius Brutus Booth was seized with the whim that he would not play "Richard III," for which he was billed. Edwin must go to the theatre and do it for him. All persuasions failing, Edwin had to. He had never studied or rehearsed the part, but he got through creditably.

Still, when he tried being a utility in a Baltimore stock company, he was awkward and confused. He did everything wrong.

In 1852, he went to California with his father—for actors had not been far behind the forty-niners. Junius Brutus returned to the "States," where he died within a few months. But for four years Edwin worked and struggled in California and Australia, this being his apprenticeship in the characters that afterward made up his repertory.

Going back to the States in 1856, he played in Richmond, Virginia, where he met Mary Devlin. Joseph Jefferson, stage manager of the theatre, introduced them to each other. She was then sixteen, and was cast as Juliet to his Romeo. This was the preface to their marriage in 1860.

In late November 1864, Edwin Booth began his phenomenal hundred nights in "Hamlet" at the Winter Garden, New York. (The record was never matched in this country until John Barrymore's hundred nights in the part during the winter of 1922-23, and only exceeded by John Gielgud in 1936-37.)

That November evening of '64 was four years to a day since Booth's first New York appearance in the same rôle. It was the same theatre, too. But much had changed for him in the interval. Mary Devlin Booth, who had been so sure that her husband would be famous and happy, had died in February 1863. Edwin was famous now, but he was not happy. In all the years that stretched ahead, he would never forget her.

Tonight he was presenting the play with a carefully selected company, and with scenery that was historically correct. Robert Stoepel, Matilda Heron's husband, had composed special music and was conducting the orchestra.

There was now no waiting for reviews in the papers; they were printed with alacrity:

> Mr. Booth gave to the very life [said the *Herald*] the picture of a reflective, sensitive, gentle, generous nature, tormented, borne down. . . . There are no inconsistencies, no mysteries, no knotty or incomprehensible points in the part. . . . As Mr. Booth plays it, all is as clear as daylight. . . .

The *Times* called his Hamlet "a part in which he has no living equal." The *Tribune's* praise was more measured:

> . . . Mr. Booth's personation is the finest with which we are acquainted. It is, indeed, the only one we can look upon with favor. It does not satisfy our ideal impression, but it exhibits many qualities which command our highest respect. . . .
>
> With the general conception we cannot agree; but the methods by which the conception is carried out

leave nothing to be desired. . . . Such tenderness, such dignity, such pathos as throng through it are seldom seen upon the stage. . . .

In this middle period of Booth's career, there were always people who could pick flaws in his Hamlet. An old newspaper clipping argues, for example, against the touches of humor which he put into the part. "Ha, ha, boy, sayest thou so! Art thou there, True penny?" had a bantering tone in it which that critic thought unsuitable. But whatever the hair-splitters might say, people did not merely admire this Prince of Denmark—they loved him. There are records of the "quick, vital, intense sympathy that prevailed between audience and actor."

He had lavished pains on his prompt-book of the drama. A comparison of it with the 'script Guthrie McClintic compiled for the production in which Gielgud appeared, shows many differences between a mid-nineteenth century presentation and such recent ones as Gielgud's and Leslie Howard's. Both of the latter gave the story much more fully and accurately. Yet Booth's version was a return to the genuine text, after the maimed adaptations which had long been played.

Booth believed that Hamlet's madness was feigned, and his impersonation was built on that.

> . . . I essentially am not in madness,
> But mad in craft,

he quoted on the title page of his published prompt-book. He did not speak those lines in the play, however, for they are in the part of the closet scene which he omitted. (Mr. McClintic told me he was sure that the habitual deletion of these lines from old acting versions was to blame for the whole controversy over whether or not Hamlet was mad.)

"This terrible success of *Hamlet* seems to swallow up everything else theatrical," said Booth in a letter written in January 1865. The hundred nights' run continued till March 22, when he left New York to fill his engagement in Boston. There, on the evening of Good Friday, April 14, he played "The Iron Chest." That night in Washington his brother, John Wilkes Booth, killed Lincoln.

For many months thereafter, Edwin Booth thought never to act again. In his home in New York—someone who saw him told me—he would sit for hours with his head bent, his hands clasped in his lap, twirling his thumbs. At last he decided "to abandon the heavy, aching gloom of my little red room, where I have sat so long chewing my heart in solitude, for the excitement of the only trade for which God has fitted me."

As Hamlet, he reappeared in New York, on January 3, 1866, and was greeted by prolonged cheers. Throughout his life tragedies befell him. Mary Devlin died; his brother was an assassin; his magnificent theatre lost a fortune and Booth toiled under mountainous debts; his second wife, Mary McVicker, went insane. But he and Hamlet journeyed together to the last.

He found relief in other parts—it was said that his Iago and his Richelieu were more consummate pieces of acting —but the public wanted his Hamlet. There grew to be a blending of his own personality with it—and his daughter wrote that in her childhood she was long in disentangling her father from the rôle. His work forced solitude and reflection upon him. Years of lofty thinking, said William Winter, made Booth's Hamlet what it finally became.

He was a master of stage technique. But the means by which he immensely moved his audiences was that ability to sink himself in the part, which had been apparent "to an eminent degree" in 1860. This natural bent, he cultivated. He suffered from insomnia, and he said that in the hours when he could not sleep he let the moods of his rôles flood through his mind. Once he wrote a friend, "I believe you understand how completely I 'ain't here' most of the time. It's an awful thing to be somebody else all the while."

It was not the public only that loved him; players in his company worshipped him. His was not a stormy nature, but sympathetic, considerate, and given to mild jollity. He had had battles with himself, for at one period he drank heavily; but he conquered, and it became a thing long past. Once when some young actresses had finished a season with him and had said their goodbyes, they asked each other disconsolately, "How can we go back to being with ordinary people?" That was what work, griefs, and successes had made of Booth.

It was as Hamlet that he gave his last performance—on April 4, 1891, at the Academy of Music, in Brooklyn. It had not been announced as a farewell; but people knew his health was poor, and they came fearing that they might never see him again. Some of them could remember the Booth of many years before; others were young people; there were small children, too, brought so that all their lives they might say they had once seen Edwin Booth.

The house was packed; extra chairs had been put into the orchestra pit. After the final curtain spectators cheered and waved handkerchiefs. They must have a speech. Booth—feeble, touched, but in control of his emotion—told them in his beautiful voice that he needed a long rest. He hoped this would not be the last time. . . . He never played again—and he died in June 1893.

Scene 3—A barn in Paradise Valley, at the foot of the Pocono Mountains, in Pennsylvania.

Time—Summer of 1859.

It is raining outside, and on the hay in the loft lies an actor, whiling away a day of his vacation by reading the published letters of Washington Irving. The actor is a small man of thirty with shrewd yet kindly blue eyes and what he himself calls a nut-cracker face. This is Joseph Jefferson, a comedian of moderate repute.

He has just come upon a paragraph telling of how Irving went to the theatre one evening and saw him— Joe Jefferson—in "The Road to Ruin." This gives him a thrill of pleasure. That Washington Irving, the distinguished author, saw him play and liked him! Then, because he is thinking of Irving, the recollection of Rip Van Winkle springs into his mind with a magic clarity and insistence. Rip. . . . Why wouldn't this be the very part for him? An odd American character for an American actor. . . .

He hurries to the farm house through the rain, finds a copy of "The Sketch Book," and brings the volume back to the haymow. Eagerly, he plunges into the story of Rip Van Winkle, which he has not read since he was a boy. He is disappointed, for Rip does not speak ten lines. How turn him into the chief character of a play? There have already been acting versions of the tale—not very good ones. Jefferson vaguely recalls them.

Still, the idea has taken a strange hold on him. Perhaps it is because this locality where he is staying is filled with farmers of Dutch descent who have seeped down here from the Catskill region.

So strong is the urge upon him that he packs up at once and goes to the city. He ransacks theatrical wardrobes for old leather and mildewed cloth; he has wigs made. In high excitement which continues day after day, he assembles his costumes for Rip Van Winkle—yet he has no play. This is the queerest situation an actor was ever in. So he sits down and writes his own drama, working at top speed, building on the old versions but altering them. Within a few days the scenes are on paper.

Back he goes to the farm, and the barn there becomes his rehearsal hall. For several weeks he studies and practices this new rôle of his, alone. Early in September, he goes to Washington, determined to try his play before an audience. Every detail is clear in his mind. He rehearses the company at Carusi's Hall, and soon the curtain goes up on his first presentation of "Rip Van Winkle."

When it is over, he knows it is not a success. The part is all he dreamed—but the play lacks substance. Does he break his heart over the fizzling out of his summer's hopes? No. He puts the plan away in some pigeonhole of his brain, and goes to New York to commence his regular season at the Winter Garden, for which he has been engaged by Dion Boucicault.

A good deal more than a year later—on Sunday, December 23, 1860—the Winter Garden inserts a certain advertisement in the *Herald*. ". . . Mr. Joseph Jefferson will make his first appearance this season in the character of Rip Van Winkle—In an entirely NEW DRAMA arranged . . . by himself . . . new music, scenery, costumes, comic tableaux." On Thursday and Friday of the week's engagement, a whole advertising column gives the story scene by scene, with comments. It reads in part:

> . . . Twenty years gone by—To Rip it is but a day. . . . This is the poetic feature of the drama. . . .
>
> The drama is strictly pastoral in its character with just sufficient plot to create an interest. . . . They who look for great sensation effects will be disappointed; but true lovers of a glorious Dutch painting . . . will look upon this great poetic creation . . . as one of the happiest dramas of the present day.

Despite that glowing—and paid—encomium, the public is apathetic. Joe Jefferson? Yes, he is delightful. But as for this play, one week of it will do.

These were the modest beginnings of a life-long partnership between Jefferson and Rip Van Winkle. Not till Dion Boucicault rewrote the play in 1865 did the partnership come into its glory; but thereafter Jefferson's Rip outlived Matilda Heron's Camille and Booth's Hamlet, and did not quit the stage till 1904.

Born in Philadelphia in February 1829, little Joe Jefferson was a child of exceptional talents, dancing and doing imitations when he was four. He belonged to the fourth generation of actors named Jefferson, his great-grandfather having played with Garrick. His grandfather, a comedian of skill, was highly regarded in New York and Philadelphia.

His father's fortunes were less exalted. He led his family from one poverty-stricken theatrical enterprise to another through the Middle West and South. An actor and manager with a taste for scene painting, he had no sense of money but was likeable and always hopeful. Once when he had gone bankrupt, his friends found him sitting cheerfully on the bank of a river, fishing. He said he had lost so much that he could no longer afford to worry about anything. There was a touch of this sunny disposition in his son's Rip Van Winkle years later.

But even as a lad, the son was a better business man than his father. Joe's vagrant upbringing gave him hard training, both in life and in acting. He played children's parts; he sang and danced; he ground colors in the paint room. At fourteen, he was a utility man in the stock company at Mobile.

At last he rose to be a comedian. By the time he was twenty-one, in 1850, he was an old young man, he said. He had played a season or two in Philadelphia, had appeared in New York, and felt himself prosperous enough to marry. His reputation grew steadily from then till that summer when he first thought of Rip Van Winkle.

For him, the fascination of the rôle was its linking of the commonplace and the fantastic.

> If the sleep of twenty years [he wrote] was merely incongruous, there would be room for argument pro and con; but as it is an impossibility, I felt the audience would accept it at once . . . from a desire to know in what condition a man's mind would be if such an event could happen. . . . This was the strange and original attitude of the character that attracted me.

He heightened the strangeness of the meeting with Hendrik Hudson's crew by making the spirits absolutely silent. They answered Rip's questions by nodding or shaking their heads; for a whole act, no one spoke but Rip.

On September 3, 1866, at the Olympic Theatre, New York, Jefferson presented a new and triumphant "Rip Van Winkle" for the first time in America. Dion Boucicault had redrafted the play a year earlier in London; and there, at the Adelphi Theatre, Jefferson had appeared in it for 170 nights. Back in his own country, perhaps he remembered that it was now seven years since that September when he had made his first attempt at the rôle.

> Those who were present at the Olympic Theatre on Monday evening—and the house was densely crowded in every part—will not soon forget . . . the strong thrill of sympathy that swept through the audience [read the *Tribune*].
> . . . It is the perception of the heart of Rip Van Winkle . . . that makes Mr. Jefferson's portraiture . . . so truthful and so deeply touching. We see that Rip is a sad dog, a weak, vacillating fellow, fond of his bottle and of idleness, but . . . we understand why all the children in the village love him, why all the dogs run after him. . . .

The Boucicault version of the play was afterward published, with carefully interpolated descriptions of Jefferson's "business" and ways of speaking. In this form, it records a characterization compact of varying moods and minutely truthful touches. Over and over, Rip starts to say something with one idea in mind, is seized with a new thought, and finishes his remark in a changed vein.

In a moment of sentiment, he recalls the day he and Gretchen were married. "My! My! Yah, we was a fine couple altogether." He holds out his cup for the schnaaps Nick Vedder is pouring, but when Nick starts to add water Rip ceases to think of Gretchen and the pretty girl she was. "Stop! I come along mitout that, Nick Vedder." He turns sententious. "Good licker and water is like man and wife. . . . They don't agree together." Now he is laughing. "I always like my licker single."

In everything Rip says or does there is this shifting, living undercurrent. He is a good-for-nothing, and he knows it; no, he is a smart fellow—nobody can get the best of him. Drink brings a man to hunger and rags. He is in deadly earnest, but his hand reaches out. "Is there any more in that cup over there?"

Only the initial nudge to his imagination did Jefferson owe to Washington Irving. With that to start him off, he created a Rip far more ingratiating and complex than the figure in "The Sketch Book." He outdid the original because his passion for Rip was greater.

Jefferson called acting a life of illuminated emotion. The secret of it, he held, lay in knowing the character's mind. The inner man, not the outer man, must be studied.

He put a high value on the player's ability to reproduce with sureness the thing he did first of all by inspiration. For it was no comfort to an audience, he said, to be told that you were good in your part last night or that you might be better tomorrow. In this difficult art of repetition, he was a master, retaining a miraculous freshness in rôles he had done for years. "At every performance, I try to look at the character as if I were meeting him for the first time," he told Otis Skinner.

He played "Rip Van Winkle" to several generations of theatregoers. There were the people who were old when they first saw young Jefferson in the part; and at last there came to be the children who never saw him till he was old. The rôle made him a very rich and a very happy man. There were other parts in his reper-

The Old Print

EDWIN BOOTH

tory, but he never loved any of them so much or played any of them so constantly as Rip. He retired in 1904, and died in 1905.

I was one of thousands of children who were taken to see Jefferson's Rip Van Winkle, but the mouldy men of the mountains diverted my attention from Rip. However, when I saw "High Tor" a forgotten impression of Jefferson came back to me. "High Tor" paralleled the Rip Van Winkle legend, and the character played by Burgess Meredith bore a resemblance to Rip. But that was not all. *Meredith was like Jefferson.* There was the same easy-going, lazy voice and manner, the same look. It was then that I remembered Jefferson's face—the glow and excitement that swept across it. His photographs are lifeless in comparison with what comes to my mind. How an actor born after Jefferson died could get the same look through touch with the same sort of story, I do not know. I only set it down as one of the queer things that happen in the theatre.

Jefferson, Booth, and Matilda Heron are extreme illustrations of the relationship which exists between the actor and the part that is peculiarly his. Some deep attraction draws them together. This does not necessarily mean that the player is like the part; he may play a drunkard or a murderer without being either. But something in the character or the theme behind it has evoked strong emotion in the actor—and that is why he afterward evokes it in his audience. "Acting is not a series of tricks, but the total of the player's reaction to life."

9.

Herne, Mansfield, Irving and Terry— in the 'Nineties

IT IS 1893. The stage in this country is veering away from Shakespeare, and now inclines toward society drama with strong emotional scenes. Actresses wear whaleboned evening gowns. Their skirts, gored and interlined with stiffening, ripple voluminously as they sweep the floor. Leading men are armored in stiff shirt bosoms, high collars, and trousers meticulously pressed.

Still, clothes make very little difference. So good and bad actors are to be found in the '90's, just as they were in the '50's and '70's. Some of them are such expert craftsmen as Nat Goodwin, E. S. Willard, Mme. Modjeska, Mr. and Mrs. Kendal, Ada Rehan, Frank Mayo, Mrs. John Drew, Sol Smith Russell, W. H. Crane, and Stuart Robson.

But there are five other names on the billboards—names of players of transcendent originality, whose work it will be no mistake to examine. They are James A. Herne, whose "Shore Acres" is winning him deserved popularity; Richard Mansfield, touring the country with varying success; and Henry Irving and Ellen Terry, on their fourth American pilgrimage. Herne represents new standards

of acting; Mansfield is the first great star not trained in
the old stock system; Irving and Terry, bred in that tradition, have created another which, in its turn, will pass.

What is going on in the theatre, in this year of the
Columbian Exposition?

An Italian actress named Eleanora Duse is appearing for
the first time in America. "She discards all tricks, all
artifice," says the *New York Dramatic Mirror* in January,
reviewing her "Camille." "She speaks, she moves, as if
spontaneously. She never makes 'points,' she never works
up situations by elaborate and transparent preliminary
devices. . . ."

Early in April the *Mirror* states:

> Charles Frohman, with his business staff, moved
> into his offices in the new Empire Theatre next to
> the Mirror building . . . last week. . . . The offices
> are furnished handsomely in hardwood, and are
> lighted by electric light. . . .

At the end of April, James O'Neill finishes a profitable
starring season on the road. "Mr. O'Neill's little son, by
the way, who had been quite seriously ill, is convalescing."
(The child is doubtless Eugene; he is less than five years
old.)

In June, Edwin Booth dies. Bishop Potter heads the
clergy at the funeral, to which there are 900 cards of
admission. Flags fly at half-mast on Daly's and Palmer's
theatres. "We loved him," people say; and they agree
that the sun has set on the classic drama. This is the
last page in the story of that boy who stood silently hand-
ing cloak and sword to his father.

A new play, "The Second Mrs. Tanqueray," is introduced to New York by the famous Kendals, in October. The public does not like the drama—feeling that Mrs. Kendal, the pink of propriety, ought not to impersonate a lady so shady as Paula Tanqueray.

John Drew is making his first road tour as a star.

— David Belasco, a stage manager and author, laments the failure of his latest play, "The Younger Son." "I made a mistake in supposing the public would find interest in . . . a mother's love. . . . The central characters of all my plays hereafter shall be young people."

In Cincinnati, says a tiny paragraph that autumn, Felix Morris' company is offering its repertory to regrettably small attendance. One of the plays is "Moses," an adaptation from the German written by Minnie Maddern Fiske. This is Miss Maddern, the actress, who married in 1890 and gave up the stage.

When James A. Herne's "Shore Acres" was presented at the Boston Museum on February 20, 1893, the *Mirror* published a telegraphic dispatch:

> . . . Much of the success was due to the thoroughness of drill under Mr. Herne as stage manager. . . . His careful attention to detail and his skill in arrangement stood in marked contrast with the methods of the regular stage manager of the house. . . .

"Shore Acres" was a homely tale of a family on a farm in Maine. It was full of genuine touches, for the author knew Maine. Boston people—who knew it, too—could see the fidelity of the characters.

But the sensation of the opening performance was its last three minutes, over which there had been argument at rehearsals. Herne wanted to end the play with a long scene in which he would not speak a word. (His was the principal rôle.) The manager of the Museum protested; when a play was over, it was over. You untangled the plot, paired off the lovers—tableau, curtain!

Herne appeared to yield. On the first night, though, he gave orders not to ring down at the cue that had been rehearsed. As Uncle Nat Berry, he stood alone in the farmhouse kitchen. All the family had gone to bed, but Uncle Nat waited to do the last "chores." He looked at the fire in the cook stove and set the dampers for the night; he wound the clock; he kicked a rug against the crack under the door so that the cold wouldn't come in. He made everything warm and safe. After that, he took his candle, lit it, and slowly climbed the stairs. Then the curtain fell.

His acting was so true and simple that people sat watching, reluctant to have the story end. This scene, of which only Herne and his wife had been confident, clinched the success of the piece. After many months in Boston, it was brought to New York for a long run—and was played for years all over the United States.

James A. Herne's ideas were upsetting in the '90's. He thought a play should be a picture lifted out of life, done so that spectators forgot they were in a theatre. Writing his own dramas and acting them with Mrs. Herne as his leading woman, that was what he had aimed at for years, but his effects were too quiet to satisfy theatrical taste of the time. The teapots of the old classic drama were gone, but there was a new stage manner which had its conventions. Like Duse, Herne wanted to discard all tricks.

At rehearsals he had a great knack in directing, and could draw abilities out of players that they scarcely knew they had. He used to urge them to regard their parts as real people—to know what those people had been doing before the play began. The whole life of the character was what the performer must have in mind. In Russia, Stanislavsky had not yet started the Moscow Art Theatre, yet here was Herne using Stanislavsky's philosophy.

"Father was a pathfinder, and his ideas were as modern as those of any of our present producers," his daughter, Chrystal Herne, told me in speaking of him. (She began acting as a child in her father's "Griffith Davenport," in 1899.) "If he were in the theatre today he would not need to change. He was ahead of his time. When I played 'Craig's Wife' in 1925, I had a long silent scene at the end; it summed up the whole story. The author, George Kelly, had planned it to do that very thing. It was considered so new. But I often thought of Father's last scene in 'Shore Acres' so many years before."

Herne discovered Will Hodge—young and inexperienced—and helped him to make his first hit in "Sag Harbor." J. C. Nugent, who also worked under Herne, likes to quote his advice to actors: "Think before you look; look before you speak." His influence would have gone on spreading—but he died in the spring of 1901, during the tour of "Sag Harbor."

To return to "Shore Acres," its success was not without a long preamble. Back in 1859, at twenty, Herne had begun his stage career in "Uncle Tom's Cabin," at Troy, N. Y., not far from Cohoes, where he was born. He was soon going through the usual apprenticeship in stock companies in Baltimore and Washington. In those years he was a wild fellow. He married Helen Western, sister of the stormy Lucille, and acted with Lucille in the West. Later, he and Helen were divorced.

At the Baldwin Theatre, San Francisco, he became associated with David Belasco. They wrote a melodrama, "Hearts of Oak"—for this was Herne's melodramatic period.

In 1878, a girl not yet twenty—Katharine Corcoran— came to Herne for lessons in acting. He saw that she had talent, and he started her on the stage. Then he married her, and she afterward did remarkable acting in his plays. (She is still living.) In the 1880's, his style of playwriting began to change; he forsook everything artificial. He made the original draft of "Shore Acres" about 1888, calling it "The Hawthornes," but he put it aside and rewrote it after several years.

Early in the 1890's, Herne was staging dramas simply and realistically at Chickering Hall, in Boston. There was little money to be made in those productions, and both Mr. and Mrs. Herne sacrificed to keep the work going. When, in 1891, they played his "Margaret Fleming" at Chickering Hall, Hamlin Garland considered it the most naturalistic, colloquial, truthful presentation of a domestic drama ever seen in America. It ran only a few weeks. Later, this work of Herne's failed speedily in New York.

Even after "Shore Acres," he had his disappointments. His "Griffith Davenport" was probably his best play—a realistic drama of the Civil War. When he staged it in New York in 1899, it was praised—but the public stayed away. My father was then dramatic critic of the *Brooklyn Daily Eagle*, and I find on looking over some of his notes that he talked with the Hernes after a performance. They were "just about heartbroken," he wrote. "I wouldn't mind," Herne told him, "if they came to see my play and said it was bad. But they won't come."

Before long, however, Herne wrote "Sag Harbor"—and everybody came. It was not so lofty as "Griffith Davenport," but it was a success.

During the run of "Shore Acres," he remarked that the play of plot was dead as a doornail and the play of theme was the new demand. He saw what was coming. It was this change in dramaturgy that would bring changes in acting.

— In 1893, Richard Mansfield was in the process of proving to the public that he was the great actor he believed himself to be. It was a long struggle—for in those days a following must be built up all over the country, not merely on Broadway. Mansfield was equal to the battle. Besides being an artist, he was a superb fighter.

He had come into the theatre from comic opera. His mother was Madame Erminia Rudersdorff, a distinguished soprano in grand opera and oratorio, who had married Maurice Mansfield, a London wine merchant. Richard was born in Berlin, in May 1857, his mother having sung in Germany that winter.

His first professional stage experience, when he was about twenty, was in musical monologues, at which he was astoundingly clever. In one of his sketches he burlesqued an opera troupe, singing everything from basso profundo to falsetto soprano, and making the singers squabble in several languages.

(Many years later, when Gilbert Miller was a beginner in the theatre, an old "road" manager said to him, "I hear you've been educated abroad and speak three languages?" Young Miller admitted it. "My poor boy," sighed the

Brown Bros.

RICHARD MANSFIELD

manager, "you'll starve to death in this business. I suppose you play the piano?" But Miller did not. The manager cheered up. "My boy, you're saved! If you played the piano, too, it would be all up with you." Mansfield, who spoke more than three languages *and* played the piano, very nearly starved to death at first.)

From entertaining, he advanced to touring in minor Gilbert and Sullivan companies, singing Sir Joseph Porter and John Wellington Wells. That was in England, from 1878 to 1881. But young Mansfield's ambition leaped beyond this. He had had a few months in a dramatic company, and he believed it was in him to act—to act better than most people. A passion to excel always drove him.

He sailed for New York in 1882—part of his bringing-up had been in Boston—and at once applied to the most important theatrical managers, A. M. Palmer, Augustin Daly, and Lester Wallack. They refused him. No, no; they didn't want a singing comedian. Lesser managers refused him, too. His funds reached the vanishing point; so he made his first New York appearance in a comic opera, "Three Black Cloaks," in September 1882.

By December, he got A. M. Palmer to give him a small part. It was in a new play about to go into rehearsal, "A Parisian Romance."

The best rôle in the drama was an old roué, Baron Chevrial, a withered, leering reprobate, who died drinking champagne at a party. This was the character Mansfield longed for; he watched it at rehearsals, and saw that the actor to whom it was assigned was having trouble. When the latter resigned, the part was handed over to the unknown Mansfield—who had not been backward about asking Palmer for it.

Richard scarcely slept or ate. He consulted doctors, for he wanted the Baron's seizure to be scientifically correct. He studied human wreckage in hospitals, on the streets. The play opened on January 11, 1883—and next morning Mansfield was famous. He was not yet twenty-six.

But his nature never let him rest. What did he do as soon as Palmer's company was through with "A Parisian Romance"? He bought the rights and started out on a starring tour. The venture failed, and everybody laughed. This was the beginning of his reputation as an egoist, yet in reality he was extremely sensitive. At about this time, a criticism in the *New York Evening Post* observed that his conceit was far too obvious, but that he was a bright young actor and would have a career when he learned to put a less extravagant estimate on himself.

That career was a fact by 1893. He had some astounding hits to his credit, including "Prince Karl," "Dr. Jekyll and Mr. Hyde," and "Beau Brummell," but it was still thought that he put an extravagant estimate on himself. He never, for instance, let anyone talk to him behind the scenes during a performance; he even offended stage hands by forbidding them to spit.

But was he as full of assurance as people insisted? During his engagement in Chicago, in April 1893, he confessed:

> I have more inward quaverings and doubtings and more horrible fears and misgivings and nervous spasms than occur to most men after fourteen years of campaigning, and I even now never face the foot-lights . . . without suffering an agony of fright. . . .

Here is his picture of himself on an opening night:

The excitement of a first night is actual suffering; the nervousness actual torture. Yet as I walk . . . to the theatre . . . and note the impassive, imperturbable faces of the passers-by, I must confess to myself that I would not change places with them— no, not for worlds. I have something that is filling my life brimful of interest. . . . It's like a battle. I shall win or die. . . .

Mansfield's acting was based on the identification of the player with his part. When he first did Baron Chevrial, he used to go to the theatre two hours before the performance, so that he would have time to work himself into the rôle.

. . . While I am playing Brutus I am Brutus [he once told an interviewer]. I am Napoleon, Nero, Beaucaire, Brummell, for the time I am playing them. I know no other way to characterize. . . .

"Do not strive to be original, strive to be true!" was his advice to young performers. "If you succeed in being true, you will be original. . . ." He worked unceasingly. Besides directing his productions, he wrote a number of the early plays he used. Taxed with being exacting at rehearsals, he used to protest that when he was a novice stage managers roared and swore at him. Whereas he was reduced to drawing someone aside and entreating, "My dear fellow, you should, you know, try, you know, to get hold of the character a little—get inside of it, if I may say so."

Up until his day, actors who aspired to be great tragedians rarely experimented with new rôles. They showed what they could do with the old standbys. He broke with this tradition; he put on new plays. His few classic parts, he approached from his own point of view. He took no pride, he said, in differing from this or that great actor of the past; still, he must do the thing as he saw it.

When he died at fifty, in 1907, he had played only a few Shakespearean rôles—Richard III, Shylock, Henry V, and Brutus. However, he had given Clyde Fitch his first commission for a full-length drama; he had introduced Shaw to the United States with "Arms and the Man," in 1894; he had set Booth Tarkington at his first job of dramatic writing with "Beaucaire"; he had been a pioneer in presenting Molière to the American public, with "The Misanthrope."

Mansfield's last season, 1906-07, was devoted to a production of "Peer Gynt"—the first given in this country, or, indeed, in English. The performance was always long and exhausting, but he never spared himself. Sometimes he said, "It takes one's life blood, this Peer Gynt. I dig a spadeful of earth for my grave every time I play the part." He was suffering with cancer, but it was not in him to stop fighting. He had a feeling for his work that was religious; he gave himself for it. Late in March 1907, he was too ill to go on. He died in August.

Although he had never played Ibsen until he did "Peer Gynt," he had long been familiar with the Norwegian's dramas. For Mrs. Mansfield—Beatrice Cameron—was a very early Ibsenite. In the winter of 1889-90, she had given special matinees of "A Doll's House"—a play then so little known that people brought children to it.

(Miss Cameron was the star's leading woman for years. They were married in 1892, and he proved a devoted husband and father. To this day, Mrs. Mansfield stages amateur plays at Christodora House, in New York.)

Not until Mansfield did "Cyrano de Bergerac," in 1898,

IRVING and TERRY

They were rarely photographed together, in character. "Olivia" the play in which they are seen here, was based on "The Vicar of Wakefield" and was in their American repertory in 1893.

did he become thoroughly popular. From then on, audiences rushed to see any play he gave. He made a great deal of money, and gradually paid off every cent of the $165,000 of debts he had incurred in some of his unsuccessful productions. But in prosperity he could never forget the hopes and disappointments of his failures. In 1900, he wrote in *Collier's Weekly*:

— Every character he [the actor] creates is a child he bears. There is labor and there is pain. He has bestowed on it his love and incessant thought, and sleeping and waking it is with him as with a mother. When it is born, it is born like the children of a King —in public. It is either a beautiful and perfect child, or he drags himself home in misery to weep away his sorrows unpitied. . . .

I have had so many children, and a number of them are dead and forgotten by everybody. Only I, their paternal mother, think of them at night over my pipe when all the world is still. Then they come out of their corners and perch upon my knee. No— they are not all beautiful. Very few of them are. But the mother always cherishes most dearly the ugly one. . . .

In September 1893, Henry Irving and Ellen Terry—he was not yet Sir Henry—were playing in San Francisco. "The Bells," "Olivia," and "The Merchant of Venice" were among their plays. According to the *Dramatic Mirror*, receipts for fourteen performances between September 4 and 16 were $90,000, "one of the greatest financial successes of a theatrical venture." After San Francisco, their itinerary included Portland, Tacoma, Seattle, Minneapolis, and St. Paul. Early October found them in

Chicago where, despite competition of the World's Fair, they drew very large houses.

This was the fifteenth year of the Irving-Terry partnership; for it had begun in 1878, when Irving had taken over management of the Lyceum Theatre, in London, and had engaged Miss Terry as his leading woman. The arrangement was not precisely a partnership; Irving was the individual always in control. He was the commanding general, but no general ever had a stauncher aide-de-camp than Ellen Terry.

As joint stars, they were complements to each other. She had grace, charm, and every natural advantage for acting. He had none. But he possessed imagination on a large scale, and tremendous capacity for sustained effort.

Both of them had been grounded in the old stock company procedure, yet neither was cramped by it. Irving conquered London in the 1870's as an innovator; as for Miss Terry, she never had a conventional mind. They both stood for "thoughtful" acting, as opposed to declamation.

Ellen Terry, ten years Irving's junior, was forty-five in 1893. She was born in Coventry, England, in 1848, her parents being Mr. and Mrs. Benjamin Terry, players of good standing. Before long they went to London, where they joined the company of Charles Kean—son of the great Edmund.

In that organization, the daughter played her first part when she was eight years old. For four or five years she continued to act children's rôles with Kean and his wife, the masterful Ellen Tree. The latter trained her well. At fourteen and fifteen, the girl had two seasons in an excellent stock company at Bristol; this gave her, she put it, the experience of her life. She returned to London. By the time she was twenty, she had spent some ten years at acting and had a basic knowledge of its technique which served her well later on.

Once when she was about thirteen, a play required her to appear at a window screaming in utter horror. A poisonous snake was supposed to be choking her. That, of course, was not a situation she had ever been in, but her cries had the greatest conviction. This was, she said, because she could imagine how it would all feel if it were real.

> Imagination! Imagination! [she wrote at sixty, in "Ellen Terry's Memoirs"]. I put it first years ago when I was asked what qualities I thought necessary for success on the stage. And I am still of the same opinion. Imagination, industry, and intelligence . . . are all indispensable to the actress, but of these three the greatest is . . . imagination.

In the '70's, Tom Taylor, comparing her work with that of another actress calls Ellen Terry's "a case of grace and spontaneity and Nature against affectation, over-emphasis, stilt, and false idealism."

Spontaneity was at the root of her playing; on this, she superimposed an eagerness for technical perfection. She had no use for ragged effects. This made her comments on acting practical and downright.

Pace was, to her, the soul of comedy. But pace meant, not so much speaking swiftly, as thinking swiftly. It took her years to be able to think rapidly on the stage—and she had observed that the thoughts of youth are long, slow thoughts. Indecision in acting she called a fatal quality. She had seen more than one good player ruin a rôle through not taking a firm grip on it—not deciding how to portray the character and sticking to this choice. To her, that was moral cowardice.

As for all the underlying technique of playing, she said the rules might be broken *if they had first been mastered.* It was one thing to discard them deliberately after having learned to use them, and quite another to toss them aside because one lacked the skill to conform.

Sympathy was so strong in Miss Terry that she cried too easily on the stage; she had to learn to hold back her emotion. If this readiness of response made acting easy for her, it complicated her life. Sympathy—"feeling with" is the Greek of it—is the artist's endowment. It is often counterbalanced by other instincts, but when it is not its possessor has fewer defenses than the average person.

Ellen Terry was like this. She was the opposite of heartless. She was interested in too many people; she diffused herself. Not one of her three marriages endured. Between the first and the second, she gave up the stage for six years and lived very happily in the country with a distinguished architect—the father of her two children. It was to provide for this son and daughter that she went back to acting, and later became famous.

She was not sufficiently self-centered to have built up a career for herself. But to be useful to someone else— that was the greatest happiness she knew. She was immeasurably helpful to Irving; and in helping his career, she helped her own.

Though she was not ambitious, she had a passion for hard work. She had been bred to work, and she never outgrew it. So she despised delinquents who let their performances sag on tour, and called it "downright dishonest." From seeing the concentration which Irving put into everything he did, she taught herself that "the artist must spend his life in incessant labor and deny himself everything for that purpose."

It was this ingrained habit of work that kept Ellen Terry playing with Irving for twenty-four years. Twenty-four years of steady output, on the part of a person who was naturally volatile! Things were not always rosy; the two stars did not always see eye to eye. Toward the last, Miss Terry wrote Bernard Shaw:

> . . . Ah, I feel so certain Henry just hates me! I can only *guess* at it, for he is exactly the same sweet-mannered person he was when I "felt so certain" Henry loved me! We have not met for years now, except before other people, when my conduct exactly matches his of course. All my fault. It is *I* am changed, not he. . . .

More adaptable than Irving, she was in touch with new currents in the theatre. He was not. That was the change she spoke of in herself. But the partnership continued for two years more, and ended without enmity in 1902. Her account of her last talk with Irving, a few months before he died in 1905, is full of touching affection.

She outlived him many years. When she died at eighty, in 1928, Dame Ellen Terry was more deeply loved than any other person of the English stage. She called out the same kind of tender regard that was felt for Edwin Booth a generation before.

John Gielgud is her grand-nephew. Edward Gordon Craig, who revolutionized scene designing and brought in a new view of the actor as related to his background, is her son.

Henry Irving was a colossal figure in the theatre. He came of farming people and was born in the village of Keinton, near Glastonbury, in February 1838, his name being John Henry Brodribb. With little facility for the stage, he nevertheless set his heart on it when he was a young clerk in London. He was already studying plays. In this period, he went with awe to a reading of "Hamlet" given by Fanny Kemble. She began by announcing, "Ham-m-lette, by Will-y-amm Shake-es-sppeere," and continued in the same vein through the tragedy. Alas, for the clerk's anticipations. In his heart he was sure there ought to be another way to do this. Many years later, his Hamlet was to Englishmen what Booth's was to Americans.

At eighteen, John Brodribb left London to join a stock company at Sunderland. That was in 1856. He called himself Henry Irving. For ten years he slaved in the provinces, playing as many as 500 parts. But he was awkward and self-conscious, with long legs and an enormous nose. Once he was offered a month's engagement in a Dublin company. He was to replace an actor whom the management had dismissed. Patrons of the theatre liked the predecessor—and so night after night they hissed and stamped, as long as Irving was speaking. But he played right through to the end of the month.

Of such dauntless stuff, Irving was made. In time this gave a quality to his acting which Ellen Terry described as "a kind of fine temper, like the purest steel, produced by the perpetual fight against difficulties."

> Henry Irving at first had everything against him as an actor [she said]. He could not speak, he could not walk, he could not *look*. He wanted to do

things in a part, and he could not do them. His
amazing power was imprisoned, and only after weary
years did he succeed in setting it free.

After those weary years, Percy Burton—the star's advance agent and manager—saw what the man had become:

> Irving had a greatness of spirit apart from his own
> calling. It was the greatness of his character and
> will, allied to a magnetic personality, which every
> really popular actor must possess. But Irving's was
> predominant in every way. . . .

He made his first appearance in London in 1866. It did
not win much approval, though—for he smacked of the
country actor, people thought. In 1867, by the merest
accident, he played opposite Ellen Terry one evening in
"Katharine and Petruchio." He took no notice of her;
he was wholly wrapped up in his work and ambition.
She was not interested in him, either—and the thought
never came to her that he would be a great actor. He was
stiff and self-conscious, his eyes had no glow in them, and
his face lacked expression.

("The longer I teach, the less I am discouraged by
unprepossessing pupils," Philip Loeb tells me. This actor,
an instructor at the American Academy of Dramatic Arts,
says there may be a tremendous artistic urge behind
defects.)

This Irving, wrapped up in his ambitions, was never
bumptious; all his life he was extremely gentle. But he
made every occasion serve him. Once when he was in-
vited to a party, he had to borrow a dress suit from a fellow actor, Herbert Standing. Irving was thus able to
attend; nor did he waste his time while he was there.
Afterward he remarked, "Funny fellows, those swells. I

watched them. I studied them a bit. They have perfect repose."

During his slow rise in London, he married Miss Florence O'Callaghan. This was in 1869. The marriage gave him two sons, but it was not congenial.

In November 1871, he created a furore when he played Mathias in "The Bells." The piece was put on as a stopgap, but Henry Irving had faith in it. Or rather, he knew what he could do with his rôle. To the surprise of the management, the play ran 151 nights in London that season.

As Mathias, Irving introduced himself to New York in 1883, and in 1893 he played the part frequently in America. Altogether, he acted it over 800 times; it was in his repertory for over thirty years.

Mathias was a man driven by remorse. Only the climax of his story was shown on the stage, but Irving's mind was saturated with the whole past of the character. The man had murdered a traveler long ago on a snowy night, and had never been suspected. He was haunted, though, by the sound of the traveler's sleigh bells. He kept thinking he heard them. In the last act, he had a horrible dream of being hanged for his crime; he woke and died strangling.

A description by Gordon Craig shows a moment in the first scene as Irving did it. It is night, and snowing. He comes in from outdoors, and sits down wearily to take off his heavy boots. Two friends speak to him of the weather; it is like that night years ago—the one when the Polish Jew was killed. . . .

Mathias' hand stiffens; he cannot go on unbuckling his boot. "Oh, you were talking of that?" he says. He sits still. Then slowly, he begins to turn his head away, in the

direction of something that has caught his attention. He
is listening. "Don't you—don't you hear the sound of
sledge bells in the road?" he asks.

This was the mood of secret suspense at the start. It
increased as the play progressed. The melancholy became terror, and the terror became immense horror. At
the end, Irving's face turned white, he grew cold all over;
he went through the agonies of dying of fright. Though
he played many death scenes in his career, this put a
heavier strain on him than any other.

The vastness of his imagination made Irving great. He
could rise to a height, maintain it, and rise still further.
His method of studying a rôle was to imbue himself with
all the person's thought and feeling, and then to add his
own emotion *about* the person. This he called passing
the character through the mind of the player.

To be natural on the stage is difficult, he owned—yet a
grain of nature is worth a bushel of artifice. How had he
found a way to be natural? The actor must think before
he speaks, said Irving—must let the idea be seen working
on him.

> Good acting is not declamation but the expression
> of character, [he told students in Boston] and the
> actor's aim is not to imitate this style or that, but to
> cultivate his own resources of impersonation.

During his tour of the United States in 1893, Irving was
at the height of his power. Two years later he was
knighted. But in 1898, his twenty years of high success
at the Lyceum began to turn on him; the plays he staged
so lavishly were now thought old-fashioned. At this
juncture he fell ill of pneumonia. The upshot of it was
that the Lyceum went into the hands of a syndicate.

He never wholly recovered from that illness; but he kept on acting, season after season. In February 1905, while he was playing in Wolverhampton, he fainted after "The Bells." The doctor told him he must have many weeks of rest. And under no condition should he play "The Bells" again; it was too great a strain on his heart.

"Fiddle! It's not my heart. It's my breath," Sir Henry told Ellen Terry when she came from London to see him. She said he looked like an old, gray, majestic tree. In the spring, he acted in London once more—but he did not do "The Bells."

The following autumn, though he was feeble, he was again in the provinces. Edith Wynne Matthison, his leading woman, said his manager and stage manager both tried to save him from "The Bells" by telling him that the scenery had gone astray. Still, he cornered them. At Bradford, on October 12, 1905, "The Bells" went on, Irving playing with all his old energy. He had to be lifted to his feet, however, to take the final curtain call. Then he agreed to let the settings go back to London.

"I've sent 'The Bells' away," he said. "I shall never play it again." The next night, he died.

But not till he had finished a performance of "Becket." When he had been lifted to his feet after the death scene, he seemed dazed and asked the stage manager, "What now?"

"You take the curtain, sir!"

In less than an hour, he was dead. They gave him a great state funeral in Westminster Abbey.

Power to convey feeling to an audience makes an actor; but it is not enough to make a career. There must be, besides, a capacity for endurance—for effort in adversity.

This was what Herne, Mansfield, and Irving possessed; and in Ellen Terry, her passion for hard work was a form of endurance. It was not by accident that Herne persisted in his own ideas even when there seemed to be no public for them; that Mansfield played "Peer Gynt," though he said he was digging his grave; that Irving was in the theatre on the last night he lived. They had schooled themselves so long that they could not yield.

That is a side of the actor's calling which audiences do not see. Work is not separate from life—it is cut off the same piece. As in wood sawed and planed from a single tree trunk, the same characteristic grain is there. So the individual's product is hewed out of his life, and the same grain runs through them both.

YESTERDAY AND TODAY

10.

Enter Our Own Century

AT THE start of the twentieth century, there was not a motion picture palace anywhere. That was to be a revolutionary development in the theatre of the near future; yet for the better part of two decades this revolution was only gathering momentum.

So actors went on as usual. When they spoke of changes in their calling, they meant that—as Herne had foreseen—the play of situation was being pushed to the wall by the play of ideas. New dramatists were coming along. With three players who made certain of these authors popular, we must now be concerned.

Every theatregoer who can look back on earlier years of this century will have his own gallery of memorable rôles. Does he recall Ethel Barrymore in "Captain Jinks of the Horse Marines" and in "Mid-Channel," or Forbes-Robertson's Hamlet? Or Warfield in "The Music Master," Cecil Yapp as the Cat in "The Bluebird," Otis Skinner's "Kismet," or Sothern and Marlowe in "Twelfth Night"? Can anyone who saw them forget John Barrymore as the bank clerk in Galsworthy's "Justice," or Frank McGlynn's performance of Abraham Lincoln in Drinkwater's tragedy? But persons whose recollections are long enough would rather fill out this list for themselves.

In the early 1900's Mrs. Fiske was, she said, in her second incarnation. Her first had been as Minnie Maddern. But as Mrs. Fiske she had come back to the stage to do plays of far greater import than any with which young Miss Maddern had beguiled her public.

"Realistic" was a word she never applied to the kind of acting she believed in. She called it merely natural, true acting. However it might be named, it turned away from conventional standards, and proved that a performer could be moving without recourse to so-called "emotional" outpourings.

Minnie Maddern was brought up in the theatre. The daughter of Thomas Davey, a western manager, and his wife Lizzie Maddern, an actress, she was born in New Orleans in December 1865. Her name at the start was Mary Augusta Davey.

She began her professional career as a handy infant-in-arms, but was soon graduated to speaking parts in support of many notable stars. One of them was J. K. Emmet, with whom she made her first New York appearance when she was four. She always said he was the most fascinating man she ever acted with.

She adored her mother, from whom she was often separated by the exigencies of their calling. Once when Minnie was eight, she was put aboard the train in New Orleans and journeyed all alone to Pittsburgh, to join her mother who was playing there. Arriving in that city, she was no bewildered youngster crying in the railway station. She knew the manager's name—as well she might, for she had acted for him. Realizing that he would be

MRS. FISKE

staying at the best hotel, she calmly took a cab to it. The manager was stunned when she presented herself. This self-directed "project" reveals the clearheadedness that was later ingrained in the woman. (Lizzie Maddern, to whom she was so devoted, died early.)

Minnie was in steady demand as a child actress. In New York in 1874, she played Prince Arthur in an all-star production of "King John," at Booth's Theatre.

"I remember her well, the little red-haired thing," Mr. Fiske told me. "I didn't know her then, but as a young boy I was taken to see 'King John,' and the scene in which Arthur begged Hubert not to put out his eyes made an unforgettable impression on me. Years afterward, Agnes Booth told me about that performance. Her husband, Junius Brutus Booth, Jr., was the King John, and she was Queen Constance. To get herself in the mood for a coming scene, she used to leave her dressing room door open, so that she could listen to speeches between Prince Arthur and Hubert. The child's voice was so real, so pitiful, Agnes Booth said, that it never failed to touch her."

Like everybody in her profession, Minnie Maddern worshipped Edwin Booth. Once she wriggled herself into an entrance to watch his Richard III. He came and stood there, waiting for his cue. She was overcome. He gave a twist to his armor, which seemed to be askew, and she saw his lips start to move. She listened for the words of this godlike creature. He swore.

By the 1880's, the child actress had become a soubrette and ingénue. She was small, with darting blue eyes, and people said she ought to be another Maggie Mitchell. At sixteen, she starred in "Fogg's Ferry"—a comedy-melodrama wherein she foiled the villain's plot to blow up a steamboat. This attraction was brought to New York in May 1882, and the *Tribune* stated:

> Minnie Maddern . . . is one of the most interesting girls that have appeared on the stage. . . . She exhibited no skill in the use of her voice, no sense of the value of repose in action, and no capacity for making the most of her dramatic points. . . . But she was seen to be full of intelligence and sensibility, and, especially, to possess piquant and charming mischievous humor. . . .

Later, she was less hoydenish in "In Spite of All," "Caprice," and "Featherbrain." During this period she married Le Grand White, an advance agent; but before long they were divorced.

Her greatest success as an ingénue was "Caprice," in which she sang "In the Gloaming," and made the song popular. At a San Francisco theatre, Kitty Molony, of Booth's company, saw Miss Maddern in this play and was struck with the everyday truthfulness of her acting. Here was a performer who listened intently to everything that was said to her. Her exclamations were not borrowed from drama, but reminded persons in the audience of happenings in life. Thus it is apparent that the actress' way of playing, later much discussed, was already in the making.

Before her twenty-fifth birthday, Miss Maddern married Harrison Grey Fiske and gave up the stage. She had been acting since she was three and believed she had had enough of it; but she had scarcely chosen a husband to help her put the theatre out of her mind. Mr. Fiske was editor and owner of the *New York Dramatic Mirror*. He did playwriting and dramatic criticism. In everything that concerned the theatre, they had a strong and enduring bond of interest. He became her manager when she eventually returned to the stage.

In the interim, however, she was a spectator. She wrote plays—among them several one-act sketches which she later produced. Early in 1893, her husband came home from a first-night and told her she must see this wonderful Italian, Signora Duse. Mrs. Fiske went and was "completely carried away."

She herself was already deep in Ibsen; for nearly a year she had been studying Nora in "A Doll's House." The Norwegian's dramas were a revelation to her. She had the highest admiration for his way of probing the motives of human beings.

On February 15, 1894, she gave a special matinee of "A Doll's House" in New York. In the round of his work as a reviewer, my father went to that performance, and years later he often told me of his impression. He knew he was watching an extraordinary actress. When he had previously seen Janet Achurch as Nora, the play had seemed to him to be enveloped in a dank mist; but Mrs. Fiske made the story clear as noon. That shows the state of mind audiences were in about Ibsen.

Without profit or too much encouragement, Mrs. Fiske put on plays, one after another, for three years. She acted by understatement. People were not quite sure it *was* acting. Then, in March 1897, she gave them "Tess of the D'Urbervilles"—and won all the critics. "Tess" established her, but it was not till the next decade that her sort of playing became popular.

Those who remember her only in comedy can have no idea how she could wring your heart in scenes of great feeling. The small, unexpected things she did were what touched the audience.

I saw "Tess" in one of her revivals of the play, and two moments in it are clear in my memory. One was Tess's meeting with Angel Clare after his long absence. She had loved him, he had deserted her, and she believed him dead. She came into the room through a door on the left. Not expecting to see anyone, all her attention was on closing the door. This kept her for an instant with her hand on the doorknob and her back toward the room. Then she turned, and caught sight of Angel.

At that, the strength ebbed out of her—you saw it go. Her hands went up weakly until they were about as high as her head. In one of them she had a handkerchief, but now her fingers were too limp to hold it. It dropped to the floor. That was all she did—but you knew that every muscle in Tess's body was as limp as the fingers that let go of the handkerchief. You knew how Tess felt; you felt it all with her.

The other moment was when Tess murdered Alec D'Urberville. She walked out of the room, through that same door on the left, with the bread knife in her hand. The stage was empty. Then came a long wait while the audience—keyed up to high excitement—listened for an outcry. There was not a sound. At last Tess came back —and you saw in her face that she had killed Alec.

This scene, like the finale of "Shore Acres," had been thought impossible by practical people of the theatre, says Mr. Fiske. They warned the actress that no one could hold an audience so long with an empty stage. But she did. She made everybody believe in the thing that was going on beyond that door.

She followed "Tess" with successes that were less harrowing. She could do tragedy; she could do comedy. Soon all Main Street went to see her.

Before 1910, she had taught audiences to listen to Ibsen and like it. To her, these plays were tales about very real, comprehensible people; besides, she could see witty implications in the lines. So her Ibsen performances had a crisp, astringent humor interwoven with the tragic themes —a happy surprise to persons who had come braced for gloom. Besides "A Doll's House" and "Hedda Gabler," she also produced "Rosmersholm," "Pillars of Society," and "Ghosts."

Though she did more plays by Ibsen than by any other one dramatist, she succeeded in the work of many authors. There were, for instance, "Becky Sharp," "Salvation Nell," "The New York Idea," "Mrs. Bumpstead-Leigh," and "Mis' Nelly of N' Orleans." In later years she adhered to light plays, for emotion put too great a strain on her.

Once she said to me, "When someone brings a 'script and tells me, 'Mrs. Fiske, this runs the whole gamut of the emotions,' I say, 'Take it away. Take it away. I've run all the gamuts I'm ever going to.' "

Her test of acting was always, "Is it true? Do people do this?" It was the tone of mind, she said, that must be true; that did not preclude some degree of enlargement and selection in the presentation.

She had a horror of boring the audience. So at rehearsals she believed in working hardest on the dullest portions of a play; they must be made to hold attention. For this, pace was indispensable. Though she had studied a part for months or even years beforehand, she felt that she never began to do it as it ought to be done until she had played it for several weeks. Even then, she was often dissatisfied. To show how she looked at her own work, I quote from a letter she once sent my father:

. . . It pained me much last night when Mr. Fiske told me you had been to the theatre & that you had deplored the continued evidence of my old besetting sin—a too rapid utterance. . . . I am ashamed —very much ashamed—whenever I disappoint these good friends who trust me & who have vouched for me!—ashamed as the singer would be ashamed if he sang falsely when truth was expected of him. . . .

And yet . . . remember that sometimes the poor player is ill or nervous or weary and then there comes a mournful & humiliating performance of his duties and a consequent heartache for many days. . . . Oh! Those detestable nights when one cowers, ashamed, all through the little hours, thinking of what beautiful, wonderful things one might have done, and alas! remembering what atrocious things one *has* done & what a fool one has made of oneself!

Believe me, every actor, from the greatest to the humblest, has known these torturesome hours. . . . I do not know why I wander on at this length—save that, as I told you before, this panic which from time to time undoes the poor actor *is* a matter of some interest—a thing not sufficiently comprehended.

In 1917, Alexander Woollcott published a series of conversations with Mrs. Fiske concerning the theatre. Fifty or a hundred years from now, when some historian of the drama comes upon this volume, he will announce that he has a find. And that will be the truth—for she told Mr. Woollcott many things out of her own observation and experience. Acting in its highest reaches is a thing of the spirit, she maintained; but she had never seen it wonderfully done without underlying technical excellence. Most of all, she cautioned the player against being cozened by the theatre. It was life that the actor must keep his eyes on, not what the stage purported to know about life:

> It is the irony of things [she said] that the theatre should be the most dangerous place for the actor. But then, after all, the world is the worst possible place, the most corrupting place, for the human soul. . . .

As a beginner, I spent a season in Mrs. Fiske's company —but I had no comprehension whatever, at that time, of the forces of will and imagination behind her work. I only knew that I never tired of watching her, or listening, every night. It was never stale to me.

Once I saw the strangest transformation in her. She was giving a matinee for some charity—a bill made up of a single act from each of several plays. One of them was "La Femme de Claude." In this, she was the wife—a creature who had something uncanny or malevolent about her. Mrs. Fiske had played the part years before. It was my heavy responsibility to speak a few lines, open the door, and let her in.

The performance came. I was in a darkish room. I lit a candle; I heard a knock outside the door at the back. Carrying the candle, I went and unlocked the door, throwing it wide open as I had been directed.

But the woman who stood there was not anyone I had expected to see. To be sure, it was the star in ordinary street dress; yet she was appallingly different—and the thing that altered her was the look in her eyes. The glitter in them was wild, evil. There was an impact from them that made me feel as if I had been struck. It was like something happening in a bad dream; and that is all I remember about it. She had wrought this change in herself before she spoke a word or stepped inside the room.

Mrs. Fiske never made a display of emotion off the stage, keeping her ready, glinting humor on the surface. She was not a disorganized genius, but a well-balanced one. Her attitude was impersonal, even toward herself. The only thing that betrayed her was her intense pity for neglected, wretched animals. In every town on tour she knew the way to the dog-and-cat hospital, and many a starving kitten had its board bill paid by her.

Early in 1932, when she was taken ill during rehearsals in Chicago, she came East and went to her secretary's home. Like the creatures she had so often befriended, she crawled off to die quietly, without having any fuss made over it.

She was sixty-six when she died, and her career had covered sixty-three years. The power and clarity of her acting came from the power and clarity of her mind. Hers was always a gallant spirit. As she grew older, she never indulged in self-pity or a backward glance.

Another actress—with a genius as shy and elusive as herself—was at her height during the first eighteen years of this century. This was Maude Adams. (Lately she has given courses in drama at Stephens College, in Missouri; but that is outside the scope of these pages.)

For years she drew bigger crowds than any other player in America. What gave her this magic hold on audiences? Some people tried to explain it as Charles Frohman's showmanship; but that was begging the question. She possessed that something special to the individual which enabled her, though she was extraordinarily diffident, to reach out to an audience and touch every person in it. In her work there was always an oddly spiritual quality.

Like Mrs. Fiske—like Gertrude Lawrence, to choose a more recent example—Maude Adams was reared in the theatre. Her mother was Mrs. Annie Adams Kiskadden, character actress of a stock company in Salt Lake City. In that town the child was born on November 11, 1872. There, too, she made her first stage appearance as a baby.

After a time her parents moved to San Francisco, where her father died when she was ten. Mrs. Kiskadden— Annie Adams was her stage name—acted at the Baldwin Theatre. The little girl played her first speaking part there, at five. She was soon regularly billed as Little Maudie. The stage manager was young David Belasco, and James A. Herne was also in the company. They had collaborated on "Hearts of Oak"—then called "Chums"— and Maudie did the child's part in it. At seven, she was spindly and not particularly pretty, according to Belasco's recollection:

> But . . . there was a magnetism about the child. . . . She had temperament. She could act and grasp the meaning of a part long before she could read. When we were beginning rehearsals of a new play at the Baldwin I would take Maudie on my knee and bit by bit would explain to her the meaning of the part she had to play. I can see her now . . . those wise eyes of hers drinking in every word. . . . She was serious-minded in her own childish way even in those days, and once she realized that you were treating her seriously there was nothing that that child would not try to do.

Little Maudie's career ended when her legs got too long. She was sent home to Salt Lake City, where she stayed in school till she was fourteen. Then she begged to go back on the stage—and to her mother. This mother is part of the story, for she made countless sacrifices for the child and believed in her future.

But the girl who returned to the stage—she was ambitious and extremely impressionable—was neither young enough nor old enough. Nobody wanted her, and the disappointment cut her deeply.

Here Annie Adams intervened. They were then on the Pacific Coast, and she decided that New York was the place for her daughter. Together, they came East. One may feel pretty certain that it was Mrs. Adams who got Maudie her first Broadway engagement—in "The Paymaster," a melodrama, in 1888.

This girl soon began to show what she could do. Two of the best directors in America—Belasco and Herne—had trained her; she was not a raw recruit. In March 1889, she was making a modest hit in the Hoyt farce, "A Midnight Bell."

Meantime, Belasco too had come to New York. He and H. C. De Mille (father of Cecil De Mille, of Hollywood) had finished a play called "Men and Women." This was to be done by Charles Frohman's new stock company, of which Maude Adams became a member. She played a small part in "Men and Women," and stayed in the company for three seasons.

When Frohman starred John Drew, he chose Miss Adams for Drew's leading woman. She was not quite twenty. Drew made his first New York appearance as a star in October 1892, in "The Masked Ball." He was a success, and Miss Adams scored a conspicuous hit with a drunken scene. She played a young wife who pretended —in a nice way—to have had too much champagne.

It wasn't easy to do [she told an interviewer from the *Dramatic Mirror*.] . . . I must study it as a sober woman trying to act intoxicated, and yet never deceiving my audience. . . . So I thought over it, dreamed over it, acted it out before the mirror over and over for weeks, entirely through my imagination. Indeed, you might call the whole business a flight of tipsy imagination. . . .

This is a rare glimpse of Maude Adams at work. Later on, she never gave interviews. "I study plays all the time, too . . . make scenes, and put myself in situations," she added.

After she had had five years with John Drew, Frohman made her a star, getting James M. Barrie to dramatize "The Little Minister" for her. She had a phenomenal success in it—the first of many in the Scotsman's plays. This was not only her start as a star, but also his as a dramatist. In 1901 she did his "Quality Street," and afterward "Peter Pan," "What Every Woman Knows," "The Legend of Leonora," and "A Kiss for Cinderella."

Her mind and Barrie's were akin; she and he saw the same light that never was on sea or land. His plays spoke to her, as Ibsen's did to Mrs. Fiske. He was not Miss Adam's only author, of course. She played Rostand's "L'Aiglon" and "Chantecler," and Schiller's "Joan of Arc," besides doing Juliet and Rosalind. But she was at her best in Barrie.

As for Charles Frohman's influence, his confidence upheld her. "Once she realized that you were treating her seriously," said Belasco of the days in San Francisco, "there was nothing that that child would not try to do." Here is a clue. Frohman took Maude Adams seriously; he believed she could do big things—and she did them.

She won audiences, she made them laugh and cry, for many years.

Under Frohman's direction, she became a mystery. People never saw her, except on the stage. Like Elisabeth Bergner and Greta Garbo, she was inaccessible; but there was something of the recluse in Miss Adams, or Frohman could not have built it up.

Once, as a schoolgirl, I met her in her dressing room after a matinee. I walked on air; I couldn't breathe. However, as I could find nothing to say when the great moment came, there was a dreadful void. She was most unassuming and kind, and tried to make conversation. But the magnetism, which she had in such an extreme degree across the footlights, was missing in this brief encounter. She was only somewhat less constrained than her caller.

Her acting was never bitter or tremendous, but it went straight to people's hearts. In comedy, she had a way of conveying two ideas at the same time. While she was laughing with the person to whom she spoke, she was having her private laugh at herself for a reason that she and the audience understood.

The charm of her Peter Pan was the utter conviction with which she did it. The actors in a fairy play, said Barrie, should feel that it is written by a child in deadly earnestness and that they are children playing it in the same spirit. This spirit, which Miss Adams put into her rôle, gave it an unexcelled zest. When she pulled the bit of gray chiffon out of the drawer in the Darlings' nursery and cried, "I've found my shadow," there was an unearthly glee in her voice.

On May 7, 1915—while she was appearing in "The Legend of Leonora" in Kansas City—Charles Frohman was drowned off the coast of Ireland. He was one of the passengers aboard the "Lusitania" when it was torpedoed by a German submarine.

For twenty-five years, Maude Adams had never worked for any other manager. He had given her opportunities, had foreseen her victories, and had sustained her in them. She continued to play for three seasons. In January 1916 she revived "The Little Minister" in New York, and she put on "A Kiss for Cinderella" in 1916-17, doing it for two seasons. In 1918, she retired from the stage for thirteen years.

In 1931-32, she toured the country in "The Merchant of Venice," with Otis Skinner as her Shylock. William Seymour, who had been Frohman's general stage director, went to the play during her Boston engagement. Afterward he wrote a friend of the pleasure the performance gave him, and of the half hour's talk he had had with Miss Adams in her dressing room. "She was so dear—and looking into her face, tears came into my eyes. I think there were tears in hers."

When Arnold Daly got together a group of actors and put on "Candida" in New York, in 1903, he started the Shaw epoch.

Mansfield had, of course, done "Arms and the Man" and "The Devil's Disciple" in the 1890's. But although first-nighters had been delighted with those offerings, the public had a dreadful suspicion that they were high-brow —and stayed away. G. B. S. belonged in the next century.

What sort of man was this Arnold Daly, and how did he come to gamble on a dramatist whose plays had done nothing but lose money?

Beginning life as Peter Christopher Daly, he was born

in the old Williamsburgh neighborhood of Brooklyn in October, 1875. His mother's maiden name was Arnold, and he adopted it when he went on the stage.

Peter Daly was expelled from no less than four public schools. He was restless, aggressive, difficult—traits which ran all through his life. At eleven, he quit the pursuit of learning. His father had died and he had to go to work, there being few bothersome laws then about child labor.

He got a job as a messenger, across the ferry in New York. Soon he was delivering telegrams at the Charles Frohman headquarters, and by 1888 or 1889 he had become an office boy there. He was never quite certain whether he or Mr. Frohman ran the office.

When the distinguished John Drew dropped in unexpectedly one day for a friendly chat with Frohman, Peter gave him a stony look. He then stated that his employer was out and the date of his return unknown. This was the youth's accustomed greeting to applicants.

Though he thus knew the unfortunate plight of players in search of engagements, he yearned to be an actor. He was now sixteen. When he was alone in the office he would sit staring at himself in the mirror, doubting whether he could act because his face was expressionless. He did not realize that he set his features when he stared.

Daniel Frohman got him a chance to serve John Drew as dresser for a short time. It is questionable if Drew cared for the young man; it is certain that he was utterly surprised later when a brilliant performer named Arnold Daly proved to be the erstwhile Peter.

Arnold began to materialize in 1892, when he got an engagement in a road company. By 1895, Frank Mayo gave him a good part in "Pudd'nhead Wilson," and in this Daly made his first New York appearance. He learned much from Mayo, whom he called "the greatest master of stagecraft I have ever seen."

In the season of 1899-1900, Daly made a hit in Clyde Fitch's "Barbara Frietchie." Julia Marlowe was the star. He played a boy who went crazy, in a moving scene of hysteria. During this engagement he married Mary Blythe, an actress in the company; but they were divorced within a few years. (Blythe Daly is their daughter.)

He was now a rising player, noted for the verity of his impersonations. He had come a long way from the lad who left school at eleven. He was a genius. School had taught him to read and write, and after that he could educate himself. This he had done.

It was in 1898 that he read two volumes of Shaw's plays, then recently published. In them he discovered a rich deposit—for what Ibsen and Barrie were to Mrs. Fiske and Maude Adams, Shaw was to Daly. They were both Irish, both intellectual, and they both throve on opposition.

"Candida" was one of the plays in those volumes, and soon Daly began to dream of staging it. But his plan fell through from lack of funds. He put the idea aside, and took such engagements as came his way.

The year 1903 was a disastrous one for him. In a little more than twelve months he appeared in eight failures. With a faith born of desperation, he turned back to "Candida." He believed the time was now ripe to put it on for special matinees. (Katharine Cornell says there is always the right time for a play, and the actor must seize it.)

Daly had $350, and he got his friend Winchell Smith to put in $400 more. Together, they borrowed $600. Daly was his own stage director. He cast himself for

Marchbanks; the Candida was Dorothy Donnelly; the Prossy, Louise Closser (long afterward, Louise Closser Hale of the pictures); Ernest Lawford was Lexy Mill.

Their first matinee was given on December 7, 1903. It created a wave of discussion, but it wiped out Arnold Daly's $350. However, each subsequent matinee lost less, and a day arrived when intake exceeded outgo. The play ran five months. Daly added "A Man of Destiny" to the company's offering, his Napoleon providing an astonishing contrast to Marchbanks. John Corbin, the critic, said no American except Mansfield could have given the Corsican such incandescent power.

Daly had a sure technique in acting. His sense of timing was unrivalled, but it was the mind of the rôle that concerned him most:

> When the public or the critic speaks of a player as a character actor, it is generally understood to mean that he does not make love to the heroine. . . . Why, pray, the term "character acting"? Each actor who is honest to himself and his work strives to give each new rôle the characteristics intended by the author. . . . In short, I have been trying to explain . . . that a true artist tries to get at the very soul of the part.

"Candida" and "A Man of Destiny" had been artistic triumphs, but Daly was not yet a financial success. In the fall of 1904 he went to George C. Tyler, the manager, for backing. Tyler, who always had a soft spot in his heart for Daly's talents, had been reading the works of this new author, Shaw, and had decided that "You Never Can Tell" was likely to be widely popular. Ac-

MAUDE ADAMS as Maggie Wylie in "What Every
Woman Knows."

cordingly, he offered to manage the actor, if the latter would put on "You Never Can Tell." Only after much demurring did Daly agree, for the play was not his favorite. It was presented in January 1905, and proved a big comedy hit.

Following it, Daly left this management—to which he later made recurrent returns. His enthusiasm was white-hot; he believed audiences were willing to accept a Shaw play as a living essay, a surgeon's knife.

But people were not ready to regard "Mrs. Warren's Profession" in this light. Alas for Daly's high hopes—he was permitted to give only a single performance of the piece in New York. That was on October 30, 1905. Anthony Comstock had refused to read the drama or attend a rehearsal, but he lodged a complaint with the authorities, and all the players were arrested. They were quickly released, save for Daly, who gave bail and finally came to trial.

This was not until July 1906. The Court then upheld Daly; but it was so long after the event that the public paid little heed.

Though he continued his other Shaw productions and was now at the height of his fame, the year 1906 was touched with a sign of his coming difficulties. Winchell Smith, who had been his silent partner, severed the connection. This was only the beginning of many shifts in the player's course.

As Peter Daly had moved from one school to another, so Arnold Daly was soon changing from one manager to another. This went on for nearly twenty years. His restlessness and love of disagreement began to undo him; yet because of the power of his acting he was in constant demand. Sometimes he played in New York, sometimes in London.

After 1907, he did Shaw only intermittently, but the list of other rôles he created is a long one. A few of the productions in which he appeared included "General John Regan," "Beau Brummell," "The Very Minute," and "The Tavern." In 1921, he was with the Theatre Guild, doing "The Wife With a Smile" and "Boubouroche."

He fell out with Shaw who, he said, got drunk on ink. He played in vaudeville. He acted and directed in pictures. But he was dissatisfied and unhappy a great deal of the time. In the autumn of 1926, he returned to the Theatre Guild and gave a brilliant performance as Marshall Bazaine in "Jaurez and Maximilian." This was his last Broadway appearance. On the night of January 13, 1927, a fire broke out in the apartment building where he lived. He was burned to death.

So closed the career of a man of the keenest comprehension. He had won battles and lost battles. But his contribution to the theatre in this country was unique; he did what no one else stood ready to do—and he knew the hour for doing it.

In Mrs. Fiske, Maude Adams, and Arnold Daly, the actor's genius worked on three diverse natures. It did not make them in the least alike. It used and magnified the traits they were born with—for magnification is a process of genius. It increases the stature of the being on whom it lays hold, and every department of his or her personality becomes involved in the final settlement.

Each of these people was an apt instrument for a dramatist new at the time. Ibsen, Barrie, and Shaw were then unconventional authors, and to make audiences like them took minds not too set in established molds.

In one thing, these three players agreed; none of them centered attention on Shakespeare and the old classic drama. That school of acting had now faded far into the past.

11.

Pictures and Radio

BY 1908, a far-reaching change was at work on the outer edges of the theatre. This was the motion picture—at first, a very poor relation indeed of the drama. Actors occasionally played in pictures without telling of it, for it enhanced neither reputation nor salary.

"The Life of an American Fireman," done in 1903, was the first motion picture narrative in this country. A cameraman compiled it. In time, ten-cent movie houses were showing dramas with such titles as "The Stolen Child," "A Sure 'Nuff Tumbler," or "Saleslady's Matinee Idol." Delicate shades of feeling were not expected of players in these offerings; projectors flickered too badly. Suspense generally involved a chase—a fat policeman, perhaps, in pursuit of an angular old maid.

But already there were attempts to do plays which depended more on acting than on muscle. Among picture studios in 1908 was the small establishment of Biograph, in Fourteenth Street, New York, where David Wark Griffith was the newly-installed director.

Griffith, who had been an actor in James K. Hackett's company, possessed artistic instinct and a superior sense of showmanship. He was feeling his way in the movies. As his studio had scanty floor space, he developed scenes in which camera came close to players. His pictures were better acted and better photographed than most productions by other organizations. As early as 1909, he did "Edgar Allan Poe," "The Cricket on the Hearth," and "The Violin Maker of Cremona." It was in the latter picture that Mary Pickford played her first screen rôle, and Lionel Barrymore did some experimental acting for the Biograph company in that same year.

Silent films improved, expanded, migrated to Hollywood, and made fortunes for movie stars—who, for the most part, had no exalted standing in the legitimate theatre. To be sure, John Barrymore first acted for pictures in 1912, Ethel Barrymore in 1914, Douglas Fairbanks in 1915, and George Arliss in 1920. (Later it was Arliss, said Bernard Shaw, who showed actors how to talk in talking pictures.) But such defections from the higher ranks were exceptional, up until 1927.

In that year came talking pictures, and soon they drew heavily on Broadway for its best players. At present, however, the score is being evened up; actors go to Hollywood—or to Ellstree, outside of London—but they come back. They now work interchangeably for stage or film. So, in little more than thirty years and from the shoddiest beginnings, the theatre has acquired an enormous new department. This development has been as rapid, as full of *élan* and energy, as that of the Elizabethan stage.

Without stopping to trace what technicians and directors have done, this chapter must limit itself to the actor. It must look at him in this jungle of new devices. How is he able to find his way around in it?

At first glance, it may seem as if talking pictures were a great labor-saving contrivance for the actor. He gives one complete performance of a rôle—and there it is, permanently recorded. His phantom will keep on endlessly reeling it off. Compare this with a stage portrayal. Its creator must go back to the theatre every night and do it over again; it is an inescapable routine, demanding all the vitality he can put into it. Sidney Howard says he never ceases to marvel at the toil of the honest, sincere, hard-working performer.

Suppose, though, the player decides that he is sick of the treadmill. He signs a contract, packs up, and goes to Hollywood for a large salary. (We assume him to be of such repute that Hollywood wants him.)

What price this new freedom of his? He is now up with the lark, presenting himself at the studio promptly each morning. Inside those sound-proof walls, he quickly discovers that he has exchanged one set of difficult demands for another. Of course he knew in advance that he would be entering a new world—but his first encounters with it are unnerving. However, a man gets used to hanging, and before long our player has taught himself an enormous number of new disciplines.

Months later, his screen characterization is released with success. He emerges from this ordeal by celluloid with an enlarged audience and increased earning powers. Thereafter, he divides his time between pictures and stage. He rarely mentions the agonies of mind he went through in adapting his acting to the cinema; or if he does, people think he is joking.

Pictures strike at the roots of what the actor in former generations used to take for granted. He assumed three things: first, that there would be an audience before him;

second, that this audience would view him from fixed positions—that is, from the front of the house; third, that he would act the story in the order in which the dramatist told it. None of these things is true in a film studio.

There, the player gets no response from spectators, to tell him whether he is conveying what he means to convey. There lenses and microphones—his substitute audience—walk around with him. They record him from any angle—from beside him, from above, from below, from a distance, from close up. He may have to play the last scene of a drama on the heels of the first, or he may start in the middle. He has no opportunity to be swept along with the story.

These are serious readjustments. Still, if an actress must arrive on the lot and go at once into Lady Macbeth's sleepwalking scene, she will find a way to do it. That is her business. Since she has this ability to give out emotion when it is demanded, pictures need her. She is obliged to work disjointedly because every sequence that happens in a certain location must be taken while that spot is available. The director is supreme. Valuable though Lady Macbeth may be, she is only one of the instruments in his orchestra; the others include crowds for the great ensemble scenes, as well as all the technical equipment.

Here, as in every form of acting, a player must comply with the rules and yet not succumb to them. He must bring such an abundance of reality that he surmounts all the unrealities.

That is what happens in every moving, rememberable screen portrait—Paul Muni and Luise Rainer in "The Good Earth," for instance, Charlie Chaplin in "Modern Times," Elisabeth Bergner in "Katharine the Great."

If pictures exact a great deal of the actor, they favor him in certain ways. The cutting room deletes his worst moments and preserves his flashes of inspiration. Then, too, screen acting gives him the delight of playing quiet scenes quietly. On the stage he must heighten them, in order to reach the audience; but the camera sees the least look, the microphone catches his least whisper.

Nevertheless, those obliging inventions pursue him relentlessly. He must go on location, where they follow him into a rowboat on a wallowing sea, into airplane or motorcar—anywhere the story sends him. He must be prepared to act in any surroundings, and under any amount of discomfort. Thus, in doing "Winterset," Burgess Meredith had to have an oily fog sprayed over him constantly. For "Captains Courageous," Spencer Tracy—who played the Portuguese sailor so beautifully—spent hours immersed in a frigid ocean.

The miracle is that players so hedged about with arbitrary requirements should give so many fine performances. There is a remarkable amount of good acting in Hollywood—along with some that is bad—and minor characters, as well as the briefest "bits," are often done with a verity that is delightful. Even to name a few film stars—say Leslie Howard, William Powell, Claudette Colbert, Gary Cooper, John Barrymore, Norma Shearer, W. C. Fields, Janet Gaynor, Warner Oland, Katharine Hepburn—is to recall the varied range of talent they bring before the camera.

Do actors like the cinema? They make contradictory statements about it; sometimes they call it an art and sometimes a dog's life. Both affirmations are doubtless true.

In 1925 a young actress arrived in Hollywood, under contract to Metro-Goldwyn-Mayer. That organization had been by no means anxious to engage her, but did so at the insistence of a director whom it was importing from Sweden—Mauritz Stiller. He said the girl had wonderful possibilities. Nevertheless, she hung around the studio for months, posing for a few advertising pictures; to the company she was just one more Swede. This was Greta Garbo.

After a while, the executives gave her a part. It was in "The Torrent," with Ricardo Cortez—and they discovered that Stiller knew what he was talking about.

Brought up in humble circumstances in Stockholm, she started life as Louvisa Gustafsson. Perhaps Greta was her middle name, or a nickname. She was born on September 18, 1906, according to rumor; official information is lacking. She dreads publicity. ("Why do they want to see me?" she once asked when she was trying to sail for Europe unnoticed. "What do they want me to say? I've said all I can.")

Her father was a machinist with a taste for music, his wife was a peasant. Greta's school teacher, looking back, remembered that she had thought the child obstinate, aloof. She was the prettiest pupil in the school, with serious eyes and little to say for herself. If she were called to come to the blackboard, she trembled.

When she was fourteen her father died, and she went to work at anything she could find. She became a millinery apprentice in a department store, which soon embarked on an advertising movie—Miss Gustafsson being the heroine. Next, we find her applying to a Stockholm picture company, which gave her a minute part in one production.

She decided to study acting, and managed to get a two years' scholarship at the Royal Dramatic Academy, continuing as a contract pupil after her graduation. It was then that she came to the notice of Mauritz Stiller, the greatest director in Sweden. He saw her play, and cast her in a picture he was doing.

He changed her name to Greta Garbo. He believed in her, he trained her, seeing what could be evoked in this shy creature. Other players at the studio used to watch him and her walking up and down in the grounds outside the building—he always talking, she always listening. They thought she was a nice young thing, with nothing remarkable about her. The director's next production was "The Atonement of Gösta Berling," and in it he gave her a leading rôle. The picture won the Nobel Prize, brought Stiller an offer from Hollywood, and transplanted Greta Garbo to America.

Stiller's subsequent career was less fortunate than hers. He was not permitted to go on directing her. A misfit in Hollywood, he returned to Sweden. In 1928, when Miss Garbo learned that he was seriously ill, she wanted to go to him; but she was in the middle of a picture and could not be released. Later, she went. He had died.

Greta Garbo spoke only a little English and her vogue was still new when talking pictures came along. People said she might continue her silent films for a year or two, but then she would be finished. They were mistaken.

She studied English, and her first speaking character for the cinema was the title rôle in "Anna Christie," in 1930. Mordaunt Hall's review in the *New York Times* told of "the low enunciation of her initial lines, with a packed theatre waiting to hear her first utterance. . . ."

Unlike most film actresses on their débuts in talking films, Miss Garbo . . . thinks about what she is saying. . . . There is no hesitancy in her speech, for she evidently memorized her lines thoroughly before going before the camera. . . .

She continued to improve her English intonations, until they became almost faultless. Her acting, too, has grown, if one compares it now with what she did in her first American film. She has those two requisites for great playing—bigness of imagination and unfailing command of technique.

Speaking of her "Anna Karenina," Richard Watts, Jr., of the *New York Herald Tribune*, called her "never quite as magnificent as she is in this drama":

> In all her dramas, including some direful examples . . . Miss Garbo has been completely and entirely superb. . . . In every rôle, she plays with an unflustered skill which hints eloquently of a tremendous emotional reserve.

That unflustered skill runs through everything Miss Garbo does. Cameramen and directors report that she is a steady, rapid worker. She has studied her part thoroughly before she begins a production, and is familiar with every detail of the story. Her instinct for truth makes close-ups easy for her; she accepts suggestions; in every way she has mastered her medium.

As Camille, from the first glimpse of her on the screen until the very end, she was deeply immersed in the character. Her eyes, with their steady, slow glance, were always filled with thought. They were as different as possible from those upturned orbs with glycerine tears oozing from them, once so prevalent in the cinema.

This Marguerite Gauthier was a rounded characterization. At the start, there she was in her carriage laughing at herself as she said, "I buy twice as many flowers as I need—but I want them." Before long, one saw Camille winding de Varville around her finger.

Then—like Matilda Heron eighty years before—as the actress warmed to her subject, she rose with the story and released her powers in one climax after another. One scene between her and Henry Daniell, the de Varville, was a splendid duet of acting. De Varville had returned inopportunely, at the very time when Camille expected Armand. De Varville, sitting down to play the piano, guessed the situation, and Camille knew that he guessed. But the two of them kept up a comedy with each other, laughing more and more excitedly while de Varville's playing grew louder and the doorbell rang unanswered.

In Camille's death scene, Miss Garbo's face had the look of a very sick person. When she was told that Armand was coming, her glance showed no comprehension. Then, little by little, she began to realize that this news was true, and tears of physical weakness came into her eyes. There was a flicker of strength, and she met Armand standing. Her last look up at him, as he was speaking, was eloquent. Her eyelids were half closed, but under them she kept her eyes on his face with all the effort that was left in her. The lids drooped—and she was dead without a word or sound.

Another cinema impersonation of great stature was Charles Laughton's Captain Bligh in "Mutiny on the Bounty." He showed you an old sea-dog—hard, avaricious, and yet heroic. In fact, he performed the feat of making you hate the man at first and admire him later.

The actor's face was the face of Captain Bligh. There was his appraising glance up into the rigging, as he spied the first hint of changing weather. There were the looks he gave his junior officers at dinner when they refused the cheese as a mute protest against his cheating the seamen of rations. Throughout the whole drama, the player's features were worked on by constantly changing thoughts. There were instants when his eyes darkened and glowed; they became luminous.

His voice, too, was filled with feeling. When the Captain was compelled by his mutinous crew to abandon his ship on the high seas, he cried, "You've taken my ship!" The words seemed to be torn from his boots; he was shaken with incredulity and outrage. Listening, one could not think of that exclamation as a speech set down for an actor to say. Later, with a handful of sailors in an open boat, he prayed, "Give us grace to quit ourselves like men in the trials and dangers that are before us," and there was a noble, blunt simplicity in the phrases. Most moving of all was his sight of land after forty days; his emotion was so great that he could not speak. The effect on the audience was enormous.

Here was a rôle which showed how far the cinema has traveled from the theatre where a player works under prearranged conditions. The film actor must, if need be, reach his highest moment as he goes down a rope ladder or tosses on a stormy ocean.

Charles Laughton was born in 1899, at Scarborough, England, a seaside resort where his family kept a—in Scarborough one says "an"—hotel. He followed his inherited calling, although he always wanted to be an actor. His ideas of characterization came from studying hotel guests. After serving in the World War, he returned to his work.

It grew irksome, but he never dreamed of giving it up until a brother volunteered to take it over. Laughton, who must have been about twenty-five by then, struck out for London, where he entered the Royal Academy of Dramatic Arts.

One of his teachers was Madame Komisarshevskaya, the great Russian player for whose ideas of acting he has the highest regard. His earliest stage appearances—in 1926—were in plays by Gogol and Chekhov. They were suburban productions, but soon he had a succession of West End engagements.

His rise was astoundingly rapid. Lacking the leading-man physique—he was overweight and had thick features —he did what is specifically called character acting. In little more than a year, he scored a London success. The power to follow one piece of good work with another is rare in new actors, but Charles Laughton had it. He kept on doing well, and in May 1931 he created a sensation in "Payment Deferred." This play was brought to New York in September; his acting became the talk of the town.

Picture producers had been watching him. He went to Hollywood for the first time in 1932 and—as he had done in London—he followed one success with another. But he felt a need to school himself in the stage classics; so in 1933, he went back to London and played Shakespeare for a season at the Old Vic.

One of his rôles that winter was Henry VIII. This led to his enacting the same personage in the British film, "The Private Life of Henry VIII"—a part which he said "stretches everything you have and then asks for more."

(The Anne of Cleves in that production was Elsa Lanchester—Mrs. Laughton. She also appeared with him in "Rembrandt.")

In a burst of enthusiasm, Mr. Laughton once told a London interviewer, "What is there that can't be done with the cinema!" Then he went on to point out that on the stage the actor must project his emotions, his thinking, across the footlights; he must make them travel to the audience. But in pictures, the camera is nearby and helps him to do the projecting:

> You can work it out with the director, "At such and such a moment my hand, trembling as it touches a table-knife, will be the most important dramatic fact." And then the camera, guided by the director, can play the part of the ideal audience. . . .

Laughton prefers rôles that have a strong psychological element, but he gets his psychology from observing people—not from books. In any biographical portrait, he tries to become "mentally at one" with this other individual, to understand his outlook on life and to know his handicaps and triumphs. After that, come investigations of the locale and the period. For "Rembrandt" he spent weeks in Leyden and Amsterdam; for "I, Claudius," he studied in Rome.

Lack of contact with an audience is the player's greatest difficulty in pictures, says Charles Laughton. His way of overcoming this is to keep feeling as if people were watching the play. He believes this is essential, because the reaction of the audience is an integral part of any performance.

With all these innovations, there is a still newer form of acting. This is radio. It is now in a stage comparable to that of movies when two reels made a picture, or when such serials as "The Perils of Pauline" were popular. So radio acting must be considered more for its possibilities than for its actualities. Its players and directors believe that a day will come when thoroughly fine dramatic offerings, written to meet the needs of this medium, will be carried everywhere by air waves. Moreover, acting by radio is a forerunner of acting by television. How far off that is, no one cares to prophesy.

In the early spring of 1924, station WGY, in Schenectady, engaged performers and commenced to broadcast plays. It was the first acting company of the sort in the United States. One of its initial presentations was "The Merchant of Venice." Other stations gradually developed their own stock companies, doing adaptations of classic and standard dramas. Performers were glad to be anonymous, just as actors in pictures had been long before.

In the pioneer cinema, no one thought of pictures as a means of advertising. This inspiration, however, was brought to bear on radio drama; so players modestly paid on a "sustaining" hour found that they worked more profitably if an advertiser "sponsored" their offering. It was thus not unpleasing to them to hear an announcer say, " 'Uncle Tom's Cabin' is brought to you by Snackettes, the breakfast food that Has Everything. Order Snackettes from your grocer, and Meet the Treat that Millions Eat."

Suppose the manufacturer of Snackettes, a convert to radio, decides that "Uncle Tom" and "Trelawny of the Wells" may be all right, but he would like to present something special. The result may be a series of scenes concerning a wholesome American family at the breakfast table, the story continuing from day to day and running

GRETA GARBO as Camille

for twenty-six weeks. If the experiment goes well, a stream of letters will come to the broadcasting station, from listeners who become interested in the affairs of that family at the breakfast table.

This correspondence is radio's equivalent for applause and curtain calls. What it reveals is that the most attentive and constant audience for plays on the air is not theatre-wise—but is made up in large proportion of people for whom stage productions and pictures are infrequent experiences. In short, it is a new public.

Innumerable series like the imaginary one for Snack-ettes have been devised in the past few years. Some have a domestic atmosphere; some are highly melodramatic and sensational. The air is thick with them every day, and in such sketches a great deal of radio acting is now done.

But broadcasting stations also present plays by the best dramatists, acted by players of high repute. These are often "sustaining" programs, provided to parallel presentations of fine music. There have been contagions of Shakespeare, Ibsen, and Eugene O'Neill on the air. Ina Claire has given a series of modern plays. Augustin Duncan has done "John Ferguson." A few of the actors in Shakespeare have been John Barrymore, Helen Menken, Walter Huston, Sir Cedric Hardwicke, and Tallulah Bankhead. Peggy Wood, Helen Hayes, and Ian Keith were among those in O'Neill casts. "Les Misérables" has been done in dramatic projections, with Orson Welles and Martin Gabel.

— Radio acting is the opposite of the silent screen. There, everything depended on pantomime; here, the voice is the actor's only instrument. Out of such limitation he discovers—or rather, re-discovers—the power of the spoken word.

Of course there is a bad side to this; you can twist the dial and hear performers resorting to all the time-worn, ready-made inflections. But there are other players who, speaking without apparent effort, manage to make you think you are overhearing real persons—and that must serve as a measure of good characterization on the air.

Besides those players already mentioned a few of many others who have done radio acting include Dudley Digges, Leslie Howard, Burgess Meredith, Ethel Barrymore, Tyrone Power, Ernest Truex, and Olga Baclanova.

Descendants of old, dignified players of long ago are among performers now heard on the radio. Anne Seymour, the Mary Marlin of a dramatic serial which runs daily, year in and year out, is the great-granddaughter of E. L. Davenport, notable in the palmy days. The Barrymores' stage ancestry goes back to the palmy days, as well—and so does Tyrone Power's. His great-grandfather starred more than a century ago.

Does acting change fundamentally, in this newest of its guises? Helen Hayes thinks not.

"Radio acting is real acting, but it is done in a different medium," she told me when she was playing a long series on the air. "The stage shows life slightly magnified; it has to, to reach people in the audience. But on the radio, the least attempt to magnify is fatal. Of course, whether you play in the theatre, or pictures, or radio, imagination is essential. It works for you. The other evening I was broadcasting a scene that had a good deal of emotion. As I stood there by the microphone, I give you my word I could see the room I was supposed to be in. I was in it."

It is evident that the player does not lose his sense of direction in the wilderness which cinema and radio compel him to explore. That is because he carries along with him the actor's old knack of getting inside the skin of his part. All other habits or preconceived notions of his craft, he has to modify; but this one process he keeps and uses.

12.

Studies of Contemporary Acting

THE time has gone by when it was possible to set sharp
boundaries between stage acting, radio acting, and
picture acting. Turning from one of these forms to another is like crossing a state line. Things seem much the
same till you start to vote or pay taxes. Then you see
unavoidable differences.

So the stage makes its peculiar test of the player. This
is the giving of one continuous performance which must
grow in interest as the play proceeds. A film drama is
pieced together, the climactic effect being a matter of
compilation. But on the stage, actors build the climax at
each presentation. They must be more compelling as the
play goes forward. There are no retakes; a bad moment
cannot be cut out. Each repetition of a rôle is complete,
with its blemishes and best touches indelible.

That is why this chapter comes back to the traditional
theatre for views of contemporary playing. It can be
examined here at close range. With the present as with
the past, it is necessary to select a few examples and to
omit others equally worth attention—those chosen in this
instance being Katharine Cornell, Leslie Howard, Pauline
Lord, Helen Hayes, Roland Young, Eva Le Gallienne,

CHARLES LAUGHTON as Captain Bligh in "Mutiny on the Bounty."

Nazimova, George M. Cohan, Alfred Lunt, and Lynn Fontanne. They stand for perhaps four times as many players now on the American stage who have pre-eminent ability to convey ideas across the footlights and evoke emotion. Theatrical producers have a plain phrase for that ability; they call it box-office appeal.

Here are ten names, and the acting of each of these persons has its own unmistakable qualities. But there are certain fundamentals that they all take for granted. These are things which good players do every evening without exciting the least wonder. Indeed, the better the things are done, the less they are noticed. Three of these fundamentals are faithfulness to the passing moment; seeming unconsciousness of the audience; and freshness in repetition.

Truth to the moment simply means that adept actors do not permit themselves to anticipate what is about to happen in a scene. Suppose someone in a play is going to trip over a foot-stool. The performer has rehearsed it; yet he lets the mishap befall him as though he were not expecting it. This is as it should be, for he is assuming to be someone who does not expect it. But watch an unskilled player try to do it. He cannot conceal his foreknowledge that he is going to stub his toe. The information leaks out of him, and the incident loses convincingness. If Roland Young were to trip over that foot-stool he would seem never to have been aware that it was there, and his mistake would be funny.

At every turn of a play, the expert at acting limits his attention to the things that can be known just then by the person he is portraying—who is living through the story instant by instant and cannot be conversant with what is coming. Katharine Cornell calls this "the thoroughly professional quality in acting—complete concentration on the reality of the thing." Though the character does not know what is going to happen to him, he knows everything that *has* happened to him. He has all kinds of memories—of his relations with people in the play, of various hopes and dreads—and some of them will affect his behavior. So the actor must know those recollections. He does not walk on to the stage and begin to act; he is already acting before he speaks a line.

The relation of a modern player to his audience is complicated to describe, but it seems simple to the actor. Let a thousand people be watching, he never intimates that he knows they are there. This is because what transpires on the stage is supposed to be actually happening to actual people. The audience is looking on, unbeknownst.

Ina Claire had her early training in musical comedy. She told me that when Belasco chose her for a "legitimate" star, she had already been going to theatres and studying dramatic technique.

"In musical comedy you are entertaining the audience," she said. "You look directly at people out in front, and even talk to them. But in a play, you behave as if the audience were not there. You are maintaining the illusion that events on the stage are real. You can still look out toward the front of the house, provided you do it as though you were looking across the room in which you are supposed to be. But you must never see the audience. It does not exist in the illusion."

Although the player thus pretends that the audience does not exist, he is alert to it. He plays *for* spectators, but not *to* them. A humbug, and a childish one? But a novel is three hundred or five hundred pages of humbug, in which the author purports to be telling a tale that happened, when everybody knows he invented it. Acting, like other arts, seeks to show a larger truth by means of something not literally true.

Repetition is another skill which modern actors have developed to a high pitch. Yet the public scarcely takes it into account, for most people go to see a play just once. They are through with it when the curtain falls on the last act.

But the curtain which descends tonight will rise tomorrow and tomorrow. The whole performance must go on eight times a week, so long as there is a line at the box-office. How is a player to retain that freshness of view, that "complete belief in the reality of the thing," month after month? This problem has to be solved by all performers but the lazy or incompetent—who are happily unaware that their playing deteriorates. The solution does not come with a mere twist of the wrist.

Here, then, are a few of the things which the trained craftsman of the stage expects of himself. Not that he or she never falls short of such standards—but they are his measures of good workmanship. To them, must be added gifts of insight and powers of projecting emotion. These latter are what audiences recognize in acting; the underlying framework is more or less invisible.

The emotions and ideas which the actor sustains on this invisible framework are things he finds difficult to discuss. They are too much a part of his own fibre. Like the pound of flesh, they cannot be severed without drawing blood. I once heard Mrs. Fiske say to an actress who had been rehearsing a scene, "That was beautiful—beautiful. Now we'll go over it lightly. We mustn't rub off the bloom."

So when players talk of their work, they are extremely

shy of rubbing off the bloom. They go over it lightly. Anyone who puts inquiries to them must respect their reserves, or run the risk of getting little enlightenment. During the past few years, I have done interviews with many of our foremost players, and at times they have talked revealingly about the practice of their craft. Some of the impressions they have given me are what I am recording here.

Once when I went to interview Katharine Cornell at her home, Flush—the cocker spaniel which (or who) had then played in hundreds of performances of "The Barretts of Wimpole Street"—rushed into the room, panting with eagerness. He had made his entrance, and would not mind being noticed. He was. But when the conversation seemed to be getting along too well without him, he turned around and began to concentrate on a ball out of his reach under the radiator. He cried for it, running the gamut of suffering from pathos to indignation, until Miss Cornell got down on the floor and rescued the ball. Flush then subsided, content.

This is an allegory. Flush, a distinctly limited actor on the stage, was shamelessly putting on a scene in private life; whereas his owner, mistress of her audiences, found it needless to display her talents in the middle of a quiet Sunday afternoon.

The first thing one notices about her is a complete absence of tension in whatever she says or does—an almost invariable trait in players of high skill. They understand relaxation. It is one of their charms; more than that, it is part of their working equipment. Without relaxation, the performer is always hampered. What he wants to express gets tied up in knots in his own physique—and though he may be thinking eloquently, little comes through. So he learns to relax. (In Joseph Jefferson's old age, Nat Goodwin described him as "a keen old man, with an exquisite repose.")

With her dark hair and dark eyes set far apart, Katharine Cornell looks like Duse. Only as Juliet and as Oparre in "The Wingless Victory" does she seem as beautiful on the stage as off. When she speaks of her playing, she does it without any air of authority; she is merely telling you, as honestly as possible, what she thinks.

"I can't remember, even at first, trying to act in the way I had seen anybody else act," she said in one of the talks I had with her. "I think my attention was always on the one part I was doing, and I was never ambitious beyond wanting to do it as well as I could. The first director who helped me was Jessie Bonstelle; I shall always be grateful to her. She engaged me for very small parts in her stock company—'fifth business,' she called it. I was with her, at different times, for about three seasons. Her way of helping me? It was by believing in me—she thought I could act. 'Of course you can do this,' she would say to me. I hadn't much confidence in myself."

This is Miss Cornell's picture of herself as a beginner. Lack of confidence was her great difficulty.

When, at eighteen, she came to New York and made her initial attempt to go on the stage, she was too frightened to speak her lines at the rehearsal, and somebody else was put into the rôle. That was in 1916. The Washington Square Players was the organization to which she applied for the part she could not rehearse. That incident, had she lived during the Restoration, would have marked her as "dash'd for an actor," and she might never have had a second chance. However, she was given a "bit" with only one speech, and in that she made her début. "My son, my son!" was what she had to say.

"The other director who has helped me most is my husband. He believes in me, too," she continued.

He is Guthrie McClintic, distinguished as a producer and stage director. When Miss Cornell was in the Bonstelle stock company, he was also a novice there. They were married in 1921, a few days before her remarkable hit in "A Bill of Divorcement"—and on their brief honeymoon they spent hours rehearsing her scenes for the play. He not only believed in her, but she believed in him as well. Mr. McClintic has directed or supervised every production in which his wife has appeared since 1925.

To this day, she says she reads her part very badly at an opening rehearsal—so badly that members of her company are sorry for her. "How an actress can give an audition of a part and convince a manager that she will be good, I don't know. It is beyond me." Miss Cornell questions the possibility of judging a player by a reading, no matter how well it is done—for, in her view, a reading and a performance are totally different things.

During rehearsals of "The Barretts of Wimpole Street" in 1931, there came a day when Katharine Cornell threw down her typewritten part. "I can never do it right," she said. McClintic picked it up. "You don't mean you can't," he told her. "You only mean you never have."

Unforgettable in this player's acting, is her power of being completely engrossed in some passing occupation. Everyone who saw "The Barretts" will recall how Elizabeth Barrett drank the tankard of porter, at her father's urging. It was a big tankard, and she hated porter—but she raised it to her lips and never put it down until the bitter stuff had been slowly swallowed. The audience

watched with an almost hypnotized belief in the scene—
a scene which served the dramatist's purpose by showing
the kind of tyranny his heroine lived under. Time and
again in her rôles, she convinces beholders by the truth
with which she does things. She is the opposite of the
person who cannot trip over the foot-stool by accident.

Exhibitionism, she insists, has no place in acting. The
player must not think, even for an instant, of the audience's opinion. This does not mean that its reactions are
not to be noted and profited by, after the performance is
over. But while it goes on, the actor must be in control.

"In your mind, worked out with all the imagination and
skill you possess, is the thing you want to do. When the
performance comes, you must be intent only on that—on
the sincerest, best thing that is in you," she said. "Nothing else counts, certainly not whether the audience will
like it. To try to please the front of the house is nothing
short of ruinous. I have noticed it many times with inexperienced players. You see them thinking, 'Now the
audience is going to laugh.' And in that instant, the whole
thing is spoiled. Nobody laughs."

A recurrent marvel in Miss Cornell's playing is the
depth of emotional excitement she can convey when
she has no lines to say. In "Romeo and Juliet" there was
a moment after the dance when Juliet stood looking off
through an archway, supposedly watching Romeo as he
left the house. Her eyes made one see the great doorway,
the darkness, and Romeo himself in the light of the
torches. Her look was glowing and prophetic.

Far more striking was something she did in complete
silence at the conclusion of the potion scene. Juliet, ter-
rified, was sitting on the edge of her curtained bed in
the shadowy room. She came to the last of the famous

lines, which generations of actresses have spoken, and she drank the poison. But this was not quite the end of the situation as Miss Cornell played it. Without word or outcry, Juliet waited to see whether the potion would work. At first, there was no change in her. Then, slowly, her hand grew weak and the empty vial dropped out of it, falling to the floor. Her head swayed to one side, and she crumpled across the bed. Only then, was the scene over. The effect of all this on the audience was galvanic. There was scarcely a breath in the front of the house. To watch Katharine Cornell is to see that the actor's argument is not solely made with words.

A rôle that put greater demands on her than Juliet was that of the Malay princess in "The Wingless Victory." In this she not only reached a high pitch of emotion—she sustained it through all the last act and a half of the play.

"Acting does not get easier as you progress; it gets harder, because you find yourself called on for constantly increasing physical and spiritual strength," she told me.

"If you ask how I study a part, I can only say that I keep mulling it over in my mind for a long time. At first I don't do anything as definite as memorizing the lines— but the person is always there in the background for me, even when I am thinking of other things. When rehearsals get under way, this character begins to fill the center of one's attention. It takes possession of you; it gives you no rest. And that goes on till the first night is over. Even then, as long as the play runs, your part is always in some corner of your consciousness."

—— Pauline Lord and Leslie Howard are two players whose acting gains poignancy through a knack of getting their speeches to convey more than is actually set down in the

KATHARINE CORNELL

words. Their simplest phrases seem to carry with them
an obbligato of ideas and memories which must inevitably
be in the character's mind at that moment; and this is done
so unobtrusively that the listener is touched on the quick
before he knows it.

Leslie Howard, born in England in 1893 and educated
there, never went on the stage until after he had served
in the trenches during the World War and had been
severely wounded. Anyone who meets him is bound to
wonder how someone so gentle endured the brutalities of
battle. But truth does not always follow the pattern of
fiction. The war did not wreck Mr. Howard. Here he
is, blond and rather slender, with keen, near-sighted blue
eyes.

He is adventurous and many-sided. He makes nothing
of flying between New York and Hollywood for a week-
end. He has written and staged his own comedies, and he
directs most of the productions in which he stars. In acting, he is always ready to attempt new things.

When he was an undergraduate at Dulwich College,
near London, he wrote for the student dramatic organization. "At that time, I thought I could never make an
actor; I was too self-conscious," he said to me. And he
added that everything he had done in the theatre had been
in spite of this handicap.

Here is an instance of a defect translating itself into a
virtue. Howard had to find a way around his obstacle.
So his acting came to be done in the manner of a person
who might draw you aside from everybody else and tell
you, in a casual undertone, the most unexpectedly moving
things. Even a plain statement like, "I was born in Osh-
kosh," would gain significance by being related for your
ear alone.

So, in "The Petrified Forest," Howard revealed the history of the part he played. He was a tragic, romantic figure—a gentleman down-and-outer, unfolding little by little all the influences which had brought him to this hopeless pass. It was all done *sotto-voce*. The man viewed his own disintegration with too much detachment for any outburst. The clue to Leslie Howard's delineation was his never forgetting things that had happened long before the play began.

(This saturation with antecedent events was also true of his Hamlet.)

In the Sherwood play, Howard purported to be living merely the last few hours of a wayfarer's life, but he let you in on the whole of it. How did he do it? By behaving as a person would behave who was thinking of the years that had gone. Here was faithfulness to the passing moment—present action being shaped by preceding causes. Without it, the onlooker would have seen nothing more than a man stepping into a lunchroom in the Arizona desert, meeting a girl, and quixotically letting himself be killed for her. That would have impoverished the author's idea, which provided the man with a past that made his course believable.

The actor knew this. He not only presented the character, but also conveyed a sense of larger meaning behind it. He gave it illumination. Illumination was of course achieved by actors long ago, but their method was usually a more outspoken one. They could take the audience by storm. With Howard, the audience does not know it has surrendered until everything is over. Anyone who wishes to study understatement should watch Mr. Howard. His is, of course, deliberate understatement backed by all the resources of a trained craftsman. Without them, the process would be ineffective.

He made his stage début in a touring company in England, in 1917. Coming to New York in 1920 under Henry Miller's management, he had no less than fourteen Broadway rôles between then and 1926—and yet he attracted little notice. His opportunity arrived in "Her Cardboard Lover" with Jeanne Eagels, in 1927. Since then the world has been his oyster.

A player so greatly in demand as Leslie Howard can choose the attractions in which he appears. This he does, giving part of his time to the cinema and reserving the rest for stage work, because he likes it best and feels the need of it.

"In acting for pictures you have to depend on memories of how an audience responds," he told me. "After a while those memories grow blurred—and then you must come back to the theatre, which is the greatest corrective of an actor's work. In pictures, it is the director who counts; in the theatre, it is the actor. The performance is in his hands. While the curtain is up, there are only two elements—the player and the audience. Nothing gets between them. Somewhere out there beyond the proscenium, they meet."

It was after a rehearsal, standing on the stage and looking out into an empty auditorium, that he said this. He is familiar with those currents which are sent out by the player and which encounter a returning surge. The demagogue or the Holy Rollers stimulate such currents to an unmeasured degree, but an artist of the theatre can both rouse and restrain them.

When Howard talks he is clear and deft at putting his thoughts into words, even though his manner has moments of diffidence. Seeing it, one believes the tradition of Edwin Booth's shyness.

"Imagination is requisite in the actor, but I wouldn't say that even that is his greatest quality," Mr. Howard insisted. "Something more is needed—that something which makes him or her different from anybody else in the world. We might call this thing personality—the individual's way of looking at life. That is the greatest thing of all. I am not one of those who think the actor should be a mere receptive substance for his part. There is something that he must give."

The word "personality" has been used often enough as a reproach to players, assuming it to be nothing more than a collection of identifying mannerisms. But here is a definition that goes deeper. A character viewed through the performer's eyes and colored by his way of looking at life—that is Leslie Howard's idea of acting. In this, his opinion agrees with Walt Whitman's that it is something special to the individual which always conquers.

Pauline Lord's family lived in a small California town and did not favor the theatre. Still, that could not prevent her being stage struck. At thirteen she played a maid's part at the Alcazar Theatre in San Francisco. This was in 1903. Her first few seasons were spent in the obscurest traveling stock companies—but that was not the worst of it. Worse, was the fact that she had no idea of how to act.

"My earliest notion of acting," she told me, "was nice speeches and beautiful gestures. I thought I must try to be like the large statuesque leading women I had seen. But the trouble was that their poses didn't fit me or the parts I played."

Vandamm

PAULINE LORD in "Ethan Frome."

She is small. Her face is small, with features that are delicately cut and impressionable.

"Before long it dawned on me that my method was all wrong. I wasn't getting anywhere. And yet, I had to act." In conversation, as well as on the stage, her words tell more than they seem to in cold type. "I had to act" was her phrase for the drive of an impulse that had not found its channel. "So I started to analyze myself. I saw that whatever acting I did would have to be done in my own way. I found that my instinct was all for being casual; but being casual was not enough. It had to be blended with other things. Learning to act is a long process. We talk about being natural on the stage, but what we mean is seeming natural. The two things aren't quite the same."

Talma said that it takes twenty years to make an actor. Burbage lavished "35 years paines" on his work. The long process of which Miss Lord spoke involves gaining that technical grasp which changes a promising beginner into a sure artist. Among the things to be acquired are a sense of timing; a confidence in the power of pauses; a clearing away of all confusion of expression. These and a hundred individual secrets of execution must be arrived at, and then seemingly forgotten—for they are not the prime concern of the player. The prime concern is to appear to be doing everything in the play as though it had never happened before.

"Actors can do too much talking at rehearsals about how they are going to play their parts and what the characters think," Miss Lord holds. "It is all there in the author's lines, and if you discuss it too much you get it talked out of you." Emotion is like the dark water in a millpond. Released through a single sluiceway it turns the mill wheel; if it spills over everywhere, it accomplishes nothing.

But to go back to Pauline Lord's early career—she first played in New York in 1912, following that with stock company engagements and road tours. "The Deluge," in 1917, brought her cordial notices, but she did not wake up famous the next morning. This happened to her, though, in "Anna Christie" in 1921. Since then some of her successes have included "They Knew What They Wanted," "The Late Christopher Bean" and "Ethan Frome."

It is not solely in sympathetic characters that she excels. As Zenobia, Ethan Frome's unlovely wife, the actress' look was transformed at moments by an overmastering hatred. One could see her face freeze with it, the muscles distorting and then growing set. Yet in her softer moods, she contrived to show that this woman had once had aspirations and tenderness. Any part she plays seems to come to life out of a long perspective.

Helen Hayes talks about her work as objectively and unassumingly as though it were somebody else's. A fortunately endowed person, she seems never to have gone through an awkward age at acting. She must always have had the secret of centering her attention on the part.

This actress' "Victoria Regina"—a remarkable study in the development of a human being's sense of power—is a striking example of concentration on the character's point of view.

The voice of the princess at the time of her accession is little more than a whisper. "They came to tell me that I am Queen. . . . Then my reign has already begun? I can do as I like?" But when the young Queen has to choose between Albert and his brother for her consort, her tone has already taken on certainty. It is gently unrelenting. The hands are firm, the footsteps short and determined. She gets rid of the unfavored suitor by urging him to his piano practice. "My dear Ernest, I wouldn't think of commanding you. But . . . as you always practice at home. . . . So do go—now." There soon follows a scene showing a clash of wills between the sovereign and the husband whom she adores. "Do not forget," she begins in a steely tone, "that though I am your wife, I am also your Queen." But on that last word, the inflection wavers and breaks between rage and hurt feelings.

With the passage of years, the Queen's German accent —predominating at the start—becomes less and less noticeable. All the while, the voice deepens with authority, until the stout widow of the 1870's has acquired a thunderous way of speaking. At the Diamond Jubilee this, too, is past; the old lady in her wheel chair talks in treble. All these gradual changes blend in the composite picture of one woman.

Miss Hayes was born in Washington, D. C., in 1902, and has been acting most of the time since she was a tiny child doing imitations. Her first New York appearance was with Lew Fields in "Old Dutch," in 1909.

The astounding thing about her acting is its continuing power of growth. In 1918 she was the sprite-like little daughter in "Dear Brutus," and thereafter theatregoers wanted her to stay like that. Managers, too, were sure she ought to keep repeating herself. To such pressure most ingénues succumb, and go on trying to be sweetly ingenuous forever.

But courage and capacity for expansion seem to have

been born in Helen Hayes. She was never aggressive; but she was quite unconvinced by all the arguments.

"Everybody kept saying to me that there was a Helen Hayes sort of part, and that I ought to stick to it. They said it was good sense to give the public what it wanted," she once told me. She added that in Hollywood, not in New York, she was first able to escape from this insistence. "The pictures gave me parts that were bigger emotionally and mentally. I think nobody on the Coast knew or cared what I had done in the East. So they began putting me into parts for which no one would have cast me in the theatre. And what was the result? I came back to New York, and the Theatre Guild engaged me for 'Mary of Scotland.' I had always wanted to grow in my art—to spread my wings."

It is probable that when this ambition first seized her, few people believed she had it in her to soar so high and far as she has come. Nor is there any sign that she has reached the limit to which she will go. An old-time performer said to me, "Helen Hayes could be a great actress, if she were only taller." Mrs. Siddons said something similar about Edmund Kean.

Miss Hayes has not acted for the films in recent seasons, being influenced by a wish to have some degree of home life with her husband and child. (She married Charles MacArthur, the playwright, in 1928.)

"There is a sort of peace in the theatre, after the picture studios," she admits. "Here the actor has a chance for long, slow growth into a part. Then too, the stage is where you get immediate response from audiences. That is why nothing can take the place of acting in the theatre."

Helen Hayes' eyes look gray-blue when she begins to

ROLAND YOUNG

talk, but as she warms to her subject they seem to turn a deep brown.

"Acting is always an inward process. It turns you in, in, in. It is the thinking and watching that do it," she told me. "Not that I was watching Helen Hayes as Mary of Scotland; I was watching Mary of Scotland herself. And not the actual Mary of history, but the Mary of the play. The worst of this habit of watching is that you get to taking notes about everything that happens to you. When I was having my baby I said to myself, 'I'm behaving pretty well.'

"When you are rehearsing a big part like Queen Victoria, it gradually gets possession of you; you can't put it out of your mind. That person is there beside you all the time. She goes everywhere with you. You ride around in taxicabs talking to yourself in the accent she uses—you are constantly speaking and thinking like her. Your concentration reaches the pitch of an obsession; it is something that owns you."

Here is a glimpse of that intense absorption which precedes effortless playing. It is a record of the creative actor's state of mind, bearing the closest resemblance to Katharine Cornell's phrase about the study of a part. ("It takes possession of you; it gives you no rest.") These are answers to anyone who asks how it happens that good acting looks so easy. It is like sliding downhill; to do it, there has to be a stiff climb beforehand.

Intentness is thus the force of Miss Hayes' playing. People remember Mary of Scotland sitting at her window in prison, because of the depth of thought she was able to suggest as she sat there. Love, plots, betrayals—all distilled to waiting. So also in "Victoria Regina," it was not solely greasepaint that aged the actress. She made herself feel old.

That rôle is another instance of her capacity for doing more than the accepted thing. It has long been customary for young, attractive stars to keep playing young, attractive parts. But Helen Hayes chose to do Queen Victoria, and she did not flinch at making herself look very old and very fat. Richard Mansfield reserved the right to be young or withered, ugly or handsome, on the stage; and so have numerous other leading actors. But among women who have played heroines, parallels are scarce.

Roland Young's father was an architect in London, and the youth served a brief term as draughtsman in the paternal office. A trace of this training can be seen in the caricatures he draws, wherein effects are gained with neat and sparing lines. They are, indeed, the kind of caricatures to be expected of Mr. Young, for he is a neat and sparing player.

Off the stage, he might be taken for a college professor, though the eyes behind his spectacles are those of an artist. An identifying trait in him is his quick and exceedingly subtle sense of humor. His vein of comedy is an extension of his own temperament; he contributes to his rôles a way of looking at life.

In "Her Master's Voice," someone asked him, "How does the old Buick go?" He answered with a quiet, breathless wonder, "I don't know. But it does." The precarious condition of that car and the worries of its owner were condensed into those six words. Young's acting is always like that. The person he plays is a complete entity, with difficulties that were going on before the curtain went up. He is not a comedian only. He has done tragic parts, but he says the public remembers the plays which have the longest runs.

It might be thought that a method so lightly touched as Roland Young's would be too Brahmin for the films, yet he is notably popular in pictures. His quiet comedy in "Topper" and "Ruggles of Red Gap," for instance, stays in one's mind; and in "David Copperfield" his Uriah Heep was a villain delineated in the same unobtrusive way. At one time Young spent five unbroken years in Hollywood, but he never intends to stay away from the theatre so long again.

"On the whole, I think screen acting has a good influence on stage technique," he said to me. "It encourages the player to make small hints count for a great deal—though of course conscious under-acting is just as bad as conscious over-acting.

"Styles in playing change because each generation makes different demands on actors—and besides, plays change. Imagine the kind of performances that were given, say, in 1869. Stages were larger, they were lighted by gas, and there was an apron in front of the proscenium. So effects had to be bigger. But with the great people who played then, the intelligence of the individual was there, just the same. They worked in the style their public expected, and we today work in the style our public expects."

Mr. Young began his career in London, in 1908—the year he was twenty-one. It took till 1916 before he made any telling impression. Then Arthur Hopkins discovered him in the Washington Square Players, in New York, and engaged him for "Good Gracious, Annabelle!" The comedy was by Clare Kummer. In 1921, while Young was appearing in this author's "Rollo's Wild Oat," he married her daughter, Marjorie Beecher Kummer—and that made him a connection of Henry Ward Beecher's family. It amuses him that the playwright whose heroes he has so often portrayed is his mother-in-law.

Eva Le Gallienne is the daughter of a poet. Her father is Richard Le Gallienne, and her mother Julie Norregaard Le Gallienne, a Danish author and critic. The girl was, as the phrase goes, conditioned to an atmosphere of artistic feeling by her rearing. This might have made an individual unfitted to cope with a hard world. But she was filled with energy; she had an instinct for doing.

Her views of acting bear traces of the idealistic and the practical. There is nothing hazy about them. "One of the plainest tests of acting is this: Does the performer seem to be talking, really talking, to other people in the play?" she once told me. "That may sound elementary, but the great people build on that.

"I have seen very great actors—Duse, Réjane, Bernhardt. I tell beginners that I don't envy them for being only eighteen or twenty; *they never saw those people.* Have you ever noticed that in back numbers of theatrical magazines it is only the great people whose photographs do not look funny? All the others are out-of-date—but not the great ones."

Born in London in 1899, and brought up in England and France by a busy yet sympathetic mother, Eva Le Gallienne took to self-reliance like a duck to water. In her childhood she set her heart on being an actress. Constance Collier was her first instructor, and it was in Miss Collier's London company that the fifteen-year-old girl first appeared on the stage. She came to America soon afterward, and her introductory part in New York was a "bit"—a colored maid. That was in October 1915. The play closed quickly, and she was out of a job.

That winter, in the midst of discouragements, she made a list of six parts which she meant to play by the time she was thirty-five. They were Juliet, L'Aiglon, Hedda Gabler, Camille, Peter Pan, and Hilda Wangel in "The Master Builder"—an oddly assorted collection. Why should a girl who aspired to Juliet and Camille also choose Peter Pan? And what could an adolescent see in Hedda Gabler? In the course of time, she acted every one of those rôles—but not till she had served an apprenticeship in plays good, bad, and indifferent.

In 1921, she made a conspicuous success as Julie in "Liliom." Four years earlier, when good opportunities were scarce with her, she had been engaged for a drama called "The Daisy." She liked the part she was to have better that any she had ever been given, and she was dreadfully disappointed when plans for the production were called off. It was just one of those griefs that had to be endured. "Liliom" turned out to be the same play, and in it she had the same part.

Starting in 1926, she conducted the Civic Repertory Company in New York for seven years—staging its productions as well as acting in them.

"If people only knew what good times we had in that old theatre in Fourteenth Street," she said to me. "Of course we worked hard; but we had so many good laughs as we went along. We didn't walk around with uplifted eyes and lilies in our hands, as outsiders sometimes imagined. You see, we were supposed to be doing something for Art, and we were expected to be solemn about it. We weren't, though.

"One of the things repertory taught me is that the public seldom distinguishes between the player and the part. Whatever your part is, the audience thinks you are that kind of person. Then, too, a showy part bowls the audience over, while something more difficult but less effective is taken for granted.

"It takes the first ten years of acting to get your technique—and the next ten to get control of your emotions, so that you can call on them and be sure they will respond. That well to draw on!"

Miss Le Gallienne's Rebecca West in "Rosmersholm" has been highly praised for its quality of living and breathing before one's eyes. It was a portrait which, besides truthful simplicity, had cumulative force. It stirred audiences.

Behind it was the actress' long familiarity with Ibsen and with this particular play. It is not for nothing that she is partly Scandinavian; the things Ibsen wrote about are in her inheritance. She first thought of Rebecca West as a possible rôle for herself ten years before she played it. Once during the interval, she planned a production of "Rosmersholm" by the Civic Repertory Company; but other arrangements interfered.

"All the parts I have cared for most, I thought of long in advance. That is how characters grow in one's mind," she said. She talks about her work without any flourishes. One imagines that she might sit down to have a tooth out with much the same composure. "To me, Rebecca West in the first two acts is a sort of question mark; she does and says very little. She is like a cat when it sits still for a long time with its paws tucked in. It keeps looking straight ahead, waiting. What is it waiting for? You don't know, but there is a strong personality there, and you feel it.   That is Rebecca West, before her history and motives open up in the story."

This was the woman Eva Le Gallienne depicted.   Like the cat, she watched and waited.   She moved about the house self-effacingly, yet it was clear that she was at home there and could have found her way around in the dark.   She made one believe in that room as part of a house that people lived in.

At every instant, even when she had only to listen, the actress' characterization gave off an emanation of the thoughts that never ceased in her—and here was the central dynamo of this performance.   Dramatic imagination, under pressure, can be turned into power.   It was as though nothing could still the rush of the stream which ran through Rebecca West's mind—a torrent of guilt, love, and relinquishment.   At last the stream burst.   One knew not only what Rebecca thought but how she felt, and was moved to tears by this creature whom one had meant to be armed against.   More than that—her experience seemed to have some connection with everybody's life.

Alla Nazimova is a past mistress at capturing audiences in ways like this.   It is more than thirty years since she learned English and became an American star, having come to New York in a company from Russia.   She had been a pupil at the Moscow Art Theatre, an institution then unheard of in America.   Her first English-speaking parts, in 1905, were Nora in "A Doll's House," and Hedda Gabler.

Her work in her first few seasons attracted wide attention—and yet it was not so deeply cut as it is now. What she had then was facility.   Now she has nobleness.

In this early period her costumes and make-up, as well as the tiny mannerisms of her parts, were almost too cleverly designing. Soon she was enjoying a vogue for sinuous, languorous impersonations.

Those things she put away years ago. Today she is the Nazimova who creates such characters as her Christine, the guilty wife in "Mourning Becomes Electra," and Mrs. Alving in "Ghosts." Trained under Stanislavsky, her acting always had the smaller fidelities to life, but years have added a touching humanity.

Her Mrs. Alving was a woman who had lived long with grief—she had not slipped into it like a coat. It was in the stoop of her shoulders, in the colorlessness of her voice. Except at one moment close to the end of the play, her emotion was never an outburst; it was just the frayed escaping edge of something she could not quite hold back. Thus, when she spoke of the endowment she was giving for the orphanage as being the amount that had made Lieutenant Alving a good catch, she added, "It was my purchase money." And Mrs. Alving's mouth and chin betrayed her feeling, in spite of her. In trying to keep the corners of her mouth from drawing down, her tongue stiffened so that she could scarcely shape the words.

This responsiveness of every muscle to the thought is so exactly what we are used to seeing in real life, that it may pass unnoticed in acting. But watch players who are not too practiced, and the absence of such flexibility is sometimes distressing. Their bodies appear to be strangely incompliant; they have not yet learned to think below their collar bones. That looks easy. But if it were, more people could do it.

EVA LE GALLIENNE in "Prelude to Exile"

"Vaudeville," as J. C. Nugent puts it, "makes good actors better and bad actors worse." That is because this form of entertainment, now largely in abeyance, is a concentrated education in the reactions of an audience. The player devises his effects for himself. If they go well, he gets bookings. If not, it is just too bad. One of the old gags which a comedian would use when spectators remained unmoved was to say, "You don't have to laugh. I can starve."

In this hard school a host of successful actors, authors, and directors got their training—and George M. Cohan is one of them.

He is a product not only of vaudeville, but also of genius. Indeed, he is an example of how genius will have its way with a human being. In spite of surface differences, his career bears a strong resemblance to that of David Garrick. It presents the same early flowering and the same abounding versatility.

Mr. Cohan was ushered into the world in Providence, Rhode Island, in 1878,

> A real live nephew to my Uncle Sam,
> Born on the Fourth of July,'

as he afterward proclaimed in a famous song. In his boyhood he appeared as a member of the vaudeville team called the Four Cohans. (Accent on the last syllable, if you please. The Cohans were Irish.) The team consisted of Jerry and Helen Cohan, and their children, Josephine and George Michael.

The boy grew into a cocky youth, sensitive and ready to fight the world. At fifteen he looked at Broadway and vowed to himself that he would stuff the street into his pocket before he was through. Subjected to professional slights, he would burst into wild tears and threaten to walk out of the theatre. He was sure he knew more than the old folks. He did. He wrote skits, plays and songs, and before he was thirty he had floated the Cohans out of vaudeville and into a fortune in musical comedy.

George M. Cohan, at that period, was the apostle of a clean and spirited vulgarity. Everything he did was shot through with his own kind of inspiration. It had speed, genuineness, fecundity. He could get songs and ideas out of the air, for there were plenty more where they came from.

Joining forces with Sam H. Harris up to the year 1920, he next became successful as a manager, dramatist and stage director. Altogether, Cohan is the author of at least fifty dramas and musical shows, in many of which he has acted.

As a director at rehearsals, he is full of excitement and kindly understanding. "Such a wonderful person to work for," say people who have been in his casts. Once, seeing an actor stiff and constrained, he drew him aside. "You don't seem at home in this," he began. "Why not?" The unhappy man could not explain. So Cohan reasoned with him quietly, and this was the argument he used: "You have been on the stage fifteen years, and you are at home in the theatre, aren't you? When you are at home you feel easy and comfortable, don't you? All right. The stage is your home, and nobody is going to make you feel strange here." In this way, Mr. Cohan relieved the player's tenseness.

During Cohan's years of crowded activity, he himself was changing. That washing away of non-essentials which accompanies the long practice of an art must have been going on in him.

And so he turned into the mellow, kindly actor of "I'd Rather Be Right" and "Ah, Wilderness"—so real that other members of a cast must beware of seeming like chromos beside him.   In "Ah, Wilderness" he was the father of a family—ageing, tolerant, a little tired—saying things off-handedly.   But his truth to life went deeper. He could be humorous, sympathetic, shrewd, worried, and caustic, all within two or three minutes.   That meant mastery.

Rehearsals of "Ah, Wilderness" were directed by Philip Moeller, who began with more than a week during which the company read the manuscript and discussed it. But having misgivings as to what the leading player might think of this slow approach, Mr. Moeller said to him, "Look here, G. M., you are a director, an actor and a playwright, all in one.   If what I am doing seems crazy to you, I wish you'd tell me."   Cohan answered, "I'm learning something every day."   And he added, "What's more, I mean it."

We come now to that remarkable acting partnership, the Lunts—Alfred Lunt and Lynn Fontanne.   Such combinations are rare.   Not that there has ever been any lack of husbands and wives who were both actors, but to find what may be called a well-matched span, is always difficult.

The Lunts supplement, rather than duplicate, each other; and that is one of the secrets of the incomparable blending in their performances.   Miss Fontanne, for instance, appears to be the one who might bear adverse artistic criticism with philosophy, and Mr. Lunt the one who would feel it before it was spoken.   It is needless to point out how valuable these separate views may be to a pair of players who have pooled their interests.

"What workers they are," says Philip Moeller. "Once I staged a production in which they had the principal parts, and after the opening night I went to Europe. I was gone three months. When I came back, there were the Lunts giving the same fine performance. Those people work on their parts all the time. They never stop. That is why they are at the top of their profession."

If Thomas Betterton and his wife could emerge out of the mists of centuries, it is pleasant to fancy that they and the Lunts might sit down and have a good chat. For the Bettertons, too, were hard workers and practical people of the theatre, achieving that adaptation to a joint career which cannot escape being a test of character in those concerned.

The Lunts have diverse backgrounds. He is of New England descent, his father hailing from Maine and his paternal forebears having settled in Newburyport, Massachusetts, in 1634. His stepfather was Swedish—and that accounts for the boy's having gone to Finland when he was fourteen. After attending Carroll College, in Wisconsin, he migrated to Boston and joined the Castle Square stock company there. That was in 1913, when he was twenty. His wife began playing earlier in her life. She was born in England and made her professional start there.

To question Miss Fontanne about acting, is to find her direct, unaffected, and very clear as to what she thinks. As she talks, she is a lesson in that repose which serves her so beautifully on the stage.

She believes in the slow upbuilding of a career. Her own record illustrates this. She began insignificantly in pantomimes, and advanced to speaking parts in "legiti-

ALLA NAZIMOVA

Here she is Mrs. Alving in "Ghosts." (The Oswald
is Harry Ellerbe.)

mate" attractions, growing into a versatile young character actress. In London, in 1914, Laurette Taylor and J. Hartley Manners were impressed with Miss Fontanne's work. This brought her to New York in their company in 1916.

"I was with them five years, playing many different parts," she told me. "Some of them attracted attention and I began to get offers from other managers, but I didn't leave Laurette Taylor. I am convinced that it is better to concentrate one's work. You are in one spot, where the public can find you and your name becomes known. This, added to increased experience in acting, is like a springboard under you when you are ready to jump."

Her real jump came when she created the title rôle in "Dulcy," in 1921. The part made her, as the phrase has it—but she also made the part. She was ready for it, with that ease and detachment which are characteristic of her playing. In May 1922, the Lunts were married. Making their first connection with the Theatre Guild in 1924, when they appeared together in "The Guardsman," they have done most of their acting since then for that one organization.

Lynn Fontanne had her initial lessons in acting from no less a person than Ellen Terry, who heard the girl recite and offered to help her.

"She taught me one invaluable thing," the actress said to me. "It was this: always to think the thought behind the words. Pay no attention to the diction or the reading, she told me, but fill your mind with the thought, and let the words burst out of your mouth. She was a *great* actress.

"Besides being a great actress, she was a great person. I'll tell you another thing she said; it was that no one could act without having religion in his heart. I don't know what she meant, but that was what she said. At sixty, she did not seem old. I remember once as I came into her room she was standing there in her chemise. She looked over at me, gave a little kick, and poised on one toe. That was not quite what you would expect of an old lady, was it?

"She coached me at odd times for about a year. The first part she drilled me in was Cordelia—never anything modern. She said beginners should always work on big parts."

Although Miss Terry was educated in the mid-Victorian theatre, her advice to Lynn Fontanne is ageless. "Fill your mind with the thought." Here is a warming-up process for the imagination, and an antidote for every fear and awkwardness.

Booth Tarkington saw Alfred Lunt as an unknown performer, believed in him, and chose him for the title rôle of his "Clarence." The author's confidence was not misplaced; it put the young actor on the highroad to fame. That was in 1919, six years after his initiation into the Castle Square company.

Lunt is one of those players who can present two strata of emotion at the same time. There is a surface mood which may be humorous, stolid, sardonic; but beneath this is another layer, painful to the least touch. It is this actor's habit to appear to make light of the pain, as though he were saying, "Pooh, that's nothing."

The method is worth noting, for a more primitive impulse is to show how much the character suffers. That soon palls on the beholder—and so the artist's way is to suggest suffering by seeming to hide it. Doing so is sometimes called playing against the scene. It was not devised yesterday. Betterton "kept his Passion under and showed it most, as Fume smoaks most when stifled."

With Alfred Lunt, in comedy or tragedy, there is a trace of something stifled and "smoaking." He can feel out the hidden turmoils which beset people.

His appetite for work is proverbial. For "Clarence," he learned to play the piano and the saxophone—for "Point Valaine," the accordion. For "Idiot's Delight," he practiced dance steps indefatigably. After one of the Lunts' plays settles in for a successful run, anyone who encounters them and asks how things are going is likely to receive some such answer as this, "Not so badly. We're working on the second act, and we are so tired that we can hardly drag around." Then the inquirer may know that everything is in excellent shape and the Lunts are happy.

They began rehearsing "Amphitryon 38" in the spring of 1937, and their delight in the rôles it gives them has grown ever since. Good parts, they insist, are not difficult—that is, not so difficult as bad parts.

"I love rehearsals," Mr. Lunt told me in the course of an interview. "In some ways, I enjoy them better than performances. That may be because I have none of that show-off confidence about walking out in front of an audience. I take my job during a performance seriously. I have no humor at all about things going wrong—somebody being late on a cue, or the curtain sticking. There are actors who think such things are funny. I don't. My idea is that people in the audience have paid for tickets, and they are entitled to the best we can do."

Petruchio, in "The Taming of the Shrew," was his first Shakespearean rôle. The production, arranged by the Lunts in swiftly-moving scenes with but one intermission, ran for many months in 1935 and 1936. It gave the stars parts which they executed with an enthusiasm that never slackened. They said they kept discovering new possibilities in the play, as long as they were in it.

When a modern actor finds himself playing Shakespeare for the first time, how does he feel in this world of an older theatrical order? To Alfred Lunt, the difference that impressed him most was the spacious atmosphere in which the player moves.

"You read a speech or do a scene, giving it a certain meaning. Then, all of a sudden, a wholly different implication dawns on you, and you say to yourself, 'Of course! *This* is what it really means. Why didn't I see it long ago?' And that keeps happening constantly. There is so much room to turn around in, in Shakespeare. No other dramatist old or new gives you so much," he said, thinking out the comparison as he spoke. "In that way, Shakespeare is like the Bible. The Bible has a great deal of room to turn around in, too—that is why there are so many opinions about it. With Shakespeare, I suppose the actor's greatest problem is how to fill up the space he finds himself in."

For players today, Shakespeare has never been worn threadbare; they see him with new eyes. That freshness inspired the Lunts' Katharine and Petruchio. They did nothing because tradition said it ought to be done. Every bit of "business" was, like the White Knight's mousetraps, their own invention.

Lunt's Petruchio was not a born blusterer, but someone who adopted bluster for his purpose and found zest in it. Lynn Fontanne's Katharine was a vixen. Yet all her retorts were touched with a savoring delight—as though her mouth watered at them. From the start, both players indicated an unacknowledged attraction which induced the couple to fight more desperately. When Petruchio,

Vandamm

BURGESS MEREDITH

in his wooing, beckoned Katharine to come and kiss him, she seemed to consent—and he believed for the moment that it was not going to be hard to tame her, after all. She approached him warily, laughing at her own secret intent. Then, getting him at close range, she bit his cheek. The whole of their first encounter was a most adroit instance of letting each successive idea work itself through the mind of the character, and emerge in action.

From the foregoing glimpses of ten players, it must be apparent that there is no one type of person who makes an actor. Some of these men and women have shown a tenacious faith in themselves, and others were deficient in that quality. Even self-consciousness or unhandiness were not insurmountable barriers to them.

But without sensitiveness, not one of them could act. ("The actor is a creature of sympathy," according to John Bernard.) Sensitiveness is a word with unpleasant connotations. We generally use it to mean a troublesome awareness of one's own feelings. The actor takes it and turns it into awareness of the other fellow's feelings, thus finding a creative outlet for this trait.

— The personality behind the work of a player who succeeds in doing this, is bigger than any single piece of his or her output, just as there is more energy in an engine than it can convert into power. That is the justification for looking at the actor, as well as his impersonations.

It would not be fair to draw on a handful of players as illustrations of contemporary acting without adding others of outstanding ability. Some of them include Ina Claire, whose lightest strokes have a sure command behind them; Noel Coward, unbeatable in the ease of his acting; Gertrude Lawrence, who has a versatility that takes one's breath away; Walter Huston, deviser of fine stage portraits; John Halliday, Tallulah Bankhead—each an expert; Grace George, deft in many parts and particularly so in "Kind Lady"; Elisabeth Bergner, not the least of whose skill lies in the way she listens to what other people in a scene are saying; Ethel Barrymore, who can make the dullest speech sound witty by implying more than is apparent on the surface; John Gielgud, Maurice Evans, and Brian Aherne—three brilliant young men from England; J. E. Bromberg and Morris Carnovsky, both with notable records in plays of the Group Theatre; Ruth Draper and Cornelia Otis Skinner, originators in monologue; Philip Merivale, whose Bothwell in "Mary of Scotland" and Washington in "Valley Forge" were masterly; Walter Connolly, who imbues his characters with a humanity that makes even a poor part seem good; Henry Travers, so completely convincing as Grandpa in "You Can't Take It With You"; Kenneth McKenna, Bramwell Fletcher, Peggy Wood, Henry Daniell, Walter Pidgeon, Margalo Gillmore, Alice Brady, Tom Powers, Ruth Gordon, Frank Craven, Raymond Massey, Jane Cowl, Leslie Banks, Walter Abel—all players in demand because of what they have done.

Any list of this sort is inadequate—but it may serve its purpose if it suggests still more names. Some of the newer players will be considered in the next chapter.

Most of those so far mentioned have been at work for a good while. Twenty years is the average span of their professional histories. Once more the long career, that mark of so many celebrated players in the past, emerges into view.

But where does the present fit into a general view of acting? Has playing today reached a higher point than it had previously attained? That would be a congratulatory conclusion to come to, but it would not square with the facts. Acting is done by individuals and shaped by what they see. So a great player may happen in any century.

Can the present be described as an era of great acting? The best of our players are chary of agreeing to this, for the standards by which they judge are more exacting than those of people who merely look on. Yet in its average level of truth and adaptability, contemporary acting does excel that of any preceding period.

The widely accepted aim of playing now is to do something that approximates life, to build on inward truth; whereas there have been epochs when only the most gifted people measured their work by this test. The spread of sincerity of intent is an undeniable characteristic of playing today.

Its other surpassing quality—its flexibility—has been forced on it by events. Performers have had to master cinema and radio; and the rapid power of adaptation they have shown is beyond belief. Since there is a constant seepage of ideas from one department of the theatre to another, this results in a stage far less arbitrary in its practices than it used to be. There probably never was a generation of actors so open-minded as to what can, or cannot, be done in acting. They have an astounding vitality and willingness to try what is new.

Moreover, when they experiment, the nature of their calling compels them to be "understanded of the people." They cannot go off into a corner and play for a little group of fellow-craftsmen; they have no other public than the big general public. All of these conditions make acting one of the most living and responsive of our arts.

13.

Influences Behind Current Playing

CONDITIONS within the theatre always set their marks on acting. The Restoration stage had its ill-mannered audiences, its endless confusions; Barton Booth's confrères were overwhelmed with the notion of "tone" and artificial dignity; in the first half of the nineteenth century, playing had to accommodate itself to the stock-and-star system.

Today is no exception. Besides cinema and radio, other demands press upon the performer. Some stimulate him, some warp or hinder him; but all of them have a bearing on the acting he does. What are some of these influences, as they can be seen in the work of new stars and younger players?

The strongest force is that of the dramatist—for the actor is not a free agent. He must act what someone has written. Until he has advanced a good way in his calling, he has no choice about whose plays he plays in. Even afterward, when he has power to select, it is far from easy to find the right part in the right drama.

But occasionally a performer falls into the hands of an author who fires his imagination—and then the public sees this player unfold before its very eyes. (That was what happened to Arnold Daly, from the time he read those two volumes of Shaw.)

Burgess Meredith has shown growth of this sort since he began to appear in Maxwell Anderson's plays. They present views of life that are wide and high, and this vision is what Meredith seems to warm to. His acting has ripened with amazing speed. This does not mean that he is limited to Anderson, or Anderson to him, or that they will continue to collaborate—but the association has been fortunate.

Meredith is twenty-seven. His stage training started in December 1929, when he entered the apprentice group at Eva Le Gallienne's Civic Repertory Theatre. In December 1932, he appeared in the disguise of the Duck with Miss Le Gallienne in "Alice in Wonderland," also contriving to be the Dormouse and Tweedledee. Later, came brief engagements in attractions which failed. How to pay for his meals was a problem.

Summer theatres gave him opportunities when he could find none in New York. Thus, in 1933, he played Marchbanks to five Candidas in various rural localities. The Broadway rôle which put him on his feet—both literally and figuratively—was in "She Loves Me Not." This comedy of life at Princeton had a long run in 1933-34, and he was cast as the youth with a passion for tap-dancing. His was an honest, engaging impersonation.

Two years later, after "Flowers of the Forest," with Katharine Cornell, he played his first part by Maxwell Anderson. He was now the tragic protagonist of "Winterset," speaking unrhymed verse. That was in the autumn of 1935, and since then he has been seen only in dramas by Anderson.

In each of them, he has improved on his own record—something which does not happen too often in the theatre. Though he was praised in "Winterset," his playing in "High Tor" had a more thoroughly human tang. The person he embodied was a half-worthless young fellow. You saw his laziness, his humor, his obstinacy; and you also saw the streak of poetry in him. In "The Star Wagon," the actor advanced further. Here, he was an odd, unworldly inventor—ageing and seedy; but the remarkable thing about his performance was that when he turned time backward and became the inventor in his youth, he had the same mannerisms, the same habits of mind. You could believe that the one man was the other, grown old.

This is a long way to have come from the Duck and Tweedledee, in five years. For the swift development of his power and scope, Meredith owes something to Anderson—but the possibilities were there in the actor. His qualities include an immense, rapid responsiveness to any character he portrays. When he was tap-dancing in "She Loves Me Not," he put his whole heart into his feet. When he sang "The Palms" in "The Star Wagon," there was that same ungrudging enthusiasm—partly humorous, partly emotional.

Another dramatist has called out some of the finest zest in players in the past few seasons. This is Shakespeare. It is forty-five years since the death of Edwin Booth, when the sun set on the classic drama—and even then, it had been sinking for a good while.

But the sun also rises. This fresh contagion for the old plays and the old parts originates not with managers, but with actors. It is a swing of the pendulum against the tradition of lounging in armchairs and saying apparent nothings that must be full of poignant meaning. A whole generation of performers has been bred on that—and so it is the old that now is novel. " 'Macbeth' is as exciting as a four-alarm fire," declared Charles Laughton.

Maurice Evans' "Richard II" and John Gielgud's "Hamlet" are two conspicuous examples of this spirit among the newer actors. Not that either of these men is new to the theatre—but to the American public, they are recent acquaintances. And neither of them has yet served those twenty years at his calling that are supposed to give the player his full stature.

Evans' first professional appearance was at Cambridge, England, in 1926. Gielgud made his début in London, in 1921, when he was seventeen. Both of them had training at the Old Vic, one of the few playhouses in England or this country where Shakespeare is habitually offered. (Both men have also done modern parts.)

The most imminent danger to the player who embarks on Shakespeare, is that the author will devour him. The performer is a good deal like Red Riding Hood, carrying her little basket to the wolf. What makes your teeth so long, grandma? What makes your mouth so big? The great verse, the great scenes, are ready to eat him up— unless he can dominate them by keeping the thought up-permost, by holding the meaning of everything steadily before the audience. This was what Gielgud and Evans were able to do throughout their performances. They combined power of thought with power of execution, a feat much more difficult than the onlooker suspects. Why is it difficult?

In Shakespeare, the modern actor is not turning his back on all that he has formerly done in acting—but his work must endure expansion. This is because of the immense background against which he is placed. How does he go about expanding his work? A photograph can only be enlarged *if* the original negative is clear and detailed; otherwise, outlines blur. So it is with the actor. In his own mind, he must have a clearly defined, detailed image of the rôle, if it is to be enlarged without growing hazy.

So this process of expansion calls for clarity of thought plus sureness of execution. Either one without the other is not enough. The clear image that he starts with is a matter of the player's searchings of the character; technique of execution comes from practice—and that is where experience at such a place as the Old Vic stands the performer in good stead.

Orson Welles is another player who has come under the influence of Shakespeare—but with him, the association developed differently. He is not yet twenty-three. Although he occasionally appeared on the stage as a child in Chicago, he had his real initiation with the Gate and Abbey companies, in Dublin, where he worked for two seasons beginning when he was about fifteen.

Even then, the Elizabethan theatre had a powerful attraction for him. At seventeen or so, in collaboration with his former schoolmaster, he wrote "Everybody's Shakespeare," a study of three plays by the dramatist, with the intent to make them alive for school children. Welles' belief was—and is—that Shakespeare speaks a universal language, though his accent may be Elizabethan.

One of the plays in that volume was "Julius Caesar"— and this is doubtless the germ of Welles' modernized staging of the drama at the Mercury Theatre, New York, in the autumn of 1937. In the production, he played Brutus. He had previously made many radio adaptations of Shakespeare, and had been concerned in the re-working of

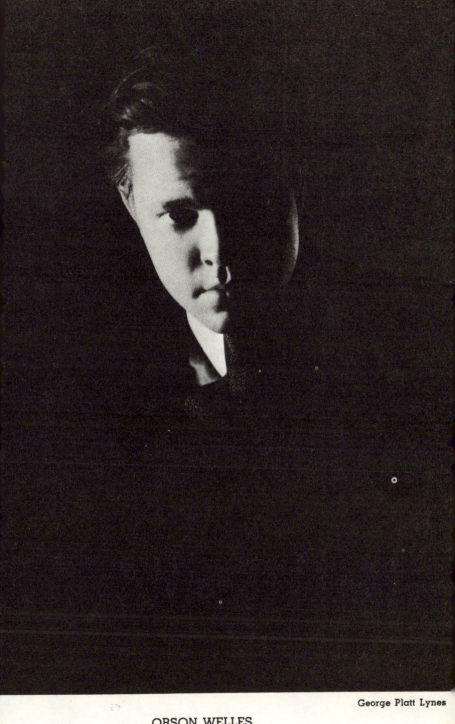

ORSON WELLES

This is a study of him as Brutus in his production of "Julius Caesar," done in modern dress and without scenery.

"Macbeth" for the WPA Federal Theatre, when it was played by a negro cast. He was also chief actor, as well as director, of the Federal Theatre's highly successful presentation of Marlowe's "The Tragical History of Dr. Faustus."

Welles is a young actor of extraordinary vitality, energy, and originality. He has done much work for radio and some in modern productions; his interest in Shakespeare is not in the least that of an antiquarian or a formalist. He simply has a tremendous conviction that Shakespeare and his contemporaries have something to say to modern audiences.

The rediscovery of this fact by many players cannot be overlooked as a force exerted on contemporary acting.

Another influence on playing is that of small theatres of every kind all over this country. They answer the young performer's need to get experience somewhere, somehow. This is, he will tell you, his most serious difficulty. He cannot learn to act without acting—and where can he get parts? There are never jobs enough to go around on Broadway. So he turns to summer theatres, Little Theatre organizations, and college dramatics to give him opportunities and help him discover his own bent.

A case in point is that of Mildred Natwick, a young character actress whose reputation has grown with every recent New York season. If it had not been for the Vagabond Players, in Baltimore, and the University Players, at West Falmouth, Mass., she might never have got a hearing.

About 1928, having finished school, she began to haunt theatrical agencies. She had studied under Edith Wynne

Matthison. But agents have to be hard-boiled; so they listened to Miss Natwick's qualifications without turning a hair. She was small and thin, and she had no technique for getting past managers' office boys. Thus she spent most of her time warming chairs in reception rooms. A week now and then in a four-a-day vaudeville sketch was the utmost height to which she soared.

Then she went home to Baltimore and joined the Vagabond Players, a Little Theatre company. "After all, you go on the stage to act, and sitting in offices wasn't acting." In Baltimore she had plenty of parts. At last Henry Fonda—also without a Broadway reputation at the time—saw her play, and introduced her to the University Players. (Of that organization, there is more to be said.) Soon after she began with them, she fell into playing old women because there was no one else who could do them.

In rôles of that sort, she made her first New York successes. Everyone who saw "The Distaff Side" in 1934-35 will recall her remarkable impersonation of a tyrannical wisp of a grandmother. She was then twenty-five, but she had that fragile, masterful look which sometimes comes to very old people. Her voice, her enunciation, were old, too. In "End of Summer" she did another grandmother. Her Prossy in Katharine Cornell's "Candida" was a young character part done with unctuous irony.

Mildred Natwick owes a great deal to out-of-town theatres. At the Westchester Playhouse in Mt. Kisco, in the summers, she has shown unusual gifts in leading parts. Her playing of the title rôle in "Elizabeth the Queen" was full of force and vitality; it glowed with the spirit of the great monarch. (Vincent Price and Harry Ellerbe have also appeared in Mt. Kisco.)

The University Players, who worked at Falmouth

and West Falmouth for five or six summers beginning in 1928, have a record for the large proportion of their members who have made names for themselves. Mildred Natwick is only one of them. Margaret Sullavan came from there; so did Myron McCormick, and Henry Fonda.

The organization was started by seven undergraduates from Princeton and three from Harvard. Among them were Bretaigne Windust, Charles Leatherbee, and Joshua Logan. Leatherbee died. This was a blow to his associates, but they kept on. Logan was lately the director of "On Borrowed Time." Windust, who has played many parts in New York, directs for the Lunts, having staged their "The Taming of the Shrew," "Idiot's Delight," and "Amphitryon 38." The University group no longer runs its own summer theatre, but it maintains a connection with the County Playhouse at Suffern, N. Y.

At the Cape Playhouse, on Cape Cod, Bette Davis and Robert Montgomery were favorite juveniles before the film public knew them. That was in 1928 and 1929. Lloyd Nolan played there in 1930.

The Hedgerow Theatre, at Moylan-Rose Valley, Pa., boasts that it is non-professional, but it has turned out many professional players. Under the direction of Jasper Deeter, this company has presented attractions winter and summer since 1923. Recruits who want to practice acting are overjoyed if Deeter will accept them. Alexander Kirkland, Ann Harding, John Beal, Libby Holman, and Van Heflin are a few of his graduates.

The Country Playhouse at Westport, Conn., has helped a number of young performers to come forward—notably Peggy Conklin and Tonio Selwart, who played "The Pursuit of Happiness" there before the comedy was seen in New York. The Lakewood Theatre, at Skowhegan,

Maine, helped Owen Davis, Jr., when he was getting a start; and it did the same thing for Mary Rogers, Patricia Calvert, Sam Byrd, and others. Before Byrd had progressed as far as Skowhegan, he worked in a Little Theatre in Florida, acting and directing while he was still in school.

To these and many other small playhouses and community theatres, stage beginners now go for practice. Oh for the good old days, they say, those good old days when people like Katharine Cornell and Alfred Lunt were starting out. There were plenty of road companies then. *There* was acting experience!

However, a realistic glance at that experience may soften such regrets. The average performer received, in that halcyon time, a thorough course in packing trunks and catching trains. Practice at acting was another matter. A novice generally had a few lines to say, and said them very badly. His was the splendid privilege of repeating his errors in every state in the Union. At the end of such a season, he had imbibed no more knowledge of acting than a few weeks in summer theatres can teach his successor.

Besides the dramatist and the small theatre, another factor in developing new actors is the New York producing group. Several such groups exist, or have existed in recent years, in the neighborhood of Broadway—each of them having been started by a handful of more-or-less like-minded enthusiasts.

That was the nucleus of the Theatre Guild, the Civic Repertory Theatre, the Group Theatre, the Theatre Union, the Actors' Repertory, and the Artef Theatre. The Civic Repertory company and the Theatre Union are both disbanded, and other ventures come and go.   But one of the things all of them have done was to bring forward new performers.

Foremost among all these enterprises is the Theatre Guild—a producing organization known all over the world.   It put on its first drama in 1919, and a list of actors of the highest standing who have appeared in its attractions would be a long one.   But the Guild has also given rôles to comparatively unknown people; that is, to people once unknown, who won early recognition in Guild plays.

Claudette Colbert was in "Dynamo" in 1929, and Miriam Hopkins in "The Camel Through the Needle's Eye" that same year.   Inside an animal suit, in 1925, Romney Brent was the Lion in "Androcles and the Lion"; also in 1925, George Abbott, the producer, played Dynamite Jim in "Processional."

The Group Theatre was started in 1931 by three people trained in the Guild—Cheryl Crawford, Lee Strasberg, and Harold Clurman.   Of young players whom the Group has developed, Jules Garfield is an outstanding example.

As a pupil in Angelo Patri's public school in New York, this boy had shown exceptional aptitude for dramatics. He became, like Burgess Meredith, an apprentice at the Civic Repertory Theatre.   That was about 1931, when he was eighteen.   After his course there, he kept applying to the Group but was not accepted till 1934.   However, once he was admitted, he made surprising strides, playing several youths with social grievances in Clifford Odets' dramas.   Later he gave a delightfully true characterization as the young hero of "Having Wonderful Time."   Following that, he returned to the Group in another Odets play—"Golden Boy."

Luther Adler, also notable in this organization, comes of a well-known family of actors.

The Group method of rehearsing is based on the practice of the Moscow Art Theatre. Scenes are done first in improvisation. This means that the author's lines are not spoken at the start, the company devising and acting incidents about the characters, to get themselves into the spirit of the story. Afterward they merge these things into the dramatist's scenes and speeches. The process is particularly good in giving reality to ensemble scenes; and it helps beginners to lose self-consciousness.

The Artef Theatre, with Benno Schneider as its guiding spirit, is a producing group which commenced in 1927, as an amateur organization. It was a protest against some of the standards in the commercial Yiddish theatre. Members of the company, who worked in factories and offices, had to learn acting from the ground up—but they soon had a director of high ability in Schneider. He joined them at first only to teach make-up, but he went far beyond that and has developed them in every way. The Artef is now a professional company, doing plays so well that English-speaking actors and directors go there to watch performances.

This has brought young people from Broadway to Schneider, as pupils in acting. One of them is Katherine Locke, who was wholly unknown to fame until the season of 1936-37. That winter she won the critics with her tenderly ironic characterization in "Having Wonderful Time," and she has since followed it with similar success in "How to Get Tough about It."

The Actors' Repertory was started in 1935 by a group of players who wanted to put on their own productions.

They attracted a great deal of attention with "Bury the
Dead," an anti-war play, and "200 Were Chosen," a
drama of the homesteaders in Alaska.

There is nothing novel about these producing groups.
The Globe Theatre, to which Shakespeare and Burbage
belonged, was just such an organization.

A force, both good and bad, which is constantly exerted on acting is that of Broadway itself—or rather, of
"show business." Show business is a term used to desig-
nate all forms of entertainment given for money, and it
includes everything from flea circuses to Euripedes.
Though it is riddled with vulgarity, though it affects to
be completely hardened, it nevertheless has its enthusiasms
for what is fine. It reaches out for the best players and
the best playwrights *after* they have proved themselves.

Broadway is no avenue of the Elysian fields. Its blare
and glare and ballyhoo have driven nearly all the first-
class theatres into comparative seclusion on side streets.
It is a region where persons understand such expressions
as "heavy sugar" and "real lettuce." Along this thorough-
fare, "Stix nix crix pix" is not Esperanto. It is merely a
statement that small towns do not support those films
most highly endorsed by the critics.

Into this atmosphere, the inexperienced player is
plunged, and he will breath it frequently if he continues
to act. Little Mabel, after initial training at school or in
some rural theatre, finds herself trudging her feet off on
the sidewalks of this part of New York, in her attempts
to impress her aspirations on managers' representatives.
Perhaps she thought in advance that the individuals she
would encounter would be glamorous. They are not.
They are simply people quite inattentive to her. Nearly

all of them are a bit hysterical over some revue, picture, play, or radio sketch that is, or eventually may be, going into production—and that is why they cannot stop to notice Mabel. Like men and women around the tables at Monte Carlo, they have stakes on the next spin of the wheel.

The theatre's great and gifted people are not accessible to a novice; they are always busy at a distance, or at least behind closed doors. So the beginner picks up the gossip and wisecracks of Broadway, learns its latest sayings, and believes that he or she is becoming an actor.

This calling seems to urge such things on the new player; it seems to want them. But it is like the villain of the old melodramas. He never did right by our Nell, if she listened to his specious persuasions. And so when show business has induced a person to adopt all its attitudes, it does not really want him or her for an actor. It gives its biggest contracts to people who understand this fact.

Among tendencies that shape present acting, there is one which gets little attention but which is at work all the time. This is the influence of the past. Playing is a contagion. It does not start with a blank page in each new epoch, but is always growing out of what went before.

Every performer teaches himself, but he also learns from others. Macready, for instance, said that playing with Mrs. Siddons when he was a very young man opened his eyes to what acting could be. Much of the player's craft is an oral tradition, passed along from one generation to the next, often unconsciously. One actor tells another of some bit of advice that somebody told him, but where that previous informant got it he probably has no idea.

The process goes on now, just as it has for centuries. There are players today who acted under Belasco's direction, or Henry Miller's, or with Mrs. Fiske or Arnold Daly. There are some who look back to Herne, a few to Edwin Booth. Noel Coward's teacher and sponsor was Sir Charles Hawtrey, and Hawtrey was helped as a beginner by a stage manager who had been with the Bancrofts.

To Arnold Daly, Frank Mayo was the great master of stagecraft. Mayo had worked with Edwin Booth and his brother Junius Brutus; and they looked back to their father, the Kembles and Mrs. Siddons.

Leslie Howard worked for years under the direction of Henry Miller, one of the best actors and directors in this country. Where did Miller get his ideas? He commenced in Adelaide Neilson's company, and afterward told of the deep impression her work made on him. Later, at Daly's and at the Lyceum Theatre, he was thrown with such skillful actors as Mrs. Gilbert and W. J. Lemoyne.

William Gaxton told me that he was greatly helped by Nat Goodwin—and Goodwin, when he was young, got his inspiration from William Warren, Stuart Robson, and Joseph Jefferson. Goodwin particularly admired Jefferson's method. Jefferson, in his turn had observed Macready and Junius Brutus Booth. Besides, in his own family there was a comedy tradition handed down from his great-grandfather who played with Garrick and repeated Garrick's sayings.

As a child actress, Helen Hayes worked with John Drew and William Gillette, both of whom knew all the mid-nineteenth century players.

In Gordon Craig's volume on Ellen Terry, he quotes a letter in which she told of talking with her great-nephew "Jack" Gielgud about imagination in the theatre. She said it stirred him immensely. Here was Gielgud, a beginner, listening to Ellen Terry, who had her initiation in Charles Kean's company. Charles Kean knew the views of his father, Edmund; Edmund's earliest training came from Miss Tidswell, who had played with Garrick; Garrick looked back to Betterton; and Betterton, through Sir William Davenant, to Taylor, the immediate successor of Burbage.

In ways such as these, players of the present can trace a genealogy of their craft running far back into the past. It is not religion only that has its apostolic succession and its communion of saints. Every science, every calling, has them too—and the theatre not least. It is never completely cut off from the great spirits of its past who, in their time, saw more clearly and spoke more truly than most of the people around them.

EPILOGUE

14.

Comparisons and Conclusions

"TIME, like an ever-rolling stream, bears all its sons away." The channels and eddies of that stream account for all the fluctuating styles of acting in the centuries since the Elizabethan theatre.

Sometimes an actor comes along who is a bit ahead of his era. His case is not so desperate, for if he can live a while events will catch up with him. Macklin was such an instance; James A. Herne was another. There is also the performer who lags behind his day. This individual's career is happy only at the start—when he fits all too easily into a vogue that is already at its height. Soon the reaction begins. From then on, time works against him. Everybody has seen a few performers of this sort, and their situation is too pitiable to dwell on.

But every now and then, players are born under lucky stars. They come into the theatre just as a new style is rising—a style to which they are especially suited. Most, though not all, eminently successful actors in any generation are indebted to the combination of talent and the right time.

In the Restoration, Betterton was such a man. Unfamiliar with theatres, he must have learned much from the battered players who had survived the Commonwealth. But he belonged to the new age—and so, with his freshness of view, he outstripped them. For a long while he was at the peak of his calling. Nevertheless, at seventy he found himself surrounded by a newer taste—the craze for declamation.

Garrick, invading London as an artistic radical, carried everything before him. For years he was copied and fawned on, retiring in 1776 amid the tears of his admirers. Yet within a decade John Philip Kemble was able, on the wings of Mrs. Siddons' glory, to revive the elocutionary style that Garrick despised.

In the 1890's, Mrs. Fiske was beginning to fight for naturalistic acting. But when her career ended in 1932, so thoroughly had everybody been converted and so long ago had it happened, that few theatregoers realized how large a share she had had in changing the trend of playing. Such cycles never arrive till the time is ripe for them. If Garrick had presented his "Richard III" twenty years sooner than he did, London would not have been ready to accept it. Declamation was then the new rage. But after many a season of mouthings and stampings, a parched soil lay ready for refreshing dew.

A recurrent rhythm of fashions in acting should be apparent to anyone who compares the playing of different periods in the English-speaking theatre. For many generations, two opposing tendencies have been at work—realism, and stylism or classicism.

Coming in slow, alternating waves, sometimes one has been in the ascendant and sometimes the other. The forms in which they reappear are never precisely the same any more than are revivals of the leg-o'-mutton sleeve. But the outlines are there. Neither style is ever in total eclipse—for in artificial eras there have been some naturalistic players, and in naturalistic periods there are performers who practice one sort or another of stylized expression.

Acting never stands still. Its innovations are not always improvements, but it cannot endure without fresh impulses. What changed directions it may take in the next fifteen years, nobody knows. After so long a period of realism, will it turn poetic and symbolic?

There is, of course, that possibility. Every recent season has had its stylized productions, though their proportion is small. Playing in "Winterset," Burgess Meredith was enthusiastic over its modern blank verse as a heightened form of expression. "The Tragical History of Dr. Faustus" was stylized, and so was "As You Like It" as it was given by the Surry Players. The Theatre Guild's "Porgy and Bess" showed what Rouben Mamoulian could do by combining stylization with realism in his stage direction.

However, Mamoulians do not grow on every bush. If the future may be judged by the past, the heightened manner can be a boon only when it is used by artists of the highest gifts. It is a method that needs to be suffused with genius. Sarah Siddons or Junius Brutus Booth could warm it in their own bosoms—but most bosoms are not so hot.

Even at present, players do not escape the two contending methods of expression which have influenced their calling for so long.

Setting aside the style which happens to be in fashion at the time a performer works, are there any more endur-

ing standards—recognizable long ago as well as now—by
which acting can be judged?

So many standards go out of date. Chatty playwriting
and small theatres undermined the authority of the player's rich, sonorous voice even before the microphone dealt
it a finishing blow. What used to be hailed as elegance
and polish are gone, too. Does there remain any least
common denominator?

Two qualities that won audiences in the past, still win
them—convincingness, and power to convey emotion.
Further scrutiny discovers that these are not two things,
but one. For convincingness comes of the player's getting inside the skin of the character he portrays; his acting
seems to act itself. And it is that very same process that
makes his emotion reach out and touch his audience. All
this was true, we have been told over and over, of the best
playing in the past; and we know it is true of the best
playing today.

Having followed the course of the actor through centuries, we see that what makes him excellent—what makes
him at times profoundly moving—is the degree to which
he can identify himself with his rôle. He is eighty-five or
ninety per cent able to be a new creature. All truly
admirable actors have a high quotient.

That, however, was fairly clear from the start. There
is a more searching question: What is the means by which
the player does this? Since that which he accomplishes is
essentially the same, whatever his generation, is it possible
that he works with the same tool? If so, what is this
thing he uses?

This brings the last mile-post within view. For it
should now be evident that there is such a tool—one of

equal efficacy to Elizabethans and to performers of today. This implement is the dramatic, or acting, imagination. An intangible yet highly practical equipment, it long ago proved its worth. In the untrained performer it is erratic, serving him on some occasions and failing him on others. But every master of acting has brought this force under control.

Here is the root of those similarities in approach to their work which are noticeable in players of different eras. These people are kin to each other.

The chapters of this book present widely varied instances of performers making use of dramatic imagination. Even at the risk of seeming to cover the same ground, it has been necessary to study players far separated in time and style. What justification could there be for assuming that certain effects are traceable to certain causes, unless it be shown that such effects do follow such conditions, and are missing when those conditions are absent? By this test, the likeness in mental processes behind acting becomes demonstrable. It is a resemblance probably stronger in fact that it looks on paper—for many a performer uses imagination as a tool without ever giving a name to what he does, or speaking of it to anybody. It is something he takes for granted.

Acting has always been a psychological art. Long before psychology was a word in our language, players divined that the underground springs of behavior are emotions and instincts, with all the swarming ideas that cling to them. The actor is an expert in the portrayal of people—and by intuition he learned that he could seize on these buried energies for the purposes of his craft. Shakespeare saw this:

> . . . this player here,
> But in a fiction, in a dream of passion,
> Could force his soul so to his own conceit
> That from her working all his visage wann'd;
>
> . . . .
>
> What's Hecuba to him, or he to Hecuba,
> That he should weep for her?

What, then, is this dramatic imagination which the actor possesses? In its most rudimentary form it is merely an instinct for feeling like somebody or something else—a child pretending to be a fire engine, for instance. Austin Strong—the dramatist—tells of how, when he was a small boy in Robert Louis Stevenson's home, he built himself an island fortress out of books from the author's shelves. Then he enacted the siege. He was the attacking force, rowing to the island; suddenly he became the defending force, the commandant, the gunners. The library door opened, and there was Stevenson looking on. At this, the boy started to run over and speak to him; but Stevenson called out excitedly, "Swim! Why don't you *swim?*"

The child's imagination and the artist's are cousins. Indeed, here is a kingdom which cannot be entered save through that ungrudging belief which children throw into their play. Not without reason is acting called playing. However, there is an enormous gap between a child's random exploits and the powerful, exquisitely adjusted impersonation given by a great performer.

Purpose is inextricably bound up in dramatic imagination. It is a working energy, and it gets things done. There is nothing spineless about it—which is the difference between it and the vagrant fancies owned by humanity in general. It represents the upper reaches of a faculty that, further down in the scale, develops idlers and day-dreamers.

There was nothing of the idler about Charlotte Cushman. As a young understudy called upon at short notice to play Meg Merrilies, she barely had time to cram the lines into her head and dress for the performance. As she stood at the wing waiting for her first entrance, she listened to the scene preceding her own. Two characters were discussing Meg. "She dotes," said one of them. In the excitement of the moment, the words struck Charlotte Cushman as being the key to the woman she was about to play. A creature whose mind was beginning to break. . . . With this flash of meaning to guide her, the actress went on and gave the rôle a haunting wildness which it had never had before. Here the dramatic imagination operated in an instant; oftener, it moves gradually.

Michel Chekhov, the Russian actor, relies on arriving slowly at this sense of illumination concerning a part. He says he does not worry or try to hasten it; he keeps thinking of the person he is to play, holding the idea of the part constantly in his mind. Suddenly, at some moment, the person stands before him—mannerisms, voice, everything. This, Chekhov calls the "anticipatory feeling of the whole," and he considers it essential to characterization. What came to Miss Cushman while she waited for her cue was that anticipatory feeling of the whole. In both of these examples, the discovery is not made by a lazy, wandering imagination, but by one that has been deliberately turned in a given direction.

But after all, it may be pointed out, every artist, inventor, or organizer of a business—everybody who takes for his goal something that does not exist and that he intends to create—is indebted to imagination for the impetus that starts him off. He, too, gets an anticipatory feeling of the whole; and toward this, he works. Is there anything exceptional, then, in the actor's use of imagination?

Yes, there is. For he handles this endowment with a peculiar physical precision. It not only starts him off; in his case, he also depends on imagination to bring about the most minute changes in his own physique. He must do this, because he himself *is* his medium of expression. He cannot be detached from it, as a composer can be from his symphony or a sculptor from his statue. Only through the performer's look and voice and ways of moving, can his ideas reach people. So, with the help of imagination, he changes himself. Audiences see those alterations and know what they mean. The hand trembles as it seizes the pen; or tears well up; or the face flushes with anger. The player can do these things, over, and over, and over.

Theatregoers who saw "Criminal at Large" a few seasons ago will recall Emlyn Williams' performance of a young man subject to attacks of murderous insanity. In the last act, such a moment began to creep up on him. One could read its advent in his eyes. First the thought amused him, then he tried to disguise it, and finally it had him so in its clutch that he cared nothing for concealment. His glance was obsessed with his wish.

Tallulah Bankhead is particularly gifted at using imagination so that she extends the reality of a scene beyond the limits of the stage setting. Every time she comes in or goes out at a door, that next room, that hallway, that sidewalk which cannot be seen, all become existent in the story. She makes you believe that they are there, just out of view. From the first moment she steps into a play, she brings with her a conviction of the reality of events that have been happening off-stage.

It is this same power of imagination that enables the skillful player actually to listen to things that are said to him, by other characters in the story. Though this looks extremely simple, it is a mark of fine command in the actor who does it. Frank Craven says most people on the stage are too concerned with their own lines to hear anything but their cues.

In the inexperienced performer this rises out of a dreadful anxiety. He dare not trust himself to relax in the sea of words around him, lest he go down with a gurgle. But if he could give himself up to the sea, it would float him. "In the destructive element, submerge," says an old German shipmaster in one of Conrad's novels. The beauty of a performer's being one with his part is that this state of mind enables him to submerge in those very things of the theatre which threaten to destroy him. He listens, he thinks over everything that is said and done around him in the drama, for the simple reason that he *is* this other person. And out of his impact with the surrounding characters, his own rôle grows.

To be sure, there was Diderot's theory which assumed acting to be completely mechanical. A person with command over the muscles that regulate voice and gesture, he argued, could reproduce every emotion with tongue in cheek. Diderot, however, was not an actor. Among people of the stage there have been some, but not many, supporters of his doctrine. When Alexander Woollcott asked Mrs. Fiske what she thought of it, she answered that there might be persons who could reach such mechanistic perfection, but it was quite beyond her. It seems, at best, a most laborious scheme for accomplishing things that acting imagination can do in a flash.

Thus it is *imagination directed by will* that one is watching every time one sees a part superbly portrayed. The actor is a master at standing in the other fellow's shoes; he knows more about how to do it than anybody else in the world. And in reaching that knowledge, he has painfully acquired better control over attention, imagination, and emotion than the average human being dreams of. This is the player's secret; this is the thing of which he is not suspected.

As inventors have made electricity work for them, as chemists have devised formulae which serve them, so highly endowed actors have discovered ways of converting imagination into an instrument of precision. The performer has been, and still is, a pioneer at that. He has taken this supposedly unaccountable, ungovernable trait and turned it into motive force. This is an achievement. The psychiatrist deals with the unemployed imagination, sullen and not a little afraid. But the actor puts imagination to work at something useful, and makes it fulfill the creative instinct.

For the present, this appears to have little bearing on everyday life. People in general do not bother themselves with the training of imagination. Yet Michael Pupin once wrote that all our feats of engineering would someday seem small in comparison with discoveries yet to be made in harnessing forces of the spirit. When that day comes, far in the future, the player will then be seen to have been an experimenter and inventor in an overlooked field.

Meantime, the actor cares nothing about being investigated as a pioneer or a specimen—in fact, he loathes investigation. He is rightly content to use his discoveries in turning out his artistic product. The goal he keeps his eyes on is his finished creation—the moving, breathing, three-dimensional portrait of a human being.

So, though imagination be his tool, the value of his output depends on the sweep and depth of the actor's understanding of men and women. That must have been what Leslie Howard had in mind when he insisted that personality is the greatest thing of all—and he described personality as "a way of looking at life." Ina Claire says the most satisfying thing about the actor's calling is that, as he studies and practices it, he grows within himself. He becomes more than he was; and so he has more to give. How much he can give, determines how well he can fill that vast space around him which is, according to Alfred Lunt, the actor's environment in great drama. Skill at handling the tool results in adept acting, but the way of looking at life adds that which is unique and compelling.

Creatures of sympathy. . . . In the end, it is the reach of his sympathies that sets the limit to each player's power. For acting is not merely an occupation; it is a preoccupation. Every estuary and backwash of the player's life is slowly inundated by the great salt sea. It is lack of caring enough to understand people that makes routine acting, and it is great understanding that makes great acting.

NOTES

Notes

(Chapter 1)

Page 3—**Importance of the actor in the theatre.** This is true, in spite of the news reel or "Snow White and the Seven Dwarfs."

Page 5—**Garrick's Richard III.** "He transformed himself into the very man," wrote Arthur Murphy, having got his information from persons who saw Garrick's début.

      Mrs. Duff. Quotation appeared in the *New York Mirror*, May 5, 1827.

Pages 7, 8, 9—**Stanislavsky.** His comments as quoted were recorded by A. L. Fovitzky, in Russian. Translated into English, they appeared in a pamphlet, *The Moscow Art Theatre and Its Distinguishing Characteristics*, 1922. For further facts on Stanislavsky, see his *My Life in Art* and his *An Actor Prepares*.

      Moscow Art Theatre. It devoted itself wholly to realistic acting in its earlier years, but later it used various forms of stylism. Present interest in stylism in America is traceable, in part, to Russian influence. A few books on the stage in Russia include *The Russian Theatre,* Oliver M. Sayler; *Shifting Scenes*, Hallie Flanagan; and *Moscow Rehearsals*, Norris Houghton.

Page 12—**Mrs. Fiske.** "Touch on the wrong note." Quoted by permission from Alexander Woollcott's *Mrs. Fiske*. (The Century Company, 1917.)

Page 13—**Garrick's Hamlet.** Phrase quoted was translated from the German of Georg Christoph Lichtenberg by Walter Herries Pollock, and appeared in *Longman's Magazine,* August 1885.

Page 14—**Byron's comment on Kean.** Written Feb. 19, 1814. From *Letters and Journals of Lord Byron.*

Page 18—**Kitty Clive to Garrick.** Dated Jan. 23, 1774. From *The Private Correspondence of David Garrick,* 1832.

(Chapter 2)

Page 27—**Letter from Lord Leicester's Men, 1572.** Quoted from the *Malone Society Collection, Volume 1, parts 4 and 5*, where it is printed from the Marquis of Bath's manuscript.

License of Leicester's Men, 1574. Quoted from Steeven's Shakespeare, 1773. This royal patent of incorporation was a distinction. Leicester could obtain it for his company because he was high in Queen Elizabeth's favor. No other company had so powerful a backer.

Page 29—**Blackfriars Theatre.** A small indoor playhouse, where performances were given by candle- or torch-light. Building had been remodeled from a dwelling, in a neighborhood then fashionable. James Burbage bought the property in 1596, but nearby residents protested against the crowds that a theatre would attract. Not till 1610 did the Globe company use the Blackfriars. Thereafter they played there in the winters.

Records of actors. Law suits, tax lists, records of Court performances, church documents, etc., are sources of information. Thus, burglars broke into Richard Burbage's home one night in 1616, and from the list of articles stolen we know that his family had many small luxuries. Shakespeare was once delinquent in his parish taxes in London.

Heywood. His *Apology for Actors* was published in 1612.

Page 30—**Leicester's Men at Stratford.** See *The Visits of Shakespeare's Company of Actors to the Provincial Cities and Towns of England*, J. O. Halliwell-Phillipps, 1887.

Page 32—**Shakespeare's plays.** As to dates of composition and production, I have followed the chronology used by Sir Sidney Lee in his *A Life of William Shakespeare*, and believed by him to be established by internal evidence as well as by other facts.

Chettle. This was Henry Chettle, both publisher

and playwright. Sometimes a collaborator with Thomas Dekker, whose *Shoemakers' Holiday* was staged by the Mercury Theatre, New York, 1937-38.

Page 33—Henslowe's Diary. Original document is owned by Dulwich College, England—a gift from its founder, Edward Alleyn, along with his other theatrical papers. (*Cf.* page 43, this chapter.) Study of this book brings one into close touch with conditions under which plays were produced.

Page 34—Rivalry between Burbage and Henslowe companies. They worked together, nevertheless, for a few months in 1592 and ten days in 1594. This was probably Shakespeare's only association with Alleyn. After the Globe opened in 1599, the latter house seems to have maintained a repertory, with only a few new plays each year, while the Rose produced a rapid succession of new pieces. Henslowe managed other theatres besides the Rose.

Page 35—"Without-book prologue . . ." From *Romeo and Juliet.*

Page 38—Gosson. Quotation is from Stephen Gosson's *School of Abuse,* 1579. Gosson had formerly been an actor.

Page 40—Kemp. His name was also spelled Kempe. There was no uniformity of spelling at that period—as is evidenced by the various spellings of Shakespeare. Burbage was written Burbadge, Burbidge, etc.; Wilson might be Wylson or Wyllson; Alleyn was also Allen.

Page 41—"Clowns have been thrust into plays . . ." From *The Pilgrimage to Parnassus,* a play acted by university students in 1598.

Page 45—Burbage in the tiring house. Quotation is from Richard Flecknoe's *Discourse of the English Stage,* 1664.

Sources.—Besides those already mentioned in text and notes, the following books and plays were also consulted in preparing this chapter: *A Dictionary of Actors*, edited by Edwin Nungezer; *British Drama*, Allardyce Nicoll; *Burbage and Shakespeare's Stage*, Charlotte C. Stopes; *Elizabethan Drama 1558-1642*, Felix E. Schelling; *English Dramatic Companies*, John Tucker Murray; *Guls Hornbook*, Thomas Dekker; *Shakespeare's Imagery*, Caroline F. E. Spurgeon; *The Alleyn Papers*, edited by J. Payne Collier; *The Return from Parnassus;* and plays by Dekker, Heywood, Jonson, Marlowe, Massinger, and Shakespeare.

(Chapter 3)

Page 47—Betterton's Hamlet. From *An Apology for the Life of Colley Cibber*. Cibber—actor, manager, and facile dramatist—was born in 1671. Going on the stage in 1690, he saw the later work of many Restoration players. He retired in 1732, and died in 1757. His adaptations of Shakespeare were in common use up to the middle of the 19th century, and parts of his version of "Richard III" were incorporated in Richard Mansfield's prompt book as late as 1889.

Page 49—Anthony Aston. Quotations of him in this chapter are from his *A Brief Supplement to Colley Cibber, Esq.; his Lives of the Late Famous Actors and Actresses.*
        Stages in the Restoration. Deep platform in front of proscenium was a survival from the Elizabethan platform stage, and important scenes were played forward on this space. There was no thought of making the proscenium arch a picture frame—as is now the usual practice. Platform gradually grew smaller, becoming an "apron." This apron began to disappear in theatres in the 1870's and 1880's, but could be seen much later in old structures. Indeed, traces of it are still to be found. In some recent productions—*e.g.* "Dr. Faustus" and "Richard II"—platform was revived.

Page 52—John Rhodes. Last trace of him was in 1663, when he was granted a license to act in the provinces.

Page 53—Charles Hart. Montague Summers, a great authority on the Restoration stage, finds no proof that Hart was related to Shakespeare.

Page 54—The King's and the Duke's companies. After more than 20 years as competitors, they united in 1682.

Page 55—Davenant. He changed the spelling of his name to D'Avenant. Some records print it in one way, some in the other.

Page 58—Betterton's Henry VIII. John Downes, prompter

of the Duke's company, said Betterton was "instructed" in the rôle by Davenant "who had it from old Mr. Lowen, that had his instruction from Mr. Shakespeare himself . . ." Quoted from Downes' *Roscius Anglicanus*, an account of the theatres of the Restoration. This is the source of information about the King and the Duke of York lending their coronation suits for "Love and Honour." Downes wrote of himself that he was "long conversant with . . . the original company under the Patent of Sir William Davenant . . . And as Book Keeper and Prompter continued so till October 1706 . . . attending every morning the Actors Rehearsals, and their performances in the afternoons." Downes is quoted elsewhere in this chapter.

Page 63—**Kynaston.** At the start of this actor's career Downes called him "a Compleat Female Stage Beauty" and said he was more moving in pathetic parts than many of the actresses who succeeded him. One can believe this, knowing how incompetent some of the women were.

Page 64—**Kynaston's Henry IV.** Quotation is from Colley Cibber.

Additional sources.—Besides those mentioned in text and notes: plays by Congreve, Dryden, Farquhar, Otway, Shadwell, Vanbrugh, and Wycherley, as well as Buckingham's "The Rehearsal"; *A History of Restoration Drama*, Allardyce Nicoll; *Diary of John Evelyn* (though his references to the theatre are scarce in comparison with those of Pepys); *Enter the Actress*, Rosamond Gilder; *Their Majesties' Servants; Annals of the English Stage*, John Doran; *The Restoration Theatre*, Montague Summers; and *Thomas Betterton*, Robert W. Lowe.

(Chapter 4)

Page 68—**French influence.** Racine's dramas were in vogue in France. They were adaptations from the Greek, and the English stage now had its adaptations from Racine. These were a far cry from the true Greek spirit.

Page 70—**Theophilus Cibber.** Quotation is from his *Life of Barton Booth, Esq.* Theophilus was born in 1703 and died in 1758; his wife was the famous Mrs. Cibber, one of Garrick's leading women when he first became manager of Drury Lane.

Page 72—**Booth's parts.** Besides Cato, some of his best were Pyrrhus, Othello, Tamerlane, Lothario, and Varanes in "Theodosius."

Page 74—**Quin.** Descriptive paragraph is from Richard Cumberland's *Memoirs.*

Page 78—**Macklin at rehearsals.** His words are quoted from William C. Macready's *Reminiscences.* Macready had them from his father, who had played with Macklin.

Page 80—**Aaron Hill.** (1685-1750) He entitled his commentary *An Essay on the Art of Acting.* Hill was a man of means, but he spent so much on theatrical undertakings that after he died an edition of his writings was published for the benefit of his family.

Additional sources for this chapter.—A General History of the Stage, (1749) William Rufus Chetwood (prompter at Drury Lane); *A Man of the World,* Charles Macklin; *Annals of the English Stage,* John Doran; *Cato,* Joseph Addison; *Memoirs,* Thomas Holcroft; *Memoirs of the Life of Charles Macklin, Esq.,* (1799) James T. Kirkman; *Recollections,* John O'Keefe; *Records of My Life,* John Taylor; *Retrospections of the Stage,* John Bernard.

(Chapter 5)

Page 84—**Garrick's manner on the stage.** Paragraph from *The Champion,* a newspaper of the time. Quoted in Percy Fitzgerald's *The Life of David Garrick.*

Page 85—**Thomas Davies.** Garrick's first biographer. He played at Drury Lane, and knew all the notable actors. Phrase is quoted from Davies' *Memoirs of the Life of David Garrick, Esq.,* 1780.

Page 86—**Lichtenberg.** This is the same person mentioned in note, Chapter 1, page 10.

Page 90—**"Of praise a mere glutton."** From Oliver Goldsmith's satirical epitaph on Garrick.

Page 91—**Garrick as manager.** Besides being a genius as actor and director, he was a highly successful playwright and adapter. His sense of the theatre never failed him, and his advice to a would-be dramatist was not to put pen to paper till he had worked out a good plot. Though his theatre was a marvel for its time, in settings and costuming his productions left much to be desired. Only such benches, chairs, or tables as were actually used by the characters were placed on the stage—all other furniture and accessories being painted on back drop or flats.

Page 92—**Dr. Johnson.** Quotation is from Boswell's *The Life of Samuel Johnson, LL.D.* (Year 1783.)

Pages 92, 93—**Grimm.** Friedrich Melchior Grimm. Translated from *Correspondence Litéraire de Grimm et Diderot.*

Page 93—**Bannister.** Excerpt is from James Boaden's *Memoirs of Mrs. Siddons,* 1827. This actor was still playing at Drury Lane when Edmund Kean made his début there in 1814. (See Chapter 6.) Unlike most members of the company, Bannister was generous in recognizing Kean's ability, from the start.

Page 96—**Mrs. Siddons' first attempt at Lady Macbeth.**
Written by her and given to the poet, Thomas Campbell,
with other material for his biography of her. See Campbell's
Life of Mrs. Siddons, 1834.

Page 102—**Mrs. Siddons' Queen Constance.** Another nota-
tion of hers, quoted from Campbell's *Life*.

Page 103—**Washington Irving.** His comment is from a letter written to his brother in 1805. Irving was thus impressed
in spite of the actress' being far too stout for any illusion of
youth. She was then fifty. Quotation is from *The Life and
Letters of Washington Irving*, by his nephew, Pierre M.
Irving.

Mrs. Siddons retired from the stage in 1812, thereafter
giving readings and appearing on special occasions. She
lived till 1831, always homesick for the theatre.

Additional sources for this chapter.—Plays by Garrick, Gold-
smith, Sheridan, and Colman the younger; *A Peep Behind
the Curtain, or the New Rehearsal; Garrick and his Circle*,
Mrs. Clement Parsons; *Garrick in the Green Room*, George
Daniel; *Memoirs of Garrick*, James Boaden; *Pineapples of
Finest Flavour*, edited and with an introduction by David
Mason Little; *Reminiscences*, Henry Crabb Robinson; *Some
Unpublished Correspondence of David Garrick*, edited by
George Pierce Baker; *The Incomparable Siddons*, Mrs. Clem-
ent Parsons; *The Life of David Garrick*, Arthur Murphy;
The Private Correspondence of David Garrick, 1832; *The
Wandering Patentee*, Tate Wilkinson; and reminiscences by
Bernard, Cumberland, Holcroft, and Macready listed in pre-
ceding chapter.

(Chapter 6)

Page 107—**Acting in America before 1800.** The first actors known to have come from England were "Charles Stagg and Mary his Wife," who signed a document at Williamsburg, Va., in 1716, agreeing to present plays in a theatre soon to be built in that town. The structure was built and plays were given, according to records now at Williamsburg. This playhouse antedated the one built at Charleston, S. C., in 1736; but it had fallen into disuse before 1752 when the Hallam company, aboard the "Charming Sally," reached Williamsburg from London. The troupe was headed by Lewis Hallam, father of the Lewis Hallam who was the foremost American actor before and after the Revolutionary War.

Page 110—**Review of Cooke's opening.** This first-night critic signed himself HAMLET. THESPIS was evidently the *Columbian's* senior reviewer, and would not write a hasty notice.

Page 112—**Cooke's childhood recollections.** Quoted from William Dunlap's *Memoirs of the Life of George Frederick Cooke.*

Page 113—**Cooke's playing of hypocrites.** The quiet, ironic humor of his villains impressed Leigh Hunt, Henry Crabb Robinson, Washington Irving, etc.

Page 120—**Kean rehearsing Shylock.** Quoted from Barry Cornwall's *Life of Edmund Kean.*

Page 123—**Kean's Hamlet.** This and other rôles of his are described by Hazlitt in his *Criticisms and Dramatic Essays on the English Stage.* See also reference to Kean's Othello, Chapter 8, page 148, of the present volume.

Page 125—**Walt Whitman excerpt.** From the *Boston Herald*, Aug. 16, 1885.

Page 128—**Edwin Booth on J. B. Booth.** Quoted from *Some Words about My Father* in *Actors and Actresses of Great Britain and the United States,* edited by Brander Matthews and Lawrence Hutton.

Page 129—**Booth's letters.** Helen Menken has a collection of these.

Barton Hill. His recollections appeared in the Christmas number of the *New York Dramatic Mirror,* 1896.

Additional sources.—Critical Essays, Leigh Hunt; *Life of Edmund Kean,* Fitzgerald Molloy; *Mad Folk of the Theatre,* Otis Skinner; *On Actors and the Art of Acting,* George Henry Lewes; *Retrospections of America,* John Bernard; *The Early Days of Edmund Kean,* in *The New Monthly Magazine and Literary Journal,* 1834, vol. 4, pp. 434-443; *The Elder and the Younger Booth,* Asia Booth Clark.

(Chapter 7)

Page 135—**Frederick Warde.** Paragraph is quoted by permission, from his *Fifty Years of Make-Believe*, 1920. He arrived in America in 1874, and later became a Shakespearean star. Toward the end of his career, he played in motion pictures.

Clara Morris. Her *Life on the Stage* reveals the routine of the old-fashioned stock company.

Page 137—**Edgar Allan Poe.** Quotation on this page is from the *Broadway Journal*, March 29, 1845.

Pages 138, 139—**Anna Cora Mowatt.** Excerpts are from her *Autobiography of an Actress*, 1854.

Page 142—**Advice to the beginner.** From *The Amateur: Guide to the Stage by a Retired Performer*, circa 1850.

Additional sources.—Study of a large number of old prompt books and "sides" in the Theatre Collections at the New York Public Library and the Museum of the City of New York; also lives of Edwin Forrest by Lawrence Barrett and Montrose J. Moses, and of Charlotte Cushman by Clara Erskine Clement; actors' reminiscences by John Bernard, Fanny Kemble, Sol Smith, George Vandenhoff, and William B. Wood; and facts told to the author by old actors.

(Chapter 8)

Page 146—Miss Heron—her arms akimbo, &c. From review in the *New York Tribune*.

"Measureless desolations, &c." Also from the *Tribune*.

Page 148—George Wilkes' critique. Originally appeared in *Times and Transcript*, San Francisco, Feb. 23, 1854. Quotation is from reprint in *Spirit of the Times*, Jan. 31, 1857.

Page 149—Matilda Heron's early life. Whether she was an actress in her childhood, I have not been able to verify, and have omitted this possibility from the text because Gilbert Miller thinks it unlikely. However, her full name was Matilda Agnes Heron—and the New York *Albion*, Dec. 18, 1847, contains a notice of two sisters, Agnes and Fanny Heron, who appeared in comedy sketches at the Park Theatre. These young girls had come from Ireland, and had acted in the British Isles. Later they studied singing under an Italian, called themselves Agnese and Francesca Natali, and gave concerts. Traces of them cease before 1851.

Page 153—Edwin Booth's Hamlet. Quoted from the *New York Herald*, Nov. 29, 1860.

Page 154—Mary Devlin's letters. Extracts quoted by permission from *Edwin Booth, 1833-1893*, by Edwina Booth Grossmann. (The Century Company, 1894.)

Page 155—Booth on Hamlet. Quoted from *Some Words about My Father*. See note, Chapter 6, page 128.

Page 159—"This terrible success . . ." Letter to Miss Carey, Jan. 10, 1865. Quoted by permission, from Mrs. Grossmann's *Edwin Booth, 1833-1893*. See note above, page 154. Quoted from same volume in letter dated Dec. 20, 1865, is Booth's phrase about "the heavy, aching gloom of my little red room . . ."

Booth after Lincoln's assassination. Mrs. Blanche Chapman Ford, who told me this, is a retired actress, over eighty. As a school girl she was a guest in Booth's home, and she remembers that the rooms were draped in black. She afterward married Henry Clay Ford, proprietor of the theatre where Lincoln was shot.

Page 160—"I 'ain't here' . . ." From letter to Miss Carey dated Jan. 10, 1865, in Mrs. Grossmann's *Edwin Booth, 1833-1893*. Quoted by permission.

Anecdote about the young actresses. This is related at length in *Behind the Scenes with Edwin Booth*, by Katherine Goodale. (Houghton Mifflin Company.)

Booth's last performance. Facts are from a touching account in the *Brooklyn Daily Eagle*, Apr. 5, 1891. This was written by Charles M. Skinner, the paper's dramatic critic.

Page 164—Jefferson on "Rip Van Winkle." From Jefferson's *Autobiography*.

Pages 165, 166—Jefferson's lines and "business." Quoted by permission from *Rip Van Winkle as Played by Joseph Jefferson*. (Dodd, Mead and Company, 1899.)

Page 166—Jefferson's remark to Otis Skinner. Mr. Skinner told me this.

Additional sources.—Besides newspaper items specifically mentioned, files of the New York *Albion* (1847 and '48) and of the *Spirit of the Times, Herald* and *Tribune* for many months in 1857, '59, '60, '61, '64, '65, and '66, as well as clippings of 1869, '75, and '77; Annals of the New York Stage, George C. D. Odell; *Darling of Misfortune*, Richard Lockridge; *Edwin Booth as I Knew Him*, Edwin Milton Royle; *Intimate Recollections of Joseph Jefferson*, Eugénie Paul Jefferson; *The Elder and the Younger Booth*, Asia Booth Clark; *The Jeffersons*, William Winter.

(Chapter 9)

Page 172—**Herne's birth.** He was the son of Patrick and
Ann Temple Ahern, who lived for years in Albany, N. Y.
James shifted his last name to Herne, but kept the A. as a
middle initial.

Page 173—**Katharine Corcoran.** When she was a child, she
adored Lucille Western who played Nancy to Herne's Bill
Sykes. The child would wait at the stage door to fling her
arms around Miss Western, declaring that she hated, hated
that Mr. Herne because he beat Nancy.

       "Margaret Fleming." This play had had a few
performances at Lynn, Mass., in July 1890. Hamlin Garland
saw it there, and encouraged the Hernes to put it on at Chickering Hall.

       Chickering Hall company. A member was Eliza-
beth Robins, who later became a noted London actress of
Ibsen. Still later, she married Joseph Pennell, the etcher.

Page 174—**Mansfield as a monologuist.** Frank Carlos Griffith, a retired manager, told me of Mansfield's giving this
monologue at his (Griffith's) benefit in Boston, and said it
was one of the most remarkable feats imaginable.

Page 176—**Quoted excerpt by Mansfield.** Used by permission of the *Chicago Herald Examiner.* It appeared in the
Inter-Ocean, in April 1893.

Page 177—**Mansfield on a first night.** From an article by
him in *Harper's Weekly,* May 24, 1890.

       "I am Brutus . . ." Quoted by permission from
an interview by Joseph I. C. Clarke in the *New York Herald,*
Dec. 7, 1902.

       "Do not strive to be original . . ." Quoted by
permission from the *North American Review,* Sept., 1894

Page 178—**Peer Gynt.** Mansfield's remark about the rôle is
quoted by permission from Frank Wilstach's *Richard Mansfield.* (Charles Scribner's Sons, 1908.)

Page 179—**Excerpt from Collier's Weekly.** Quoted by permission. Article was entitled *My Audiences and Myself*, Oct. 6, 1900.

Page 181—**Two quotations.** Used by permission; from *Ellen Terry's Memoirs*, with a preface, notes, and additional biographical chapters by Edith Craig and Christopher St. John. (G. P. Putnam's Sons.)

Page 183—**Miss Terry to Bernard Shaw.** Nov. 7, 1900. Quoted by permission from *Ellen Terry and Bernard Shaw: a Correspondence*, edited by Christopher St. John. (G. P. Putnam's Sons, 1932.) The volume is often called *The Shaw-Terry Letters*.

Page 184—**Miss Terry, about Irving.** Quotations are by permission, from *Ellen Terry's Memoirs*. See note, page 181.

Page 185—**Percy Burton.** . His estimate of Irving quoted by permission from an article in *The Sun* (New York) May 28, 1916. Mr. Burton has been manager for many stars.

Herbert Standing. Anecdote quoted by permission from his *Recollections of Irving*, in *The Morning Telegraph* (New York) Sept. 6, 1908.

Page 187—**Irving to students.** Quoted from the *New York Dramatic Mirror*, March 3, 1888.

Page 188—**Irving's last performances.** From an interview with Edith Wynne Matthison in the *Toledo Blade,* Nov. 13, 1908. Quoted by permission.

Additional sources.—Files of the *New York Dramatic Mirror* for the entire year 1893, as well as many other issues of the magazine; Robinson Locke scrapbooks, in the Theatre Collection, New York Public Library; an interview with Mansfield in *Leslie's Weekly*, Jan. 21, 1897; *Ellen Terry and her Secret Self*, E. Gordon Craig; *Personal Reminiscences of Henry Irving*, Bram Stoker; *Shore Acres and Other Plays*, James A. Herne, with Biographical Note by Julie A. Herne.

(Chapter 10)

Page 201—Quoted excerpt. This is from *Mrs. Fiske: her Views on Actors, Acting, and the Problems of Production,* by Alexander Woollcott. (The Century Company, 1917.) By permission.

Page 202—Maude Adams at Stephens College. Persons who saw Miss Adams' work report that she obtained remarkable results from students, and was unsparing of her own skill, tact, and energy. For an account of her at Stephens, see Eunice Fuller Barnard's article in the *New York Times Magazine,* Nov. 7, 1937.

Page 203—Belasco's memories of Little Maudie. Quoted by permission from *Maude Adams,* by Acton Davies. (Frederick A. Stokes Company, 1901.)

Page 208—Peter—afterward Arnold—Daly. He had no connection with Peter, or Pete, Daly—a musical comedy star.
    "Pudd'nhead Wilson." Daly played the white twin, and made a striking impression, says George C. Tyler, who saw the performance. His belief in Daly dated from that.

Page 209—Money borrowed for "Candida." William Gillette lent it to Daly and Smith, though this fact was not known at the time.

Page 210—Quoted excerpt. From a newspaper clipping without date or name of publication. Written by Daly when he was playing in "The Girl from Dixie."

Page 211—Autumn of 1905. Shaw's "Man and Superman" —with Robert Lorraine—was playing to packed houses, even though "Mrs. Warren's Profession" was banned.

Sources (in addition to those already mentioned in text and notes).—Files of the *New York Dramatic Mirror* at various times in 1903, '04, '05, '06, and '15; of the *Theatre Magazine* for some of the same periods; of the *Bookman,* 1904, and of *Harper's Weekly,* 1905; reviews of plays mentioned in this chapter; Robinson Locke scrapbooks, at New York Public Library; *Arnold Daly,* B. H. Goldsmith; *Mrs. Fiske,* Frank Carlos Griffith. (Mr. Griffith was for many years Mrs. Fiske's company manager.)

(Chapter 11)

Page 215—**Early talking pictures.** The first talking picture was "The Jazz Singer," in 1927. By 1929, the migration from New York to Hollywood was well advanced.

Page 220—**Greta Garbo trained by Stiller.** In 1936, Henry Albert Phillips visited Filmstad, near Stockholm, and interviewed players who worked with Miss Garbo when she was unknown. See his article in the Drama Section, *New York Herald Tribune*, Dec. 20, 1936.

Page 221—**Excerpt from Mordaunt Hall's review.** From *New York Times*, March 15, 1930. Quoted by permission.
　　　　Richard Watts, Jr. Quotation is by permission. *New York Herald Tribune*, Sept. 8, 1935.

Sources.—Much of this chapter is based on facts gathered by the author from players and other persons connected with pictures and radio. For a very full list of film periodicals and of books and articles on motion pictures, see *Film and Theatre*, by Allardyce Nicoll. (Thomas Y. Crowell Company, 1936.)

(Chapter 12)

Note: Statements quoted in this chapter were made to the author, in the course of interviews for the Sunday Drama Section of the *New York Herald Tribune*. Wherever possible, such quotations have been submitted for verification by the persons concerned. Further facts are based on many talks with actors and actresses which are not included here, as well as on the author's own observation and research.

(Chapter 13)

Page 266—**Influence of dramatists on acting.** This subject, which would make a book in itself, can merely be touched on here. Every dramatist of standing influences the work of players. Anderson and Shakespeare are used as examples.

Page 271—**Little Theatres, summer theatres, college dramatics.** These activities interlock—summer theatres often being established by college or Little Theatre groups, the members of which become professional actors and producers as speedily as possible. The growth of university influence in the professional theatre started in the first decade of the present century. Brander Matthews, at Columbia, and George Pierce Baker, at Harvard, were among pioneers who taught their students to consider practical problems of the stage.

Page 273—**Summer theatres.** Besides those mentioned in this chapter, some others which have been in operation for a number of years include: Abingdon, Va.—Barter Theatre; Arden, Del.—Robin Hood Theatre; Brattleboro, Vt.—Brattleboro Players; Carmel, N. Y.—Rockridge Theatre; Cohasset, Mass.—Cohasset Players; Denver, Col.—Elitch's Theatre (a very old institution); Ivoryton, Conn.—Ivoryton Summer Playhouse; Locust Valley, N. Y.—Red Barn Theatre; Matunuck, R. I.—Theatre-by-the-Sea; Newport, R. I.—Newport Casino; Ogunquit, Me.—Manhattan Repertory Company; Pawling, N. Y.—Starlight Theatre; Peterborough, N. H.—Peterborough Players; Putney, Vt.—Repertory Playhouse; Stockbridge, Mass.—Berkshire Playhouse; Tamworth, N. H.—The Barnstormers.

The above organizations are conducted, for the most part, on a professional basis. As to community theatres and Little Theatres, two outstanding authorities are Mrs. Edith J. R. Isaacs, editor of *Theatre Arts Monthly*, and Barrett H. Clark, of the Dramatists' Guild.

Page 280—**Gordon Craig.** Book referred to is his *Ellen Terry and her Secret Self*.

(Chapter 14)

Page 284—**Realism and stylism.** For convenience, the term stylism is used here to cover all forms of acting in which the player's voice and manner greatly transcend those of everyday life. This method has sometimes been called declamatory, sometimes classic or classicized, sometimes "idealized."

In it, the player aims at action which sums up or symbolizes life, yet which does not copy it. But in realism, or naturalism, he tries to present a character who—to the spectator—shall look as nearly as possible like an everyday person. There is no complete demarcation between these two methods, for actors generally color one with a touch of the other. However, in extreme cases the difference is highly apparent.

Behind the rhythmic ebb and flow of these styles in our theatre are three simple causes. (1) The kind of drama in favor during an epoch. It is obvious that verse is susceptible of a manner which would not fit "You Can't Take It With You" or "Golden Boy." (2) The vogue of some great actor. He or she is temperamentally inclined to realism or stylism, perhaps without applying these names to acting; but the work he or she does is so compelling, so full of originality, that it sets a fashion. Other players follow it. (3) The desire for change. When the public has seen one style carried as far as it will go for a long time, some degree of reversal sets in. That is because nothing newer or better can be done, for the time-being, in the established direction.

INDEX

Abbreviations: Eliz. = Elizabethan.   Rest. = Restoration.   Cent. = Century.

These and other comments in parentheses are for convenience in identification.   Periods indicated are merely approximate, and for fuller information the reader is referred to text and Notes.   Explanations have been omitted where they seemed superfluous.

The term "Elizabethan" is here applied broadly—as it often is in classifying Elizabethan drama—and includes the reigns of Elizabeth, James I, and Charles I, ending with the closing of the theatres in 1642.   The term "Restoration" here covers the period from 1660, when theatres were re-opened, to the death of Betterton in 1710, when the Restoration style of acting had already begun to wane.

Titles of plays are in italics, film productions being so designated.

Index

A

323

G

J

K

U

V

W

Y